THINGS AREN'T RIGHT

THE DISAPPEARANCE OF THE YUBA COUNTY FIVE

TONY WRIGHT

Genius
Book Publishing

Milwaukee Wisconsin USA

Published by:
Genius Book Publishing
PO Box 250380
Milwaukee Wisconsin 53225 USA
GeniusBookPublishing.com

ISBN: 978-1-958727-20-1

231231 Trade

Contents

... and you will know the truth, and the truth will set you free.
—John 8:32

*This book is dedicated to Ted Weiher, Jack Madruga,
Bill Sterling, Jackie Huett, and Gary Mathias.
May the world know you and your story.*

AUTHOR'S NOTE

The following book is a true crime story involving people with intellectual disabilities and mental illness. At times, some antiquated terminology will be used, and it is important to inform the reader of this in advance. The inclusion of the terminology was by no means to shame or ridicule anyone, but to shed a light on a different era and to see how we have progressed in certain ways when it comes to treating others with intellectual disabilities and mental illness. Also, certain individuals who were interviewed for this book or were interviewed by investigators in 1978 will be under pseudonyms for privacy.

FOREWORD
by Shannon McGarvey

Anyone who has touched the case of the Yuba County Five understands how intriguing—and impossibly sad—it is. For nearly half a century, the mysterious disappearances of Ted Weiher, Jackie Huett, Bill Sterling, Jack Madruga, and Gary Mathias have haunted their families and confounded law enforcement. With each passing year, another memory of the men seemingly fades, another clue gets lost to the annals of time, and another answer drifts beyond our grasp.

If you're going to research the Yuba County Five case, you've got to accept the ache of uncertainty. Not knowing is the hardest part. The realization [is] that for all the research, the hours of interviews, and the data collected, we will likely never know what happened to those five young men that night. What drove them into the mountains, seventy miles in the wrong direction, amid subfreezing temperatures, wearing only spring clothes? What then made them abandon the safety of their vehicle and hike further into the wilderness instead of turning around and heading back home?

No one can theorize explanations to these questions or sit within the void of doubt better than Tony Wright.

I met Tony in the fall of 2021 when I began researching the story for the *Yuba County Five* podcast. From the beginning, Tony was the definitive go-to for all the ins and outs of the case—the person everyone pointed to as knowing the most. He was meticulous in his research and had an almost encyclopedic recall of names, dates, and places related to the men's chronologies. Tony took on this book in complete earnest, out of a virtuous interest, working in his spare time, and, in turn, it transformed into a passion for him. It was not hard to latch on to his enthusiasm and follow him into the depths of this investigation. Tony had collected more research than any resource I'd previously encountered. However, he still lacked one integral piece: a digitized copy of the Yuba County Sheriff's Department (YCSD) case files.

Tony had seen the case files once before when he traveled to Yuba County on a research trip, but the YCSD had only permitted him to take notes—photographs and copies of the files were forbidden. There were hundreds of pages of documents, so getting digitized copies was paramount to thorough case research. But it takes time to push requests such as these through the public sector pipeline, especially when the nature of some of the documents therein are sensitive and require redaction.

When I submitted my request for case files to the YCSD in the fall of 2021, Tony had already been waiting for months. That is why, when I received a response within two weeks of my initial request, we were suitably shocked. I'd developed a friendliness with a YCSD records clerk, who had helped prioritize my digitization request. Within a month, we had the files and went back and forth about all the new data we [had] gleaned. This type of collaboration, accessibility, and transparency punctuated my professional relationship with Tony and continues to this day.

Beyond simply wanting to solve this mystery, it is clear that Tony Wright truly cares for the people affected by it. He has developed lasting relationships with nearly all of the men's close surviving relatives and continues to do the daily emotional legwork required to move this story forward.

This book is the product of his journey into the maddening world of this case. It is a culmination of Tony's dogged research, all the tedious pulling of threads, and all the mental labor of translating archival data into real-life events. This body of work stands as the definitive literary account of case details. Truly, this is a bible for the Yuba County Five.

—Shannon McGarvey

INTRODUCTION

Since 1997, I have worked in local government as an archivist, and during that time, I have assisted local officials, citizens, journalists, filmmakers, researchers, and authors. The work is fascinating and incredibly rewarding because I provide access to historical reports, images, and maps for those seeking answers to questions. Some of the information I find has been considered lost or forgotten.

It was March 2016 when a retired professor of biology who was writing a book about the history of streetcars in Grand Rapids, Michigan, stopped by the archives to review some historical streetcar reports from the 1930s. His eyes lit up when he saw the reports because they contained some valuable data for his research. With a bit of a laugh, the retired professor told me that, initially, he never had an interest in streetcars. He was researching the logging industry in Michigan, and it was linked to the railroad and streetcar industries. An interest was sparked, and now he wanted to know more about the use of streetcars in Grand Rapids and why the system was scrapped in the 1930s.

That retired professor told me that the books people end up writing find them and not the other way around.

☙

It was 2018 when a missing persons case that was considered long forgotten was somehow unearthed. It spread like wildfire across social media. Podcasters, video content creators, internet sleuths, and writers became completely fascinated with a forty-year-old mystery that was once described as "bizarre as hell."

On February 24, 1978, Ted Weiher, Jack Madruga, Bill Sterling, Jackie Huett, and Gary Mathias left the Yuba County, California, area to attend a college basketball game in Chico, California. It was a relatively easy fifty-mile drive, and the five men had reportedly made the trip previously without incident. But on that February night, they never returned home. The friends were traveling in Jack Madruga's pride and joy, which was a 1969 light blue, two-door Mercury Montego. Sometime after 11 p.m., the car became stuck on a desolate snow-covered road in the Plumas National Forest situated in the Sierra Nevada mountains. The location was sixty miles in the wrong direction from where they lived. Weiher, Madruga, Sterling, Huett, and Mathias emerged from the vehicle and disappeared into the frigid darkness of an unforgiving land. They were never seen alive again.

These men lived in the Yuba County area some forty miles north of Sacramento. Weiher, Madruga, Sterling, and Huett were considered intellectually disabled, while Mathias had been diagnosed with schizophrenia. The five collectively were referred to as "the boys." They were all adults who lived with their parents, held jobs, and were incredibly passionate about sports, especially basketball. Weiher was the oldest of the group at thirty-two, while Huett was the youngest at twenty-four. Weiher,

Madruga, Sterling, and Huett had known each other for several years, while Mathias was somewhat of a newcomer to the group.

The five were members of the Gateway Gators, a basketball team for the Gateway Projects, a local organization for people with disabilities and those living with mental illness. The Gateway Gators were scheduled to participate in a Special Olympics basketball tournament near Sacramento on Saturday, February 25, 1978, where the winning team would advance to the state Special Olympics event in Los Angeles during the summer. It included a trip to Disneyland. Some of the men were so excited about the tournament they decided to lay out their uniforms early.

Sometime around 6 p.m. on February 24th, they departed for Chico State University to watch their favorite team, the University of California, Davis (UC Davis), play an away game. Believing it could be the last time they could catch a UC Davis game that season, the five decided it was worth staying up late the night before their big tournament. Their parents agreed, perhaps some very reluctantly, to allow them the opportunity to make the trip. There were previous occasions when they had successfully traveled out of town together to watch UC Davis games, participate in their own basketball tournaments, or enjoy an evening of roller skating or miniature golf. If anything were to go wrong, the five knew they could phone home for assistance. But for some unknown reason, they never called for help, and they never returned home.

Hours passed, and the mothers of the five were up all night worried sick. Some called each other to see if there were any updates on the whereabouts of their sons. Family and friends spent Saturday, February 25th, frantically searching Yuba County, the highways, and Chico for the missing men. Jack Madruga's mother would report them missing to the Yuba County Sheriff's Department that Saturday at 8 p.m. Days of no leads ended on Tuesday, February 28th, when a forest ranger alerted authorities that he had found Madruga's car in the Plumas National Forest. The result was a major search and rescue operation during a time of record snowfall. Months dragged on with no sign of the missing men, and by June of that same year, the bodies of four of the five were discovered roughly twelve miles away from the Mercury Montego. The families, the members of law enforcement who worked on the case, the media that reported the story, and those who have had an interest in the disappearance have been frustrated and heartbroken for nearly forty-five years. The story about the disappearance of Weiher, Madruga, Sterling, Huett, and Mathias became known as the case of the Yuba County Five.

What is known is that the five attended the game in Chico, and afterward, they made a last-minute stop at a local convenience store for drinks and snacks. It is believed they got on the road shortly after 10 p.m. to head home, and over an hour later, the five somehow ended up in the Plumas National Forest. The location where they disappeared was far from their homes in the foothills of the Sierra Nevada. Temperatures in the forest were well below freezing that night, and there were snowdrifts that were reportedly ten to twelve feet in areas. Earlier in the day, it was unusually warm in Marysville, and that evening was supposed to be cool and comfortable. Some of the men were last seen wearing light jackets, short-sleeved shirts, jeans, and tennis shoes, which would have provided little protection against the elements in the Plumas National Forest.

When the investigation was launched the following evening by the Yuba County Sheriff's Department in Marysville, it was theorized that Madruga's car broke down, and they were stuck on the side of the highway somewhere waiting for a tow truck or assistance from a passing motorist. Alerts were sent out to law enforcement agencies from Sacramento up to the Oregon state line. Nothing was reported. No car. No men.

Four Northern California jurisdictions of law enforcement ended up working together to search for the missing men in the forest with the aid of family, friends, the community, and additional law enforcement agencies. The story was picked up by the media, and it spread quickly across the U.S., Canada, and beyond. Days turned into months. On June 4, 1978, Ted Weiher's body was discovered in a US Forest Service trailer some twelve miles from where the Montego was abandoned. The remains of Jack Madruga, Bill Sterling, and Jackie Huett were discovered shortly thereafter in the vicinity of the trailer, but Gary Mathias's remains were never found. The story of the five saw sporadic national and local reporting until the end of 1979, and from that point forward, the news story was nothing more than a distant memory buried in newspapers. Until recently.

☙

My interest in the Yuba County Five began in March 2018 when I watched an episode of *Criminally Listed* on YouTube. The series, narrated by creator Robert Grimminck, had caught my attention months earlier because each episode dealt with incredibly compelling true crime cases. Each episode had a specific topic. There were episodes about cold cases with strange voicemails or haunting deathbed confessions, and I was a faithful subscriber waiting for the latest weekly episode to be posted. I was watching a viewer's choice episode of *Criminally Listed* featuring three requested cases. The first two I cannot recall, but the third was titled "Gary Mathias and the Boys." It was an incredibly bizarre and heartbreaking story that took place in Northern California, where five friends mysteriously vanished in the Plumas National Forest. That story struck a chord, and I could not stop thinking about the fate of "Gary Mathias and the Boys."

After watching the story on *Criminally Listed*, YouTube recommended some more true crime channels, and they too were talking about this 1978 case, but the stories were titled "The Yuba County Five." A channel called *Bedtime Stories* covered the story but did so with an animated black-and-white style, and it fueled my fascination with the case. Something mysterious occurred that night; I absolutely needed to investigate what really happened to Weiher, Madruga, Sterling, Huett, and Mathias.

The Yuba County Five had also become a popular topic discussed on true crime podcasts. There were articles I read online at *Mental Floss* and the *San Francisco Chronicle*. Perhaps the biggest post-1978 article for the story was published in 2019 by the *Sacramento Bee*. Benjy Egel was the reporter, and his story was a two-day front-page feature that included an interview with Jack Beecham, the undersheriff for Yuba County in

1978, and a few people who knew the five. People like me were becoming interested in a case that had been dormant since the late 1970s. Someone had brought it back into the spotlight, which allowed a group of people with internet access to further investigate the fate of the Yuba County Five.

Until 2019, the case had not been covered by a network show. As a fan of true crime, I wanted to find a book about the Yuba County Five and discovered during a search on Amazon that no books were available. I knew there was a story to be written about the case. I had assisted researchers who were working on books for years, I wrote numerous research papers as an undergraduate and graduate student, and I had experience writing comic books and graphic novels. Perhaps it was up to me to write a book on it. My goal was to do a proper deep dive into one of the most intriguing disappearances in American history. Most importantly, I wanted the stories of Ted Weiher, Jack Madruga, Bill Sterling, Jackie Huett, and Gary Mathias shared with the world. It was important that people knew the five as individuals and as a group of friends.

❧

Since 1978, theories have developed concerning the fate of the Yuba County Five, including an encounter with deranged basketball fans from Chico or a possible wrong turn that had them hopelessly lost and panicked. On the surface, these seemed to be plausible explanations, but when one digs further into the case, there is something more bizarre and perplexing, only leading to more questions. It is nothing short of a journey into madness.

From the very beginning family members believed something or someone forced Weiher, Sterling, Madruga, Huett, and Mathias off the highway up into the Plumas National Forest. There were plenty of opportunities for the car to turn around and get back on the highway. Madruga was familiar with the area where they disappeared, so it should have been obvious they were going up into the Sierra Nevada and not heading home. The road on which they abandoned the car was unpaved, rutted, and didn't connect to any major roads. Plus, they slowly drove it up into the snow, which led to the car being stuck. Why did they drive up the road instead of turning around to find another way home?

The 1970s were a dark period for the Marysville-Yuba City area where the men resided because it was where Juan Corona murdered some twenty-five people. The Gateway Projects that the five attended was the target of numerous mysterious arson attacks, which included the horrific murder of the executive director. The senseless murder of two young girls would shock the community. Then, a local school bus tragedy that turned out to be one of the worst in history seemed to be yet another cruel turn in events. (More on these to follow.) Crime was rampant, and law enforcement seemed to have their hands full daily. The case of the Yuba County Five would be another addition to an area linked to tragedy.

Questions have piled on top of questions. Family members and those who have fully studied the case believe there was something sinister behind the disappearance, but that something is uncertain. Those who knew the five have stated that Jack Madruga was a trusted and responsible driver who knew the highways of Northern California.

Fingers have been pointed, names have been whispered in gossip circles about individuals rumored to be involved with the disappearance, and possible motives have been theorized. These theories have remained as merely theories, but some who were interviewed for this book say the truth is out there in the Yuba County area or beyond. Perhaps someone knew something, refused to come forward, and took it to their grave. Perhaps someone knows something and is still too afraid to come forward. Others are of the opinion that they simply got lost on the way home and it was nothing more than an unfortunate tragedy.

For the surviving family members, it has been four incredibly difficult decades. All the parents of the five have died, and some of their siblings have also passed away. When the five disappeared, a few of them were uncles and are remembered fondly by their nieces and nephews. The five never saw some of their siblings or nieces and nephews get married and start families. Tears come in waves for reasons unknown, and days of depression and pain are all too common for those who knew and loved the five. Answers are needed on why they disappeared on the evening of February 24, 1978. It was not like the five to drive off into the unknown because some in the group feared the dark, disliked the snow, and despised the wilderness. Impulsive trips were not something the five did, especially the night before an important tournament. As Melba Madruga, the mother of Jack Madruga, told a reporter in 1978, "Things aren't right."

YUBA COUNTY SHERIFF'S DEPARTMENT

MISSING PERSONS

CASE #CR 78-534

WILLIAM LEE STERLING
WMA, 29 years, 5'10",
160 lbs., black hair,
brown eyes.

THEODORE EARL WEIHER
WMA, 32 years, 6'0,
200 lbs., brown kinky
hair, brown eyes

GARY DALE MATHIAS
WMA, 25 years, 5'10",
170 lbs., brown hair,
hazel eyes.

JACK CHARLES HUETT
WMA, 24 years, 5'9",
165 lbs., brown hair,
green eyes.

JACK ANTONE MADRUGA
WMA, 30 years, 5'10",
190 lbs., brown hair,
hazel eyes.

Courtesy of the Yuba County Sheriff's Department

Jackie Huett and unidentified child
Courtesy of the Huett Family

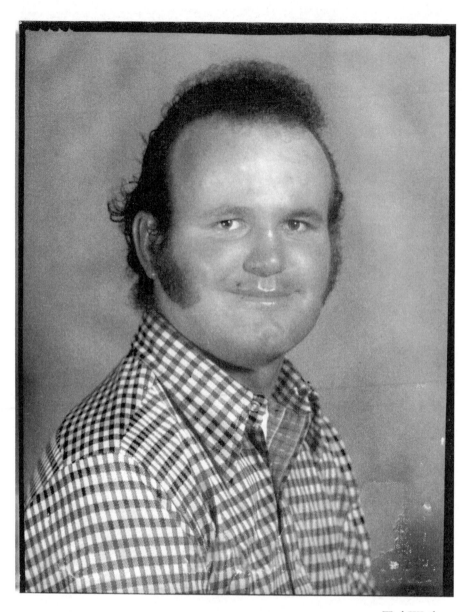

Ted Weiher
Courtesy of Dallas Weiher, Jr.

Gary Mathias
Courtesy of Tammie Phillips

Jack "Doc" Madruga
Courtesy of the Madruga Family

Bill Sterling
Courtesy of the Yuba County Sheriff's Department

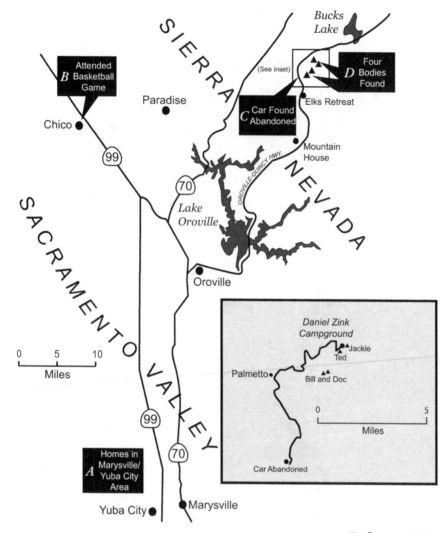

Reference Map
Copyright © 2024 Genius Books & Media, Inc.
See copyright page for distribution rights.

PART I: THE FIVE

CHAPTER ONE:
THEIR WORLD

Working on this book required a great deal of research about the five men and the case itself. I also needed to gain a better understanding of intellectual disabilities and mental illness. Countless hours were spent watching videos and documentaries about people living with schizophrenia or an intellectual disability. A majority of what I watched was created by people diagnosed with a mental illness or an intellectual disability. What I learned is that there are challenges, but people live productive lives. Some have careers and families. People might count them out, but they have proved their critics wrong.

While Gary Mathias was diagnosed with schizophrenia, there was not a clear diagnosis for Weiher, Madruga, Sterling, or Huett. All four were rubber-stamped as "disabled." Some information was provided about Madruga and Sterling. It is difficult to understand a disability if you have limited resources. Family members clarified the disabilities of the four to the best of their abilities, but they wish they had an actual diagnosis at the time.

Weiher, Madruga, Sterling, Huett, and Mathias grew up in a time when intellectual disabilities and mental illness were swept under the rug or treated with complete disdain. Special education classes were available to some but not everyone with a disability. Some were sent away to institutions that ranged from acceptable to downright inhuman.

The 1970s were a time of deinstitutionalization for psychiatric hospitals due to legal and economic factors. Another change was the 1973 Rehabilitation Act passed by Congress. Section 504 of the act stated that employers and organizations that received federal funds had to provide equal opportunity benefits and services to people with disabilities. It was in the books, but it did not mean life changed instantly for those with disabilities. For the five, they had dealt with years of obstacles and other personal difficulties long before that law was signed.

In 1975, Congress passed the Education for all Handicapped Children Act. At the time, it was estimated that there were eight million children with disabilities in the United States, and one million of those children were excluded from the public school system. The act would provide a free "appropriate" public education to these children. The five were out of high school when that was passed. Their families do not recall if the men faced major obstacles with their education.

During the interview process, I didn't press the families too hard about intellectual disabilities or mental illness. Some discussed the topic without me bringing up the issue, and for others I knew it wouldn't be a good idea to press my luck. From what I gathered, the men's families dealt with their intellectual disabilities to the best of their abilities. The men were not treated differently from their siblings. I spoke with someone about this, and they wondered if it was the parents treating their children as equals or some sort of unconscious denial that there was something wrong.

Discussing mental illness was harder since Gary Mathias's schizophrenia was viewed by many as the reason behind the men's disappearance. His family was on the defensive, and rightly so. It's hard to know if the person interviewing you is using the information to shed light on mental illness or to use the information as data to prove Mathias was the villain.

Without a doubt, the families of Weiher, Madruga, Sterling, Huett, and Mathias did their best to raise their children. During the 1960s and 1970s, Yuba County and neighboring Sutter County provided certain services for the five, and they were part of programs including the Gateway Projects.

∽

I grew up in Ohio, which is basically a Midwestern state where people drive through or fly over to get to somewhere more interesting or exciting. My hometown of Springfield, Ohio, was once a city with the potential to be something bigger, but it never happened due to a variety of circumstances. In 1983, the 50th anniversary edition of *Newsweek* featured a story about some families in Springfield. "The American Dream" was the title of the article, and some 30 years after that *Newsweek* story ran, Springfield was in the press again, but this time, it was being examined as the American city with the biggest decline of middle-class residents from 2000-2014.

As I began studying the history of Yuba County for this book, I noticed some curious similarities. Marysville, the county seat for Yuba County, and my hometown were visioned at one time as becoming major cities, but it was not their destiny. Both are very blue-collar and pretty much filled with conservative, God-fearing folk. Perhaps Springfield and Marysville had already experienced the best of times, but both towns have citizens who believe that the best is yet to come.

My research also focused on the histories of neighboring communities like Olivehurst and Yuba City in Sutter County. As I studied the Yuba County area, I realized that my understanding of California was just Southern California and the Bay Area. Sure, I was familiar with Napa Valley, the mountains, and the giant sequoias in Northern California, but I knew nothing of the communities north of Sacramento. I began to expand my knowledge of a region of California that's not always depicted in movies or television.

ↄ⌀

At the time they went missing, Weiher, Madruga, Huett, and Mathias resided in Linda and Olivehurst, communities in Yuba County east of the confluence of the Yuba and Feather Rivers. Sterling lived west of the Feather River in Yuba City. Located some forty-five minutes north of Sacramento, life in the Yuba County region was vastly different from the faster-paced lifestyles of Southern California with its glitz, glamour, sun, surf, and beaches.

"I grew up in Marysville when it was a vibrant and diverse regional 'hub' of an agriculturally rich three-county region," said Mike Geniella, a former employee of the *Appeal-Democrat*, the local newspaper for Marysville and Yuba City. "Marysville had a vibrant business center, great restaurants, a bar on practically every corner, and a rich history dating to the gold rush era. It was a mercantile center for the northern gold mines."

Agriculture was a way of life for many, and some residents were descendants of the old gold rush while newer residents left places in the Central Plains or South, with a few considered true "Okies" from the Dust Bowl. The five may have had a small-town upbringing, but they lived over an hour's drive away from the Plumas National Forest, while Lake Tahoe, San Francisco, and Reno were anywhere from two to three hours away by car.

Marysville and Yuba City have been part of an area of great agricultural importance known as the Central Valley. From Redding down past Bakersfield, the Central Valley covers some twenty-thousand square miles and is bounded by the Cascade Range to the north, the Tehachapi Mountains to the south, the Sierra Nevada mountains to the east, and the Coast Ranges to the west. Two major rivers, the Sacramento and San Joaquin, run through the Central Valley.

To the west of Yuba City, the Sutter Buttes are visible to those in the region. Remnants of an ancient volcano, they are two thousand feet in height and run roughly eleven miles going north to south while measuring roughly ten miles from east to west. The Sutter Buttes are not classified as a mountain range, although they are referred to in the area as "the world's smallest mountain range."

Marysville was named in honor of Mary Murphy, a survivor of the infamous Donner Party. A group of settlers, led in part by the Donner family, left Independence, Missouri, during the spring of 1846 to claim fertile land in California. By the time they reached Fort Laramie (in modern-day Wyoming), they had learned of a shortcut to California, which turned out to be a lie that cost numerous lives and allegedly resulted in some of the survivors choosing cannibalism to survive. One of the factors that brought them to that last resort was the same unforgiving winter conditions of the Sierra Nevada that sadly also took the lives of the Yuba County Five.

Gold put Marysville on the map during the 1850s, and some believed the town had the potential to be the state capital of California. Marysville was along the Feather River that flowed to Sacramento, and it became a popular shipping route for miners. A lust for gold led to the practice of hydraulic mining, which caused an environmental disaster that raised river levels. Flooding became an issue. A levee system was built in Marysville for protection, but it boxed in the city, limiting its growth. Hydraulic mining also made the rivers less navigable, leading to Marysville, which ended the fairytale for the town that some envisioned as "the New York of the Pacific."

When the gold boom came to an end, the area would turn to a new business. Agriculture flourished in the region and is still a major business today. Rice, almonds, walnuts, plums, and peaches are a few examples of the hundreds of crops that are grown in the Central Valley. Orchards are visible in the region to this day, along with the rice fields that make up most of the rice produced in the state. Yuba City is home to Sunsweet Growers, Inc., a major producer of dried tree fruits.

Marysville's neighbor to the west is Yuba City, the county seat of Sutter County. Located along the banks of the Feather River, Yuba City had similar beginnings to Marysville. It was an area of interest during the California Gold Rush. By 1856, it would become the seat of Sutter County, which was one of the original twenty-seven counties in California.

To the Southeast of Marysville is a census-designated area known as Olivehurst. It was settled mostly by people looking for work in California to escape the Great Depression. Some of those people were true Okies, and there are streets in Olivehurst named after communities in Oklahoma. This is where some of the Yuba County Five resided.

"Social tensions existed for a long time between the townsfolk and the new arrivals, the 'Okies,'" said Geniella, who added, "Even though we were blue-collar, my parents, their families, and neighbors scorned anyone from Olivehurst."

Agriculture would drive the economy of both Sutter and Yuba Counties. Commercial agriculture would be successful in California during the late 1800s, and the state would lead the way in exporting grain. Technology and innovation allowed California to thrive, but it was also at this time that many farmers saw the potential in growing other crops like fruits and vegetables. Refrigerated cars and an impressive irrigation system were contributing factors to their success.

It was mid-December of 1955 when a historic rainfall hit Northern California. Beginning on December 18th, the Sierra Nevada had areas that measured over thirty inches of rain, while the valley and coastal regions would record twenty inches of rain in areas. Runoff from the Sierra Nevada flooded the region, and the result was roads being washed away, farmland destroyed, and towns flooded.

The floods did a great deal of damage from Christmas Eve into the new year, where some eighty people were killed, over four thousand injured, some fifteen hundred homes were destroyed, while an additional estimated four thousand were badly damaged beyond repair, resulting in an estimated $225 million in property damages. Marysville and Yuba City would be the worst hit cities during this flood.

∾

For ten years, I taught modern American history classes part time at a community college. It covered our nation's history from 1865 to the present, and students learned about topics such as the migration West during the late 1800s, the Great Depression, and the post-World War II era. After doing some genealogical research on all five families, I learned that the Yuba County Five were born to families that hoped to find a better life in California. Some of the five's grandparents and parents came from places like Oklahoma, Arkansas, Missouri, and Virginia. A few were Okies leaving areas of the United States known as "the Dust Bowl" during the Great Depression, while others were just dirt-poor individuals sold on the dream of success in California. The families knew how to work the land, and their skills were a definite advantage in living in the Central Valley. It was a place where the families could escape poverty and live an idyllic American dream type of life. During the late 1960s and early 1970s, however, there were some disturbing incidents in the Yuba City-Marysville area that shattered the quiet, all-American appearance of those communities.

It was May 20, 1971 when a shallow grave was discovered in an orchard north of Yuba City. The victim was believed to be a transient worker in their mid-thirties, and they died a horrible death by a hatchet or machete. A freshly dug hole was found by the property owner on May 19th, and the next day, they noticed the hole had been filled with dirt. The police were contacted immediately.

As investigators searched the area days after the discovery, they found more graves. One body became a dozen, and it was just the beginning. A grand total of twenty-five victims were discovered, and clues found during the investigation were linked to a man named Juan Corona. Married and the father of four children, Corona was a farm labor contractor who had been committed in 1956 to the DeWitt General Hospital in Auburn, California, where he was diagnosed with schizophrenia. Apparently, the horrors of the 1955 flood had disturbed him greatly. He later found work recruiting farmhands, which was the way he met his victims. On January 18, 1973, Corona was convicted of the deaths of twenty-five men, and he would later be sentenced to life in prison. At that time, Corona was considered one of the worst serial killers in the history of the United States.

Less than ten months after Corona was sentenced, the Yuba City-Marysville area was shocked by the murders of two young girls named Doris Derryberry and Valerie Lane. Both were thirteen and were close friends who attended the Yuba Gardens Intermediate School. Derryberry and Lane had left their homes sometime on Sunday, January 11th, and were reported missing the next day. Their bodies were discovered in a wooded area southeast of Marysville, and both had been shot at point-blank range and were assaulted. Very little was found in the way of clues, suspects were nowhere to be found, and the case would remain cold for decades.

Somehow, the area could not release itself from the grasp of tragedy. On May 21, 1976, a school bus carrying some fifty-seven Yuba City High School students and adults crashed through a guardrail on an on-ramp and plunged some thirty feet, landing upside down. The crash occurred in Martinez, California, and twenty-nine people on the bus died. It would end up being one of the worst bus accidents in United States history.

Murders and tragedies should not be the legacy of a community or region, but Yuba City and Marysville had their fair share of heartbreaking incidents. Although the area had a rich agricultural history and was seen as a quiet getaway from bigger cities, Yuba City and Marysville also faced issues with unemployment, illegal drug activities, and crime during the 1970s. Ted Weiher, Jack Madruga, Bill Sterling, Jackie Huett, and Gary Mathias lived in the area, were educated in the area, worked in the area, and enjoyed many sports-related activities in the area. They were loved and respected by family, friends, and coworkers. Their families were hardworking people proud to be blue-collar and, in some cases, proud to be devoted to their faith and God. Somehow, through some cruel twist of fate, an incident on February 24, 1978, added their names to yet another tragedy linked to the area. They would forever be known as the Yuba County Five.

CHAPTER TWO:
TED WEIHER

Writing this book required a great deal of patience when it came to locating family and friends of the five. One challenge was finding a working phone number for people I wanted to interview. I discovered some people on Facebook and tried to contact them via Messenger, but they either never saw the message or simply ignored me. There were a few where I had no choice but to take the old-school route and mail a letter, hoping someone would write back or even call. That also did not work. My guess is that they saw my letter and thought it was some sort of junk mail or scam.

There were moments of success when I found an actual working phone number. The next step was for me to introduce myself over the phone with the hopes of sounding confident and compassionate. I wanted the families to know I wanted to write the real story about the five and their case. Some were happy to talk; others were not interested. A handful were beyond shocked that their phone number and mailing address were easily found on the internet.

The Weiher family was the first to be contacted and interviewed. They were, and have been, very kind and patient. The same can be said about the other families I interviewed, which made this experience especially rewarding.

∾

Theodore ("Ted") Earl Weiher was the oldest member of the Yuba County Five and was remembered as a kind but fun-loving individual. He stood six feet tall and weighed two hundred pounds at the time of his disappearance. He had brown hair and brown eyes. Weiher's hair was curly, and at times he sported a mustache, which made him look like the average drinking buddy. With a good haircut and a shave, Weiher had a strong all-American look.

He was born May 26, 1946, to Robert and Imogene Weiher in Prescott, Arizona, a small town of roughly six thousand residents located over one hundred miles north of Phoenix. A once-prosperous place for mining, Prescott served as the Territorial Capital for Arizona, and at one time, it was an important location for the local cattle industry. It was a temporary home for the Weiher family.

Ted Weiher's parents had married six years before his birth in Warner, Oklahoma. His mother was only seventeen at the time, while his father claimed to be forty-seven. Hazel Haight, Imogene's mother, signed their marriage license, giving consent to the union. Records indicate that Robert Weiher was likely born in Arkansas sometime in 1889, and if that information was correct, then that would have made him fifty when they married. He had previously married in 1910 and raised a family, but his first wife died in 1936 in Oklahoma. How Weiher's parents met is lost to history, but despite the difference in age, they would raise five children together. From oldest to youngest, it was Delores, Dallas Sr., Ted, Perry, and Dorothy.

Dallas Weiher Jr. is Ted's nephew and spoke over the phone about his memories of "Uncle Ted" and the Weiher family. His voice is golden for radio, and Weiher Jr. has a Kurt Russell look with a perfectly waxed mustache. He recalled some family memories of Robert Weiher passed along to him.

"He drove a truck that was hauling flagstone. From what I understand, he took the doors off his truck so he could jump out easier if it lost control." The work in Prescott was temporary as the Weiher family decided to head out to California a little over three weeks after Ted was born to join the family from Robert's first marriage in the Marysville area.

Dallas Weiher Sr. is Ted's older brother and a respected softball player in the Marysville-Yuba City area. His voice is gravelly, but he is one comical soul. Weiher Sr. was asked why his parents moved, and he responded, "Because they were poor (laughs)." He went on to add, "My half-sister and her husband was here." The success of the children from his first marriage in California was probably enough motivation for the Weiher family to relocate.

During an interview for the 2022 *Yuba County Five* podcast for Mopac Audio, Dallas Weiher Jr. stated that Robert and Imogene Weiher "bought two acres, built a little tar paper shack, and that's where my uncle Ted grew up."

Weiher's father was employed as a well digger in Marysville. "They did dig wells here. The water level would only… some wells only went fifteen feet and there was plenty of water," said Dallas Weiher Sr. He recalled that the wells for water were dug by hand. Weiher's father provided irrigation for plum orchards, and those plums would be dried and turned into prunes. Robert Weiher would also dig holes on properties in the area for septic tank use.

Before the Weiher family settled in Northern California, they were aware that something was different with their son. Dorothy Weiher-Dornan, the younger sister of Ted Weiher, stated that the discovery had been made "at birth" but did not elaborate. The file on Ted Weiher from the Yuba County Sheriff's Department stated that he had always been viewed by his family as "very slow." However, that was not the only challenge Weiher faced as a child.

"When Ted was born, he was born without knee joints, and they took him up to Paradise, which is up near Oroville, when he was two," recalls Weiher Sr. "They had a [holy roller] camp meeting, and everybody prayed for him." Weiher Sr. remembered sometime circa 1948 that his mother was out hanging diapers on a clothesline and God told her that Weiher would walk in the spring. When the season arrived, the revelation turned out to be true because one day, he got up and took off walking. Weiher would be an avid walker up until the day he disappeared, and his mother continued to be a devoted servant to God for the rest of her days.

Ted Weiher entered the public school system in Marysville as a young child, and at times, he would face the torment of bullies due to his disability. "People would pick on him," said Weiher Sr., who added, "I got in a fight in grammar school a couple of times." Dallas Weiher Sr., and Perry Weiher attended school with their brother and had to "protect him from harm and to keep him out of trouble."

Even Dorothy Weiher-Dornan had to join in on fights. She is Ted's younger sister. Her stories of Ted are told with a smoker's voice and a "kiss my grits" kind of attitude. She has many great memories of her brother, and she still laughs when thinking about their escapades. "He was our baby. We fought over him."

A few friends also had Ted Weiher's back. As a student at Marysville High School, Weiher was picked on at times. One student was relentlessly picking on him, but a guy named Russell Mitchell saw what was happening, grabbed the bully by his shirt, and slammed him against the wall. The student learned a hard lesson about messing with Weiher.

People who knew Weiher knew better than to press his buttons. "You didn't want to get in a rock fight with him. He was left-handed and threw like a major leaguer," said Weiher Sr., who went on to add, "We'd get into broom fights out in the orchard. If he'd hit you with a broom, then it would hurt." The Yuba County Sheriff's Department file reported that Ted Weiher was not a violent person, but "it would not take much to make him mad." When Weiher was a kid, his siblings knew it would irritate the hell out of Ted if they sang "Why Do Fools Fall in Love?" by Frankie Lymon and the Teenagers. So they did it frequently.

Ted Weiher's strength was also on display when he played sports as a youngster. Weiher Sr. noted that there was a scar on his own knee because he was trying to catch a pass from his brother in a field but ran into a barbed wire fence because "he could throw it a half mile." Weiher even set a school record for a softball toss. "He had the Yuba County grade school softball throw record for a long time," recalled Weiher Sr., who believed it was somewhere in the ballpark of two hundred feet.

Being active was something Ted Weiher enjoyed. He was known to walk all over town, and he could walk for miles. He owned a beachcomber-style bicycle with a basket in the front. He also had a sweet tooth, as his nephew Dallas Weiher Jr. remembered. "He'd ride his bike up to the store to get an eight-pack of Pepsi or some Langendorf cookies or cakes." Pepsi was his drink of choice and the fridge had to be stocked with it or the Weiher household would not hear the end of it. Weiher Jr. could remember his uncle getting angry with Imogene Weiher, yelling, "Damnit, Ma, why'd you let them drink my Pepsis?!"

Weiher's ability to walk a good distance was reported in the press, but his mother told the Yuba County Sheriff's Department that her son also possessed a poor sense of direction, especially at night. Not only that, but he was afraid of the dark and would need someone to be with him just in case. According to his mother, if Weiher were to get lost, then he knew how to call home from a pay phone as long it was not a long-distance call. Weiher would sometimes phone his mother and ask her to get him a cab. She believed that Ted only knew his telephone number and that of one or two ladies he liked.

Although Weiher attended Marysville High School during the early 1960s, he did not earn enough credits to graduate. He earned his diploma by taking night school classes. It is unclear what challenges he faced academically, but his brother, Dallas Weiher Sr., had his own theories, including Ted possibly being on the autism spectrum.

Weiher Sr. admitted that they really didn't know anything about autism when Weiher was younger, but with what they know now, it could have been a possible diagnosis. "He could remember stuff, movies, and stuff that the rest of us couldn't remember. He could spell and write as good as [people his own age] could." Weiher Sr added, "He was artistic, too. He could draw, write, and spell, but he didn't understand stuff."

"Common sense eluded him," said Dallas Weiher Jr., when asked about his uncle's faculties. One example of Weiher's inability to comprehend basic situations happened circa 1967 when the Weiher family home on Star Avenue just east of Linda caught fire. It was either Perry or Dallas Weiher Sr., who tried getting Weiher out of his bed because the flames had covered the ceiling of his bedroom. Weiher could not understand the commotion and was more interested in getting a good night's sleep because he had to be at work the next morning. The result was Weiher being forcibly dragged from the burning premises by one of his brothers.

Another example of this type of behavior occurred years before. The Weiher family was living in a home with a gravel driveway, so Weiher decided to throw a rock from the driveway at someone who was walking along the road. According to Weiher Sr., that person returned with some others to explain to his brother that it wasn't a good idea to pelt people from the driveway with rocks. Weiher apparently did not understand why someone did not want to be pelted with gravel.

Weiher would also wave happily at random people in public and was perplexed when they did not wave in return. He also had no issue talking to strangers, and it was very important to Weiher that he was liked by everyone since he was friendly to people. Imogene Weiher told the Yuba County Sheriff's Department that her son could be easily persuaded by friendly people, and she added that he was also known to be passive but would fight if he were scared or hurt by someone. There was a time when Imogene Weiher asked Ted what he would do if someone broke into the house while he was home. He told his mother he would hide in his bed or somewhere in his bedroom.

Dallas Weiher Sr.'s family nickname was Wayne, and he remembered his days sharing a bunk bed with his brother. Ted Weiher was full of questions, and it would keep Weiher Sr. up some nights. "He'd say, 'Wayne,' and I'd say, 'What, Ted?' 'How come Mickey Mantle can hit a ball farther than I can?' 'Because he practices, he's bigger, and he's stronger. Now shut up and go to sleep.'"

Coming to a complete stop at a stop sign was another concept that Weiher could not comprehend despite his family trying their best to explain the basic rules of driving and safety. "I tried to teach him to drive once," said Weiher Sr., who remembered the session was difficult because he was trying to show his brother how to drive stick on some dirt roads in an orchard, and they ended up in a ditch. "I'm not a good teacher," he added with a chuckle.

Ted Weiher may not have been ready to drive a car, but when interviewed for the *Yuba County Five* podcast, Dallas Weiher Jr. recalled a near-disastrous story involving his uncle and aunt Delores Weiher. She was driving, and Weiher was in the passenger seat when they pulled up to a stop sign at an intersection. She asked Weiher if there were any cars coming, and he told her no cars were coming. As she started to drive, Delores Weiher noticed a truck coming down the street from her brother's direction, and she had to slam on the brakes to avoid an accident. A frustrated Delores asked her brother why he didn't warn her about the truck, and Ted grumpily informed her that she had asked about *cars* and not *trucks*.

ↄ

It was June 1966 when Robert Weiher died at seventy-six years of age. He left behind his five children from his marriage to Imogene Weiher, along with the children from his first marriage. Robert Weiher also left behind sixteen grandchildren and ten great-grandchildren.

Imogene Weiher was a widow overnight, but she was not alone. Her mother, Hazel Haight, was living with her in California. It was up to the matriarch of the Weiher family to be a provider and a rock. "She was a short order cook at a café or diner type of thing. Good grief, that woman could cook," said Weiher Jr., who remembered her yeast rolls being "five inches high and fluffy" and paired beautifully with her recipe of pinto beans and potatoes. The Weiher family would eat like kings even at times when money was tight, which was common in their household. Weiher Jr. believed her skills came from her hard life growing up poor in Oklahoma. Weiher Jr. referred to Imogene Weiher as a "real *Grapes of Wrath* type of person that lived close to the earth." It was a lifestyle where you grew your own food and raised hogs or cows for meat and milk. Adversity was no stranger to Imogene Weiher.

Ted Weiher also went on with life without his father. We do not know what impact this had on him as a twenty-year-old, but he was making the most out of life. Weiher worked odd jobs and spent his free time bowling, roller skating, riding his bike, walking, dancing, playing miniature golf, and participating in Special Olympics events, although he never understood why he was put in those events with people with disabilities. Weiher's family recalls he did very well in the Special Olympics and was a gifted athlete.

Employment varied for Ted Weiher, but one of his jobs was as a janitor at the Yuba Gardens Middle School. Micromanagement was the key to success in supervising Weiher, and it was noted in the Yuba County Sheriff's Department investigation that Weiher did a good job cleaning the school if he was carefully supervised. That job was perhaps the best fit for him because his mother told investigators that if he had a job and was left unsupervised, then he did not do it well.

Dallas Weiher Jr. said that his uncle had earned the nickname Bat Man working at the Yuba Gardens Middle School because he'd play baseball with the kids during recess and "hit the ball a mile." Weiher was also remembered as a kind worker at the school, and he was known to smile and nod at the children in the hallway. He was even remembered as someone who would make a basketball shot in the gym if a child handed him the ball.

One time, Weiher worked part-time at the snack counter at a local office building. Dorothy Weiher-Dornan remembered that his coworkers were dumbfounded at times after counting money from the daily sales. "They [would] always come up with more money than they should. They come to find out that it was his tips, and he didn't take them because that was stealing. He didn't realize they were tipping him for what he had done for them."

Around the time he went missing, Ted Weiher was a laborer for Pacific Gas and Electric (PG&E) in the area. His work involved packaging, winding, or repairing cable, and it was made possible by his involvement with the Gateway Projects in Yuba City. They were a nonprofit that allowed people with disabilities and those living with mental illness to earn job skills through their training centers. Ted Weiher was involved with the Gateway Projects from roughly 1973 until the time he disappeared in 1978.

Ted Weiher was an incredibly kind, fun-loving individual. At first, my understanding of Weiher, just like the other four, was from podcasts, videos, and articles. Speaking to his siblings, sister-in-law, and nephew allowed me the opportunity to know the true Ted Weiher.

One of my goals with the book was to make sure what had been reported concerning the five was correct. There had been a story floating around about Weiher spending $100 on pencils for no apparent reason. Allegedly, it was a memory from his brother, Dallas Weiher Sr., but during a 2020 interview with me, he stated, "I don't remember that." Weiher Sr. thought that it didn't seem a likely story since their family was poor and his brother, or anyone in the Weiher house for that matter, likely did not have $100 to spend freely.

While researching Ted Weiher's background at the Yuba County Sheriff's Department, I found a statement in his file that read, "If he has money, he will spend it freely on things he doesn't need, such as one hundred pencils, etc." There was nothing in the file that stated it was an actual incident, but it was possibly used as an example of Weiher's lack of common sense.

One person who gave me the best opportunity to know the real Ted Weiher was his nephew, Dallas Weiher Jr. Twenty years younger than his uncle, Weiher Jr. was allowed to pal around with his "Uncle Ted." "He was my buddy. He was just the fun uncle. He'd play catch with you. He'd do the airplane thing, pick you up by your arms and legs, and swing you in circles." Weiher Jr. said in an interview for the *Yuba County Five* podcast that his uncle was very kind and loved to laugh, and, most importantly, he had a heart of gold.

Weiher Jr. was the child of his father, Dallas Weiher Sr.'s, first marriage. When he was around the age of three or four, his father remarried a woman named Nelda and she became Weiher Jr.'s mother. She was also the chauffeur when Weiher Jr. wanted to join some of the five for a night at the roller rink or bowling alley.

There were times when Ted Weiher would walk to Jackie Huett's house, which was over a mile away from his home. Huett was eight years younger than Weiher, but the two were inseparable friends. They met during the early 1970s, and Weiher ended up being a protector of Huett's. Gary Mathias lived in the same neighborhood as the Weihers, so it would not have been uncommon for the two to run into each other from time to time. Weiher would also reportedly walk to Bill Sterling's home in Yuba City, which was an estimated seven miles away, and it would have taken Weiher some two hours to complete.

Weiher did find plenty of time to go out and have fun. When Weiher was twenty-one, he attended a party at a local hangout known as "the river bottoms" and purportedly did quite a bit of drinking. At some point, someone threw a full can of beer at Weiher, and it hit him directly in the head, leaving a permanent scar. According to Imogene Weiher, her son wouldn't drink because it gave him headaches.

Ted Weiher, according to his mother, was a man who enjoyed good food and clean clothes. Dallas Weiher Jr. said on the *Yuba County Five* podcast that he remembered his uncle in the shower with a radio blasting. Weiher Jr. remembered hearing Ted Weiher singing in the shower to "Rubberband Man" by the Spinners.

A food favorite of Weiher's was boxed macaroni and cheese. At Christmas, Dallas Weiher Jr. would get four boxes for his uncle. He would ask his mom to tape the four boxes together and wrap them. Every Christmas, Uncle Ted would open his present of macaroni and cheese and be overjoyed.

The report from the Yuba County Sheriff's Department shows that he was dating a woman named Shirley Lancaster (a pseudonym) at the time of his death. There is a possibility that Weiher met Lancaster at the Gateway Projects since she was also linked, possibly romantically, to Jackie Huett. Weiher and Lancaster had planned on having a date sometime in February of 1978, roughly two weeks before he disappeared. Lancaster's telephone number was one of the numbers that Weiher knew off the top of his head.

CHAPTER THREE: JACK MADRUGA

As a child, I enjoyed playing with friends. We would ride bikes, play football, or go to the mall and hang out at the arcade. I also enjoyed being alone and just being in my own little world. Nobody was yelling at me in that world, and I felt appreciated.

Most if not all of us have had that experience as kids or teenagers where we feel like people do not understand what we are going through. Also, we feel misunderstood. Some look at us as young and inexperienced, but at times, we possess a certain amount of wisdom that surprises others.

From reports, I knew little about Jack Madruga, other than being the driver of the car the night the five went missing. People outside his family knew him as kind, but that was all. His file at the Yuba County Sheriff's Department merely stated he was shy and withdrawn. The real Jack Madruga would be found from talking to his family

Sometimes, I have found some fascinating bits of information about the five while researching this case. My map skills were put to good use in studying the origins of the Madruga family because I learned they were Portuguese. However, I was pleasantly surprised to learn that they were from the Azores.

When I was younger, I was a huge fan of encyclopedias and world almanacs. They were full of fascinating information, and some included a world map section and a world flag section. I would spend hours studying maps and flags. We also had a globe, and I would enjoy studying different continents and oceans. If my parents saw a flag on television, they'd ask me to identify it, and I would.

That passion returned when I studied Jack Madruga's family tree. A simple task of research turned into a deep dive into the history of the Azores. Located roughly one thousand miles west of Portugal are the Azores, an autonomous archipelago featuring nine main islands in the Atlantic Ocean.

Sometime during the 1880s, a man named Antone Madruga left Pico Island in the Azores and made his way to Boston. The story the family was told was that he was a stowaway on a ship and would find work as a fisherman in Massachusetts. Eventually, he married a woman named Maria, and they ended up traveling to California to start a life together. Antone and Maria Madruga would have two children named Antone and Manuel.

The younger Antone Madruga met Melba Wiley, and on November 24, 1933, they married in Carson City, Nevada. Within a year, they were living in the Marysville area, and they would raise four children together. From oldest to youngest, it was Arlene, George, Janet, and finally Jack, who was born on June 18, 1947.

Cathy Madruga is the niece of Jack Madruga. She is a caretaker for a family member and is only available via phone call during certain hours. Madruga recalled many wonderful memories of her family, including her grandfather, Antone Madruga. "He was known as Tony, and he was reportedly a bootlegger during prohibition." According to family legend,

Antone Madruga was supposedly jailed for his illegal activities and was known for having a bad leg due to an accident where he was badly burned by tar. Also, he was employed as a truck driver for a company involved with road construction.

"I was five years old when he passed away," said Cathy Madruga about her grandfather. "I remember him. I remember being on horses with him, and I can remember him bouncing me on his leg at the Madruga ranch." The location of the Madruga ranch was in Loma Rica, California, a quiet community outside the Plumas National Forest fifteen miles north of Marysville.

Jack Madruga was eleven years old when his father died at Franklin Hospital in San Francisco. Cathy Madruga recalled that Antone Madruga died on the operating table of a heart attack before a surgical procedure to fix his injured leg. Like the Weihers, the Madruga family had to adjust to life without a husband and a father. Cathy Madruga remembered those were difficult times for Melba Madruga. "She was up the hill with the kids." She also recalled that her grandmother loved her garden, enjoyed walks, and fed the cows and chickens at the Madruga ranch. "She lived up there with Grandpa forever."

Melba Madruga relied upon her son Jack, nicknamed Doc, following the death of her husband. "Doc was my standby," she said to the press in 1978. She also told them that her son was "emotionally introverted."

What Cathy Madruga remembered the most was the time she spent with her uncle Jack Madruga. A quiet, kind, but introverted person, he was remembered as someone very special. Not only to her but also to her brothers, Rick and George Madruga. "We were all buddies," said Cathy Madruga, who added, "We did everything together. We hiked, we camped, we fished, we went to the movies, we went to concerts, we went to games."

Cathy Madruga could not recall the origins of the Doc nickname. "I knew him growing up as Doc," said Cathy Madruga, adding, "We all had nicknames." Her family nickname was Muffet.

George Madruga Jr. is Jack Madruga's nephew. He was interviewed for the *Yuba County Five* podcast and remembered the origin of the Doc nickname. Madruga Jr. said that his uncle would go around the house saying, "What's up, Doc?" It was the famous line from the *Bugs Bunny* cartoon, and he would be forever remembered as Doc by friends and family.

Sports was a love for the Madrugas, especially Jack. He enjoyed basketball and baseball, and his nephews Rick and George Jr. were good athletes as well. Jack Madruga was also a swimmer and enjoyed taking trips with family to a local spot for a day of swimming and relaxation.

Cathy Madruga remembered going with Rick, George, and Doc to some "kegger parties" after football games. "He was a lot of fun. No B.S. He did not drink, and he watched out for us. Our limit. He knew our limit."

Music was another love of Madruga's. "He liked all kinds [of music]. He liked Neil Diamond, country western, he loved the Supremes, and rock and roll," said Cathy Madruga. They attended concerts together and had a wonderful time.

Jack Madruga attended Marysville High School and was a few years younger than Ted Weiher. Like Weiher, Madruga didn't have enough credits to graduate. While Weiher's family understood that their son had some sort of cognitive issue, the same could not be said about Madruga. Information from the Yuba County Sheriff's Department of the investigation of the Yuba County Five shows that Jack Madruga was allegedly never diagnosed as having an intellectual disability but was considered slow in his thought process.

"He was a quiet guy. He was very sensitive and very smart, too," said George Madruga Jr. in an interview with the *Yuba County Five* podcast. "That's one thing that never comes out is he was smart. People assumed since he was so quiet that he was not all there, but he was extremely intelligent and fun-loving."

There are some who believe Madruga may also have been diagnosed on the autism spectrum if they knew more about it at the time. It is uncertain if he took the night school path like Ted Weiher after high school, but he would somehow graduate and attend Yuba College, a community college in Marysville. Although his life was moving in one direction, the United States of America had other plans for a young Jack Madruga.

Sometime before or during 1966, Madruga received a notice in the mail that he had been drafted. "I remember the day he got his draft notice," said Cathy Madruga. She recalled him being scared and she remembers crying because she had a feeling that her uncle would be going into combat in Vietnam.

Jack Madruga would spend roughly two years in the military. His basic training was completed at Fort Dix in New Jersey, but information about Madruga's stint in the Army is mixed. According to records, he did not have any special training, especially survival. A newspaper article when he went missing stated he served in Vietnam, but his file at the Yuba County Sheriff's Department notes that he was stationed at one point in West Germany and was responsible for driving trucks. It seemed he was a chip off the old block, like his old man when it came to driving.

Records also show that he may have spent time at the Oakland Army Base in the Bay Area. Sometime during 1968, Madruga was honorably discharged from the Army. The Yuba County Sheriff's Department investigation file for the case included the reason for Madruga's discharge. Under Chapter 5, AR-635-200, the Army was permitted to discharge Madruga due to physical or mental conditions that would prohibit him from performing his duties properly. His military record also stated that he had an "average capability of responsibility." Although he was honorably discharged, Madruga would be on reserve status until 1973.

Madruga earned money during his time in the Army, and he put those funds toward the purchase of a personal vehicle. Madruga would eventually become the owner of a two-door white-over-light-blue 1969 Mercury Montego sedan. It would be his pride and joy, and Madruga would take great care of his car. As he began hanging out with Ted Weiher, Bill Sterling, Jackie Huett, and Gary Mathias, he became the official driver. Madruga would take friends and family to the bowling alley or mini-golf courses or a stop at his favorite fast-food restaurant, Taco Bell. What is known about Madruga and his car was that beer was not allowed in the vehicle, and Madruga did not appreciate backseat drivers barking orders telling him where and how to drive.

During this time, Madruga moved back in with Melba Madruga, and they lived in a mobile home community in Olivehurst. They had decided to leave the family house in Loma Rica. Madruga was either encouraged by family or by his own volition to seek mental health services at a local outpatient facility. Madruga would meet with a doctor, and they reported that Madruga was a very withdrawn and shy individual. The doctor also noted that Madruga was someone who needed guidance in his life. Sometime in 1975, Madruga ended his visits to the facility for unknown reasons.

Also in 1975, Madruga found his way to the Gateway Projects and was assigned to some work-related duties. By 1976, he was employed as a dishwasher at Sunsweet Growers in Yuba City and was working there with Bill Sterling for approximately one year. Following his termination at Sunsweet, Madruga began receiving unemployment compensation.

During the investigation by the Yuba County Sheriff's Department, it was noted by Melba Madruga that her son was not really a leader or a follower in life. He would speak his mind if pressed to do something outside of his comfort zone. There were never any disciplinary issues for Madruga when he was at Gateway or Sunsweet. Melba Madruga said her son could make reasonable judgments and would not do something just to follow the crowd. Most importantly, Melba Madruga told investigators that her son would always tell her his plans for going out, and he would call her if he was ever running late.

∞

There have been unexpected surprises with this book, and one of them was discovering that I had some things in common with Jack Madruga. Both of us have been viewed as quiet people who seem withdrawn or off in our own little worlds. Our hearts are in the right place, but sometimes, it is difficult to connect with the real world because it's overwhelming.

Like Madruga, I washed dishes at a job and, for me at least, it was a truly miserable experience. Perhaps my worst memory of being the dishwasher was the way I smelled after a shift. My shoes were wet and covered with food waste, plus I had this smell of dirty dishwater. Also, there was an unrealistic demand to be always working at top speed, and a simple "thank you" was nowhere to be found. Perhaps Madruga couldn't keep up, or he may not have cared that much about a crummy job that probably paid a crummy wage. I know the feeling.

When I was researching the case in Marysville, I stopped by the Yuba County Library to do research at their archives. I perused some yearbooks for Marysville High School and found a picture of Jack Madruga. It was his senior year photo. He isn't smiling, but there's a kindness in his eyes, and he's a handsome young man.

Another thing Jack and I had in common was his passion for music, which has been something that has been part of my life since my teenage years. You might have had a bad day, and everyone is breathing down your neck, but there is music, and it is a wonderful escape.

When I think about Doc, I think about the music of Neil Diamond. I don't know if he ever had someone in his life who didn't play games behind him, but I know he was more than a solitary man.

CHAPTER FOUR:
BILL STERLING

Many of us have a friend who likes to remember former classmates or coworkers. Hours are spent reminiscing about the past, and occasionally, we will bring up the name of someone we have not remembered in years. Sometimes, there will be a moment of silence followed by someone saying, "I never really knew them that well."

That is the way I've felt about William ("Bill") Lee Sterling because he has been the true unknown of the Yuba County Five. What I do know is that he was born in Marysville on Tuesday, April 5, 1949, to Jim and Juanita Sterling and was one of four children. He had a brother named David and twin sisters named Deana and Debbie. Little is known about Sterling and his family as they have been the most private of the Yuba County Five. They did speak to the press and law enforcement during the 1978 investigation, but following the discovery of Sterling's remains, they have politely remained out of the spotlight.

Finding someone outside the family who knew Sterling was a challenge. Those who did know Bill Sterling only had a few interactions, which were all positive. Like Ted Weiher and Jack Madruga, he was remembered for his kindness. While it is nice to hear people speak highly of Sterling, he is someone I only know on the surface.

⌘

Juanita Johnson was born in Short, Oklahoma, in 1923 and was the oldest of seven children; William ("Jim") James Sterling was born on January 14, 1921, in Tupelo, Oklahoma. At some point in time, they each made their way out west. Juanita Sterling's obituary from 2017 stated she worked in a machine shop at McChord Field in Tacoma, Washington, during World War II, and it also mentioned that Jim and Juanita met at Robinson's Corner, an area south of Oroville, California, in 1948 at a dance and married soon thereafter.

The Sterlings would reside in the Yuba City area, and Jim Sterling would be an attendant at local service stations and would become the owner of Jim's Mico and U-Haul in Yuba City. Juanita Sterling would be employed by companies like JCPenney and Pacific Bell. They raised their four children in Yuba City and were a typical blue-collar family.

Information about Bill Sterling's early years was only available from the 1978 Yuba County Sheriff's Department report. Juanita Sterling was interviewed and stated that Bill Sterling, from ages eight to nineteen, spent an unspecified amount of time in two mental institutions, first at Napa State Hospital, then at DeWitt General Hospital. Sterling was living at home at the time of his disappearance, and records do not indicate if he was ever institutionalized in his twenties or if he sought any additional treatment.

Juanita Sterling's interview with the Yuba County Sheriff's Department sheds light on why Bill Sterling was institutionalized various times over a span of eleven years. She stated that her son had issues with hyperactivity, plus he could be viewed as a danger if people got in his way. It was decided by the Sterling family that he be sent away so that he was not a threat to others. What is not clear in the file is if Sterling was institutionalized for ten years straight or if he was periodically sent to these institutions for various stays.

During Bill Sterling's time at the Napa State Hospital, he was discovered to be partaking in a violent confrontation with another patient in a laundry or kitchen area. A custodian caught him a moment or two away from possibly taking someone's life. Juanita Sterling explained that the person her son was in the confrontation with had possibly sexually assaulted or sexually harassed her son at Napa. The staff at Napa then put Sterling into "custody." However, according to the interview with Juanita Sterling, this was one of many reported cases of him being put into "custody." No additional information was provided by Juanita Sterling to investigators about her son at Napa or DeWitt. She did state that Bill Sterling had been living with her and her husband "continuously" since the age of nineteen without incident.

❧

This was the first major surprise about the five that I discovered while researching the case. It was something that had to be examined and discussed to a certain point. Those familiar with the story of the Yuba County Five are aware of the troubled history of Gary Mathias, which was public record because he was arrested and it was reported in the newspaper.

Sterling's incident took place behind the walls of a mental institution, and records for patients are not public. The incident was told by his mother to investigators during the 1978 investigation. Within the case file for Bill Sterling, there are no records from Napa or DeWitt, so it is impossible to determine what really happened during that violent confrontation.

It must have been difficult for a minor to be admitted to a mental hospital. Bill Sterling did not have the chance to publicly defend his actions, so his confrontation at Napa was both troubling and disheartening. One of the oldest mental health facilities in California, Napa had a reputation for housing dangerous individuals staffed with what some critics viewed as a skeleton crew. The number of patients there varied from an estimated fifty-six hundred in 1958 to an estimated twenty-five hundred in 1972.

∞

Also included in his file with the Yuba County Sheriff's Department are some notes of incidents from 1960 to 1977 involving Sterling. On April 25, 1960, an eleven-year-old Sterling was reported missing but showed up later that day. A report stated that on July 19, 1972, a conviction of petty theft was recorded, but it did not state if Sterling was a victim or the thief. There was also an incident in Olivehurst in 1975 when someone stole Sterling's ten-speed bike. Also, Sterling contacted the Yuba City Police Department on August 19, 1976, to report that he was being followed. A note of a report from November 15, 1977, provides little detail on Sterling or why law enforcement was contacted.

There was reportedly an autobiography written by Bill Sterling that was in Juanita Sterling's possession. She did not share it with law enforcement during the investigation because it was poorly written and contained some "family things" that were never specified.

Bill Sterling managed to graduate from Placer High School in Auburn, California. His year of graduation was not reported, but he was later employed at a restaurant at Beale Air Force Base near Marysville circa 1970 as a dishwasher at the age of twenty or twenty-one. Sterling would often fraternize with the airmen at the base and would go drinking with them on various occasions. Juanita Sterling told investigators in 1978 that her son would be taken advantage of by the airmen because they would get him drunk and take his money since he was viewed by them as "not bright." She told her son to quit working there and to stop drinking, so he quit his job after a year and a half.

Bill Sterling and Jack Madruga would work together in the dish room at Sunsweet Growers in 1976, but their time working there was short. Madruga was hired first and eventually helped Sterling get a job there in the dish room. A year later, Sunsweet decided to let Sterling go because they were overstaffed, but Madruga was let go because Sunsweet had installed new equipment, and they believed Madruga could not learn how to work it properly. Plus, they felt Madruga could not keep up with the pace of the dish room. According to Juanita Sterling, this decision by Sunsweet upset Sterling because he felt Madruga was a good worker.

Sterling and Madruga were close friends and spent time together watching television and listening to music. Melba Madruga would tell the press in 1978 that "Bill [Sterling] was my boy's special friend." The two were close in the way that Ted Weiher and Jackie Huett were good friends.

Bill Sterling and Ted Weiher were also close friends. A 1978 *Washington Post* article stated that Weiher would call Sterling and share a funny story he read in the newspaper. Weiher would also call Sterling if he found a silly name in the phone book.

Sterling enjoyed bowling and would go out with Ted Weiher, Jack Madruga, and Jackie Huett to bowl or play miniature golf. He also loved basketball. Sterling was also an avid walker, and his mother told investigators that her son could easily cover nine miles in a day because of his fast walking style. Sterling also enjoyed going to the library to research people with disabilities.

He was a member of a bowling league known as the Pin Pickers, which was a team comprised of individuals with disabilities. It was sponsored by a local foundation and a local bowling club. Sterling's name would occasionally be listed in the newspaper during their bowling tournaments.

Dallas Weiher Jr., Ted Weiher's nephew, spent time with the Yuba County Five as a youngster and tagged along for some of their bowling excursions. "Bill bowled a lot. I remember Bill giving me tips and trying to help me. Showing me what to do, how to hold my hand, and to make sure my hand was at a certain spot when I released the ball."

Another interest of Sterling's was religion. The notes from the Yuba County Sheriff's Department states that Sterling was involved with various churches in the area and may have been friends with a "Pastor Russell" in Yuba City. Juanita Sterling had told law enforcement that their family was not overly religious, but it was reported that Bill Sterling would read Bible quotes to patients in mental institutions. Sterling was a member of the Community Church of Marysville at the time of his disappearance.

Sterling was also involved with the California Christian Singles, and Sterling's name would be listed in the *Appeal-Democrat* in 1977 as the group's spokesperson. There were various events for singles in the area, like banquets, concerts, and weekend seminars. It is unknown if Sterling had a steady girlfriend or just casually dated at this time.

Juanita Sterling told investigators that her son never worked with Gateway Projects but was involved with their basketball team.

❧

There's an image of Bill Sterling from 1977, taken at his sister Deana's wedding in Yuba City. In the image, Sterling has offered his arm to his mother, Juanita, possibly to walk her to her seat. Sterling is wearing a tuxedo with a yellow flower pinned to the lapel. He appears dapper with his dark hair and his clean-cut look, perfect for *Leave it to Beaver* or *Ozzie and Harriet*. Sterling is looking at his mother, who is wearing a white dress with a yellow flower. She has a big smile, and Sterling is the spitting image of his father.

Bill Sterling has remained the mystery person within a mystery. I spent over three years researching the case, and what I know about Sterling is what was printed in the papers or told to me by people outside their family. While it is great to hear the positive memories, I wonder what his dreams were in life and what goals he had for himself.

CHAPTER FIVE:
JACKIE HUETT

Obituaries in newspapers are valuable resources when researching families. When you find one with the names of family members you're researching, then it is the equivalent of striking gold. "How did you find me?" is a typical response following an email or telephone call. It was the way I met Tom and Claudia Huett.

When it came to researching the Yuba County Five, I only had what was written about them in the press from 1978 or what was discussed in the podcasts and articles following the 2018 resurgence of the case. Basically, what was said was that Jackie Huett was the most disabled of the group and possessed an extremely low IQ. It was reported that Huett hated talking on the phone and that he relied on his good friend Ted Weiher to be his rock.

Tom and Claudia Huett were not only able to help me better understand Jackie Huett, but they made sure the inaccuracies reported about him were corrected. The bottom line is that Tom and Claudia Huett are Jackie's advocates. They would not grant me an interview unless I was able to prove to them that I was dedicated to writing the truth and that I understood the case from beginning to end. I respected their tough love, and we developed a wonderful friendship while I was writing this book.

We spoke for the first time over the phone in January 2021, and I learned a great deal about Jackie and the Huett family. I was surprised to learn that Jack Huett Sr., Jackie Huett's father, had passed away a few years before our first conversation. What also amazed me was that Tom and Claudia Huett were dedicated to the story and wanted to be sure that podcasts, articles, and videos got the facts correct not only on Jackie but for all five of the men. What I discovered during the writing process is that the Huett family has no problem raising some hell from time to time.

 env

Jack Huett Sr. was born in Missouri in 1931 and lived in St. Louis and Williamsville. When he was seventeen years old, he made the move to Eureka, California, a coastal city roughly one hundred miles south of the Oregon state line. It was an easy decision for Jack Huett Sr. because wages were higher in California. Apparently, his uncle was making good money in a sawmill, so he decided to join him. While living in Eureka, Jack Huett Sr. was driving down a road and saw two teenage girls walking. They flagged him down and told him they needed a ride into town. One of the girls was Sara Graham, who was born and raised in Colorado. Jack and Sara courted for a few years and then were married. They would go on to raise four children together. From oldest to youngest, it was Jack Jr. (Jackie), Connie, David, and Tom.

Tom Huett was Jackie's younger brother. One memory he had of their father's family was that they were a household of eight known for more than being a handful. "When the Huetts came to the bar on the weekends, there was always a fight. Nobody would mess with the Huett brothers."

Jack Huett Sr.'s toughness would show up from time to time while courting Sara. There were instances when Jack and Sara went out together, and Jack would wait around for a guy to hit on Sara, which gave Jack the opportunity to beat the guy up. Tom Huett recalled, "He hung a guy out a second-story window one time by his ankles until he apologized to my mom just for asking her to dance."

Jack and Sara Huett would settle in Eureka, California, but circumstances beyond their control took Jack Huett Sr. overseas. During the early 1950s, the United States was involved in a military conflict in Korea, so Jack Sr. was drafted. He was initially sent to Korea but was reassigned in 1953, possibly due to Jack ("Jackie") Charles Huett Jr. being born in March. Huett Sr. would be stationed in West Germany for a few years and would not be around for the early years of Jackie Huett's life.

When he returned, Jack Huett Sr. would meet his son for the first time. Huett Sr. was the last of the Yuba County Five's parents to pass away. During an interview in 2018, he remembered his earliest memories of Jackie. "I never seen him 'til he was two years old. I was in Germany, and I knew the minute I was home, he wasn't right. Because he wouldn't have nothing to do with me at all." Jackie Huett would scream when his father entered the room, so they decided to take their son to a doctor to get a better understanding of their son's condition. According to Huett Sr., the doctor advised him that their son was "retarded."

Jack and Sara Huett accepted the diagnosis and decided to raise their son like they did the rest of the Huett kids. Claudia Huett, Tom Huett's wife, got to know Jack and Sara many years after the Yuba County Five case ended. They shared with her the Huett family history, and Claudia Huett is something along the lines of their family historian. Claudia would say in an interview, "Jack and Sara raised Jackie no different than they raised their other three kids. Jackie did everything they did." She added, "He participated in everything they did as a family, from hunting to fishing to camping."

While in Eureka, Jack Huett Sr. found a new career. "He was a plumber pipe fitter," said Tom Huett, who recalls the family moving to Marysville in 1969 because Jack Huett Sr. was offered a better paying job. "So, we packed up, and I was ten years old—it was right after my tenth birthday—and we moved to Marysville."

Another reason for the move was Jackie Huett's asthma. Jack Huett Sr. would tell an interviewer, "When he was fourteen years old, he only weighed about one hundred ten pounds. They told us move to hot country and it would help him. Well, a year later, he weighed two hundred twenty pounds, so we had… I was glad we did, in a way, but if [we'd] have stayed [t]here, he'd have probably died anyhow because they said that there was no cure for it." Jackie Huett would use an inhaler for his asthma for the rest of his life, according to his father.

Jackie was enrolled in special education programs in Eureka around the age of seven or eight and would continue in a similar program when the family moved to the Marysville area. Jack Huett Sr. told interviewers, "And he liked it. He couldn't write; he could print. Not very good, but he could do it."

A pillar for Jackie Huett was his mom, Sara Huett. Both were very close until the time he went missing. Jackie Huett never spent an evening away from home or his mother. Known for her sense of humor, Sara Huett was an "ideal 1970s stay-at-home wife," according to Claudia Huett. Sara would earn extra money picking peaches every summer to buy school clothes for her children. Claudia Huett also remembered, "When Jack went to work, she'd have his breakfast ready. When he came home from work, dinner was on the table. She had his paper next to the chair."

When asked to describe his brother, Tom Huett said, "Very loving, caring, funny… nowhere near as slow as the papers and everybody else said." When the investigation took place in 1978, Jackie Huett was viewed as the most disabled of the group, which Tom Huett disputes to this very day. It was reported that Huett had a speech impediment, but his brother said it was more like something of a lisp, and he was easily understood by family. There were reports that Huett had a very low IQ, but Tom Huett disputes those reports as well because his brother was a talented athlete who would join the family on various hunting and fishing trips and held his own like a pro.

Huett even worked odd jobs to bring in some income. At some point, Huett asked to mow his neighbor's lawn, who was remembered as an "old-timer" from Oklahoma. Huett spent hours working on the lawn and was paid a quarter for his work, which completely knocked the wind out of his sails. It was a life lesson, but Huett would find his way to the Gateway Projects, where he palled around with Ted Weiher, and they would be assigned jobs. Ted Weiher became Huett's closest friend, and they were inseparable.

Huett and Weiher had met sometime in 1970, and by 1974, Huett was enrolled in the Gateway Projects. Tom Huett has fond memories of Ted Weiher. "He was like Jackie's best friend. He was a real temperamental guy, and he waved to everybody, loved everybody, and he was like a big brother to my little brother." The Huett family not only saw Ted Weiher as Jackie Huett's big brother but also as a protector.

At one point, both Weiher and Huett were also enrolled at the Alta Regional Center. It was a place that aided individuals with developmental disabilities, and it's uncertain how often they would go and what services were provided. Tom Huett believes his brother learned about the Gateway Projects when they lived in Eureka. When they moved to the Marysville area, the Gateway Projects gave Huett the opportunity to be employed, and he would do a variety of jobs for PG&E alongside Ted Weiher. Interviews and reports stated they would pack and wind cable for the company. It was Jack Huett Sr.'s understanding that the Gateway Projects and PG&E split the costs for hourly wages, and the money Huett earned from his work was put toward a major purchase: a motorcycle.

There's an image from the 1970s of Jackie Huett in his backyard on a Yamaha motorcycle, and to his left is Tom Huett on a Yamaha motorcycle with Sara Huett seated behind him. A six-foot wooden fence is visible in the back; it was no match for Jackie Huett's first time riding a motorcycle. The family story is that Huett's first ride saw him go plowing through the fence. Later, he completely wrecked their above-ground swimming pool. This did not deter Huett from continuing to ride his motorcycle.

Jack Huett Sr. told the *Yuba County Five* podcast about another incident with his son and the motorcycle. This time, it had to do with Jackie not having a license. "The cops caught him riding down the highway one time, a highway patrolman, and he brought him home. Says, 'Is this your son?' I said, 'Yeah.'" The patrolman questioned Huett Sr. about his son and inquired if his son had a disability, and Huett Sr. confirmed. The patrolman looked at Huett Sr. and said, "Ah, forget it," and drove off.

Not only could Huett ride a motorcycle, but he had the ability to drive a car. However, he did not possess a license. Tom Huett remembers a relative who was an alcoholic, and they would bring Jackie Huett along as something of a designated driver because there were times when Jackie would end up driving the relative home.

Huett also enjoyed roller skating, mini golf, bowling, and basketball. If someone was not available to take Huett and Weiher bowling, then they would walk for miles to get there themselves. Huett joined his family for camping or hunting trips at the Plumas National Forest. He also spent time at a local lake waterskiing.

Huett happily participated in the Special Olympics. Tom and Claudia Huett have Jackie Huett's medals and ribbons, and they proudly show images of what he accomplished as a competitor. Huett and Weiher were both eager to join in Special Olympics events. They participated in the 1977 State Special Olympics in Los Angeles at the University of California Los Angeles (UCLA). Both Ted and Jackie won silver medals in the senior division of basketball. That year, some twenty-five medals were won by people from the Yuba-Sutter County area.

While Huett and Weiher were the best of friends and coworkers, they both had a romantic link to Shirley Lancaster. The report from the Yuba County Sheriff's Department showed that Huett was dating or was interested in dating Lancaster. A picture of her was in his wallet at the time he went missing, plus there was a piece of paper with her name and number written on it. Jack Huett Sr. told investigators that his son would spend time on the phone talking to Lancaster, but Huett Sr. believed that they were not a serious couple. However, Weiher was also to have scheduled a date with Lancaster in February 1978.

Something that had been reported about Jackie Huett was his reluctance to use a telephone because he did not understand the basics of how a telephone worked. It would befuddle Huett that he could say something into the phone, and someone else on the other end of the call would respond. Tom Huett said that Jackie's aversion to phone calls was a bit overblown. "He really didn't talk much on the phone," said Tom Huett. If Jackie had to call home, then he would enlist the help of Ted Weiher, who would make the call and let the Huett family know they were on their way home or running a bit late.

∞

Tom and Claudia Huett were a tremendous help with my Yuba County Five research. If I had a question about the Huett family, Claudia was a text away. If a name I'd never heard before came up in my research, I'd text Claudia to see if it rang a bell. Same with Tom, most of the time, Tom would know the person or know something about them. Sometimes Tom needed "a minute" to remember, which ranged from a few minutes to a few hours. They were kind enough to take my calls, and we spent about an hour per call on the phone talking about the case, my research, and our families.

Claudia Huett keeps an eye on social media and still sends me links to podcasts and videos about the Yuba County Five. She knows the story from the Huett family's point of view. There are days when she shares pictures of Jackie, Tom, Sara, and Jack Sr. I have images of Jackie Huett's awards from the Special Olympics and pictures the items that were in his wallet when he went missing.

CHAPTER SIX:
GARY MATHIAS

Gary Mathias had something to do with their disappearance was one of the first thoughts I had about the fate of the Yuba County Five. My opinion came from a place where I knew little about schizophrenia. It also came from a negative experience from twenty-five years ago.

During the late 1990s, I worked at a county archive in Ohio. One of our regular researchers was a man who was schizophrenic. There were times when he was fine, but there were instances when we needed to have security escort him from the building. His belligerent attitude and screaming fits were common on what we referred to as "his bad days."

When I researched the case of the Yuba County Five, I took time to learn more about schizophrenia. I read various articles about the condition and watched some YouTube channels created by people living with schizophrenia. That research changed my opinion regarding Mathias.

I understood more about how people manage their lives with medication. It was important to learn how people with schizophrenia deal with delusions and hallucinations. Psychosis was another issue that I needed to understand.

Gary Mathias is the scapegoat of this case due to his schizophrenia. There have been instances where I have discussed the case with people who are unfamiliar with the story of the Yuba County Five. When I mention Mathias's schizophrenia, I've heard responses like, "Oh, well, there you go. He must have snapped or something." Many people assume that Mathias had a psychotic episode the night the men went missing.

It was 2020 when I reached out to members of the Mathias family for interviews. My initial thought was that they would not be interested or would be standoffish. It wasn't easy finding Gary's living relatives, but I found people who were more than willing to talk about the good times— and the bad times.

※

Gary Dale Mathias was born October 15, 1952, in Scotia, a small community less than thirty miles from Eureka. Mathias was the child of Garland and Ida Mathias. Garland Mathias was born in 1927 in Myra, Kentucky, located in the southeastern part of the state near Virginia. Ida Mosley was born in Taloga, Oklahoma, and ended up in Olivehurst. She decided to leave behind the poverty of the Dust Bowl to enjoy a better life in California. Garland and Ida married in 1951, and they raised four children together. From oldest to youngest, it was Gary, Sharon, Mark, and Tammie.

Tammie Phillips, Gary's youngest sibling, is a one-woman army determined to let the world know the truth about her brother. She has been through some incredibly difficult times, including recovering from a near-death traffic accident. Phillips claimed Gary was the one who named her. According to the family's story, Gary was a fan of the song "Tammy" by Debbie Reynolds. It was a number-one hit in 1957 and was from the soundtrack of *Tammy and the Bachelor*. According to Phillips, when her mother was pregnant, Gary said, "If the baby is a girl, then I want her name to be 'Tammy.'"

Mark Mathias, Gary's younger brother, is a man of few words. When he has something to say, it is direct and to the point. Mathias remembered his father working at a sawmill and their early years together as a family in Scotia. "[It] was the last of the logging towns. You had to be an employee of Pacific Lumber to live there." The Mathias family would soon make the move north to Eureka, where Garland Mathias would continue to work for the Pacific Lumber Company.

The profile on Gary Mathias from the Yuba County Sheriff's Department shows trouble between Garland and Ida Mathias in Eureka starting on August 1, 1956, when Ida left town with Gary (age three), Sharon (age two), and Mark (five months) without telling Garland. Law enforcement was contacted, and an investigation was conducted. It was August 7, 1956, when Ida was found in Bakersfield, California, with the kids. Her family lived in the area, and she either needed a break or wanted to start somewhere new. There was a definite strain in their marriage.

"My parents split up when I was pretty little. I remember moving back to Olivehurst when I was three or four," said Mark Mathias. When Ida returned from Bakersfield, she tried to make things work with Garland, but he eventually left the picture. Mark Mathias does not remember much about his father. The exact date is not known, but it was probably 1960 when Ida and Garland Mathias divorced.

The family has conflicting stories about Garland's life after the split. Mark Mathias remembers occasional letters from his father. "He used to write us letters from a place called Neon, Kentucky." Mark Mathias would go on to say that Mathias lived in Pound, Virginia, which was south of the Fleming-Neon area of Kentucky.

Another individual interviewed for this book claimed Garland Mathias was committed to DeWitt General Hospital by Ida Mathias sometime during the early 1960s. It was rumored that Garland Mathias's family had money in the lumber industry, and Ida put her husband away to secure his funds. Alcoholism was the alleged reason Garland was institutionalized. The individual interviewed for this book also stated that Garland Mathias was at DeWitt for over a decade and was treated poorly during his stay.

Life for the Mathias family would change in 1964 when Ida Mathias met a man named Robert Klopf, pronounced "kluff." Robert was previously married, and the two apparently met at the Olive Club, a restaurant/club that Klopf owned and managed. Ida was working at the time as well. "She was an escrow officer in a title insurance company for a long time, and then she was self-employed after that," said Mark Mathias.

The early years of Gary Mathias were full of youthful mischief and adventure. Tammie Phillips recalled her brother's love of the beloved children's television show *Howdy Doody*. She said that her brother wore a Howdy Doody cowboy suit around the house constantly. Another television show that Mathias loved was *Superman*.

"He thought Superman was great," said Phillips, who added that her brother "jumped off our great-grandma's house and jammed his legs." The fateful jump landed Mathias in the hospital, where he was placed in a body cast for close to a year. However, that was not the only scary jump that Mathias performed as a youth.

Phillips recalls a time when Mathias jumped out of a moving car and hit his head on the road, which sent him to the hospital. The injury to his head could have been worse, and Mathias's family was told that he could have gone blind from the damage. "He wore strong glasses after that to see," said Phillips.

When he attended Marysville High School, Gary Mathias was the lead singer of a rock and roll band called The Fifth Shade. "Don't ask me what it means, but it sounds cool," said Mark Mathias. The Fifth Shade performed covers of popular music for the time. Gary Mathias was a huge rock music fan and loved The Rolling Stones. Mark Mathias recalled their material included "The Doors, Eric Burdon and the Animals, just the hits of the 1960s." The band won a Battle of the Bands competition in 1969, but they would later split up.

Mark Mathias said there were times when Gary was hanging out with his old bandmates and jamming with them at Marysville High School.

One instrument Gary Mathias could play was the harmonica, and Mark Mathias remembered his brother played "some awesome blues."

Gary Mathias was also an athlete at Marysville High School. Tammie Phillips remembers her brother playing football. Mathias was athletic and spent time bowling, going roller skating, and enjoying time in the snow.

"He had three girlfriends I knew of," said Phillips when asked if her brother dated in high school. She does remember his "true love" from high school, but she dumped him following graduation.

Ida Klopf would inform the Yuba County Sheriff's Department during the 1978 investigation that Gary Mathias began experimenting with drugs when he was a sophomore in high school. Klopf remembered a time when her son experimented with a hallucinogenic drug that resulted in Mathias admitting himself to a hospital because the effects of the drug scared him.

Months after his graduation from high school in 1971, Gary Mathias decided to enlist in the Army. He was stationed in West Germany and may have been a supply clerk. During his stint, Mathias was suspected by the Army of being under the influence of drugs and was eventually diagnosed as schizophrenic. The Army sent Mathias back to California sometime in 1972 for hospitalization at the Letterman Army Hospital at the Presidio in San Francisco because of the suspected drug use. By November of 1973, Gary Mathias was discharged from the Army.

"He was different," recalled Mark Mathias when asked about his brother following his discharge. Life for Gary Mathias from 1972 to 1975 would be very difficult for him and his family. It should be noted that Gary Mathias was diagnosed with schizophrenia but would not be properly medicated from 1972 until 1975. Mathias was at the mercy of the disease, and his actions were part of the psychosis, delusions, disorganized thinking, and hallucinations associated with schizophrenia.

Misunderstood by many, schizophrenia develops at certain periods in life. For men, symptoms usually are seen during the late teens into the early twenties. People can live productive lives if they manage their schizophrenia. Those who live with schizophrenia are generally not more violent than those not living with it.

When asked about his brother's issues during that time, Mark Mathias replied, "I'm not going to candy-coat it: He wasn't a model citizen." Ida and Robert Klopf would be overwhelmed with the task of taking care of Gary Mathias, and Mark Mathias recalls the toll of it all. "Well, they had to deal with it. They dealt with more than most parents dealt with in a lifetime. It was always something, but they were there one hundred percent."

Before he joined the Army in 1971, Gary Mathias had minor run-ins with law enforcement. His file at the Yuba County Sheriff's Department shows that as a juvenile, around 1968, he was investigated for possibly pulling stop signs with a group of teens. Mathias was also a suspect in some local burglaries, but he was not arrested.

Mathias was back in the Olivehurst area sometime in 1972, but he would be involved in an altercation in downtown Marysville with a gang of youths. It was around 1 a.m. on June 27, 1972, when an intoxicated Mathias was thrown or pushed into a window at Flurry's Buy and Sell, which resulted in no major injuries for Mathias. The incident was investigated by the Marysville Police Department, and no arrests were made, although they knew who committed the act against Mathias.

Following that incident, Mathias was sent to the Letterman Army Hospital in San Francisco. He escaped and reportedly walked some one hundred thirty miles back to Olivehurst. By this time, Ida and Robert Klopf were living in the same neighborhood as the Weiher family. The Army would report Gary Mathias as Absent Without Official Leave (AWOL) on January 13, 1973. His whereabouts were discovered on the morning of February 3, 1973, when a citizen contacted the Yuba County Sheriff's Department about an attempted rape.

Al Schaffer (pseudonym) was an acquaintance of Mathias's. Mathias stopped by Schaffer's home on February 3, and they watched television. Mathias stood up and told Schaffer he was going to the bathroom. When Mathias never returned, Schaffer went to check on him and discovered Mathias was not in the bathroom. Al Schaffer's wife, Veronica (pseudonym), was asleep on her bed, and Al found Mathias on top of her, fondling her breasts. When questioned, Schaffer said he could only see Mathias's back and could not see if he was exposed. Mathias jumped off the bed with his back to Al Schaffer and took off.

Later that day, the Yuba County Sheriff's Department discovered Mathias at the Klopf residence. They attempted to question Mathias, but he wanted his attorney present. The Yuba County Sheriff's Department arrested Mathias, and he was booked into their jail. Some eight days after his arrest, Mathias had an altercation with officers.

It was the evening of February 11, 1973, when Sgt. Gerald Glasgow, Sgt. Lloyd "Pat" Finley, and Deputy John MacDonald attempted to speak with Mathias because he was reportedly causing a disturbance. Mathias wanted to speak with the shift sergeant. Glasgow, Finley, and MacDonald went to the cell where Mathias was, opened it, and they were met by a naked Mathias. He escaped from the cell and went down the hallway. Finley caught up with Mathias and asked him why he had a problem. Mathias sucker punched Finley in the face.

Mathias had damaged Finley's nose and mouth, and when asked why he did it, Mathias replied, "I don't like fuckin' cops, that's all." However, Mathias was not finished with the officers. He would then make a motion toward Glasgow, who was behind Finley, and try to hit him. All three officers subdued Mathias and took him to another part of the jail for questioning.

When asked what was going on, Mathias told the officers, "I've been in the Army and I don't like it, and I thought if I hit a cop, maybe they'll let me out." Mathias was placed in an isolation cell based on his actions that night.

Mathias was sentenced on May 21, 1973, after pleading guilty to battery of a police officer while the second charge of intent to commit rape was dropped. Mathias had made a plea deal, which resulted in him being sentenced to six months in the Yuba County Jail.

It was December 1973 when Mathias was reported as a prowler at Delores Elliot's (pseudonym) home. There may have been a relationship between the two in the past. Elliot had a child who was three years old.

It is not known if the child was from a previous relationship or Elliot's current relationship, but Mathias reportedly told the child, "I thought I'd kill you once, but I'll do it again."

Two days later, Mathias and an acquaintance were doing "bennies" or Benzedrine, which was an amphetamine sulfate. According to the acquaintance, Mathias had told them that they had been poisoned. The acquaintance became highly agitated with Mathias and would seek treatment at a local hospital.

Mathias was admitted sometime in 1974 to a state hospital in Stockton, California. He may have been at the Stockton State Hospital, also known as the Stockton Developmental Center. It was not reported why he was admitted, but Mathias was picked up by the Stockton Police. After two days, he was able to escape from the facility by climbing down an external drainpipe. Wearing his hospital gown, Mathias was able to hitchhike and made his way back to Olivehurst.

The next incident involving Mathias and law enforcement occurred after 2 a.m. on July 20, 1974, when Mathias was arrested for multiple charges following a traffic incident. Mathias was driving around Marysville in a 1963 red Plymouth sedan that was missing headlights and taillights. The vehicle had Oregon plates and had become involved in a hit-and-run with another vehicle driven by a thirty-five-year-old resident. At some point following the incident, Mathias was pulled over by law enforcement and was questioned about the hit-and-run. It was soon discovered that Mathias did not have a driver's license on him. According to the report, Mathias became more belligerent while being questioned and would not stop saying "fuck" around an unidentified female witness and members of law enforcement. Mathias then said, "Fuck you, cops. You are all motherfuckers." Mathias was arrested and booked at the Yuba County Jail for driving without a license, driving at night without headlights, and disturbing the peace.

Mathias had a grandmother named Viola Watterman, who lived in Eddyville or Portland, Oregon. They were very close. The vehicle Mathias was driving during the hit-and-run may have belonged to Watterman.

However, Tammie Phillips recalled Mathias was dating a woman from Oregon around that time.

"She claimed Gary was the father of her child," said Phillips. Either Phillips forgot the name of the woman or refused to name her in an interview. She said that Gary never saw the child, and the woman never took a paternity test to prove Mathias was the father.

In 1975, Mathias decided to enroll in Yuba College. His parents assisted Mathias with enrollment. Mathias decided to take on a challenging course load. His father warned him it would be too challenging, but Mathias refused to listen. He could not keep up with the demands of college, and ended up failing his classes. Mathias grew concerned that he would face the wrath of his father, so he decided to visit his grandmother, Viola Watterman, in Oregon.

His parents contacted Watterman, but she was mum on Mathias's whereabouts. At some point, they were able to get Mathias on the phone and asked him to come home. It would be five weeks that the Klopfs were without Mathias. Mathias showed up to the family home in Olivehurst worse for wear. Mathias admitted he survived by stealing milk from porches and eating dog food. If Mathias had left the Portland, Oregon, area and walked back home to Olivehurst, he would have walked five-hundred sixty-two miles. If he left from Eddyville, Oregon, he would have walked five-hundred twelve miles.

April 1975 saw Mathias in trouble with the law once again. He was now twenty-two years old. In the early hours of April 25th, Tom and Rebecca Metzger (pseudonyms) were awoken by a crashing sound in their home. Tom asked Rebecca to get his gun, and they suddenly discovered that Gary Mathias was in their bedroom. Tom Metzger asked Mathias what he was doing in their house, and Mathias replied, "I want my ring. I'm looking for Satan. He's got my ring." Mathias was scared off by Tom Metzger and made his way to the family's backyard.

The Metzgers stayed inside and contacted law enforcement. They were able to find Mathias in the backyard. He did not have any identification on him. He claimed he had torn it up so people could not steal it from him.

Mathias gave his information. Apparently, one or more of the responding officers knew Mathias from his past incidents. When asked why he broke into the house, Mathias told the officers that he was the landlord and he was there to collect the rent. Mathias then discussed recovering the ring and made a comment about the pool in their backyard. It was Mathias's opinion that they did not keep it clean, and it was "very black." The officers soon discovered that Mathias had punched out a small window in the front door at the Metzgers to gain entry. The only explanation Mathias could give for his actions was that the voices in his head told him to go there, and he informed the officers he didn't mean to harm anyone. Mathias then asked the officers to send him to jail because he had nowhere else to stay.

Officers sent Mathias to a local hospital for a seventy-two-hour mental health hold. While in the hospital, Mathias told the staff, "They came to my house first. I went to their house second." Mathias wanted to be at that house, which he referred to as "Barnaby's house," because Satan had his ring and he needed it back to "save his marriage." He also shared that he was tired of living in a graveyard.

Gary Mathias did know the Metzgers. They once lived near the Klopf family some ten years earlier. An individual who was interviewed for this book believes Mathias may have dated Rebecca Metzger at one time or was possibly infatuated with her. It is the only reason they can think of as to why Gary Mathias broke into their home.

Sometime around 9 p.m. on May 26, 1975, a security guard at Sierra View, a local cemetery in Olivehurst, saw an old classmate resting on the ground smoking a cigarette. It was Gary Mathias, and he told the guard that he wanted to get into one of the mausoleums because there was an attic full of Bibles. Law enforcement was called, but no charges were made against Mathias.

The next day, the California Highway Patrol in Chico reported a stolen vehicle in the West Linda area. The car was parked in a church parking lot and was running. There were three men that had been in the vehicle, and one of them was Gary Mathias. One of the men from the vehicle stated that he and the other man had been offered a ride by Mathias earlier in the day. Mathias was going to take them where they needed to go, and he told the two that he needed to stop by his sister's house. Mathias parked the car at the church and walked to his sister's house. Both men in the car noticed it was running, but there was no key in the ignition. Mathias took the blame for the stolen car and was booked by law enforcement for grand theft auto. The owner of the car would later be identified as a Yuba City woman who had parked the car at the local mental health clinic.

ↂ

"People don't understand what families go through when they have a child with problems," said Mark Mathias. He remembered this as a time when Robert and Ida Klopf had no choice but to get Gary Mathias back on track. "As things progressed, that's when [Robert] got him into these programs to help him out." Mathias was cared for by a doctor at Sutter-Yuba Mental Health Services.

Mathias would be put on certain medications and follow his medication schedule to the best of his abilities. He was taking Prolixin/Plixen, Stelazine, and Cogentin. If he missed any of his doses, then he would become irrational, plus he would experience hallucinations and talk to himself. Ida Klopf would tell the Yuba County Sheriff's Department that Mathias could not drink alcohol while on his medication because it made him ill. Mathias's last appointment for medication was February 21, 1978, and his next session was scheduled seven days later.

Also, he would eventually become involved with the Gateway Projects because they assisted people living with mental illness. It was supposedly recommended to Mathias by his doctor at Sutter-Yuba Mental Health Services. This doctor also saw Jack Madruga as a patient. The doctor had also worked at the Napa State Hospital and may have had contact with Bill Sterling.

Mathias would also do some part-time work for Robert Klopf's lawncare business. Mark Mathias remembers his brother taking control of his life and his schizophrenia. "That's when Gary was in the program. He was on his medications, you know. When he did good, he did great. No problems whatsoever."

Tammie Phillips remembers Gary Mathias joining Gateway as well. She recalled that it was a step in the right direction for her brother. Phillips also remembers an employee there "threw a fit" when Mathias was brought on board. The employee claimed that Mathias didn't belong in the program due to his schizophrenia, but the director at the time was not swayed.

✧

My main contact for the Mathias family is Tammie Phillips. It took forever to find a working number, but when I got in touch, she stayed in touch. We talk about Gary Mathias over texts, and I have a better understanding of her brother and his battle with schizophrenia. He wasn't in control of himself, and it was incredibly hard for Gary and his family.

Phillips is on social media and looks for videos and podcasts about the Yuba County Five case. She wants to know what people think about Gary Mathias and if he had anything to do with the disappearance of Weiher, Madruga, Sterling, and Huett. There are times when she reaches out to me because she is tired of people calling her brother "crazy" or something worse.

There are days when we discuss the little things. We talk about the weather, and I keep an eye on wildfire reports in California. I check on Tammie to see if she is safe and staying cool during the summer. We both have the same kind of inflatable pools. We also both enjoy classic rock.

Phillips has been an amazing resource like Tom and Claudia Huett. She remembers names and recalls certain businesses in Marysville and Yuba City. One place we talk about often is the Gateway Projects.

The Gateway Projects was a place that had a positive impact on the lives of Ted Weiher, Jack Madruga, Bill Sterling, Jackie Huett, and Gary Mathias. It was developed to help others, but it wasn't a place without controversy, including murder.

CHAPTER SEVEN:
GATEWAY PROJECTS, INC.

When I started researching the case of the Yuba County Five, I knew nothing about the Gateway Projects. It seemed like a program that had the best of intentions, but I had no idea it was, at one time, an incredibly dangerous place to work.

During the 1990s I had a job at a county archives facility. Our department was part of a local program that hired people with disabilities. One of my fellow coworkers from the program was a man named Chad. He was incredibly kind and a hard worker. If I am not mistaken, he had cerebral palsy.

One of our tasks was delivering records to other county buildings. We did not have a vehicle, so we had to walk. The job was in the Midwest, so we enjoyed the coldest winters and the hottest summers during our deliveries. Chad was assigned the morning deliveries, and I would go with him if we had to drop off a bunch of files or boxes. Most of the time, he was alone.

An office manager pulled me aside one day. He told me some guy was harassing Chad during his deliveries. The guy was making fun of the way he walked and spoke. The office manager was explaining the situation while punching one hand with the other. He told me that we should escort Chad for the week, and if that guy started bothering him, then we would take care of business. Those were my orders. It sounded like a good plan.

We joined Chad for his deliveries for a week, and we didn't have any run-ins with the guy. I was mad that Chad had to deal with that kind of harassment. It was the only incident that I could remember where one of the employees was harassed.

⁊

Robert Sutherlin made the news in October 1966 when he obtained a California hunting license at a store in San Francisco. Sutherlin paid the $4 fee and was not asked any questions about his vision. After they handed Sutherlin his license, he apparently grabbed his white cane and used it to find his way out of the store. Sutherlin was legally blind, and his purchase was a way to bring attention to the fact that a vision test was not required for hunters. His visit was something of a publicity stunt done in conjunction with the San Francisco Optometric Society.

The story was picked up by various newspapers, including the *Appeal-Democrat*, the local newspaper for the Yuba City-Marysville area. A few years after the story was published, Sutherlin would come to the area with a plan to put the differently abled to work. Sutherlin understood what it meant to be dismissed from job opportunities for being labeled as "different."

Sutherlin was born in Portland, Oregon, in 1935 and was abandoned by his parents when he was eighteen months old. His adoptive family noticed he had trouble with his vision, and a diagnosis showed that Sutherlin had 20/300 vision in one eye, which made him legally blind.

As Sutherlin grew older, he landed employment at a variety of jobs, including a gas station attendant, a disc jockey at a country station, a hotel manager, and a dance teacher. His employers did not realize he was legally blind until he informed them of his condition. When interviewed by the *Sacramento Bee* in 1971 about his work experience, Sutherlin said, "When I would try and level with an employer, tell them about my vision, they'd say, 'We don't need you.'"

Sutherlin's plan was to be one step ahead of management to avoid being fired. He mentioned in his 1971 interview that "There was always this fear that the boss is going to find out, and I'd move on before I got caught up with." There were times when Sutherlin went to great lengths to hide his blindness.

Sutherlin was able to become a truck driver in the Portland area. He was hired with the aid of a friend who gave Sutherlin information in advance about the letters on the eye chart and the route involved in the driving test. Sutherlin had no problem and passed.

During the early 1970s, there were some one hundred fifty rehabilitation workshops in California that employed an estimated fifteen thousand workers with disabilities. Those workers made an estimated $13 million in wages.

At some point, Sutherlin enrolled in a business school in Oregon, which led to a nine-month program at the University of San Francisco. Sutherlin's education allowed him to become involved in the field of rehabilitation training. While attending the University of San Francisco, Sutherlin was a member of a 1969 survey team to write a proposal for Yuba and Sutter Counties for reviving a training program for people with disabilities. Sutherlin had experience with the San Francisco Lighthouse for the Blind and Goodwill Industries in San Francisco.

Sutherlin saw a need in Yuba and Sutter Counties. In 1971, Sutherlin told the press, "I estimate we have about one thousand persons in Yuba and Sutter Counties who can benefit from rehabilitation." His goal was to have these adults make the move from receiving welfare assistance to earning a wage so they could have a sense of independence and pride. He received an estimated $50,000 in grants from the federal government, the State of California, and private donations (most of it federal money) in the early 1970 to get Gateway Projects, Inc. up and running as a nonprofit agency.

"It's a chance to repay what rehab has given to me," said Sutherlin in 1971. The plan was to train people with disabilities and mental illness so they could get jobs. The Gateway Projects wanted to employ fifteen to thirty people during the first year and have some sixty employed within five years. At first, they made items for companies like wooden survey stakes and wooden bins for the local agricultural businesses, which was part of their plan to provide basic job skills that eventually led to meaningful employment.

By the spring of 1972, the Gateway Projects employed a full-time staff of five people, and they had some twenty-seven adults in their program that offered job training and special education classes. They successfully placed fifteen trainees in jobs during their first two years of existence. Their main facility was an old hardware store's warehouse in Yuba City, and they had earned contracts with local businesses to reupholster furniture and to build items like steps for mobile homes. They also provided education to those who were part of the program.

Donations and grants were desperately needed to keep Gateway Projects, Inc. on solid financial ground. Sutherlin would tell the *Appeal-Democrat* in 1972 that they didn't realize early on that there would be additional costs for warehouse repair. "That money came out of our own pockets," said Sutherlin.

Those interested in being part of the Gateway Projects had to undergo a series of tests, physical and mental, to determine if they were a good fit. Some individuals were required to be part of a trainee work evaluation program where they could be closely monitored. It was important that the trainees worked well with their coworkers and supervisors.

The average age of a trainee at Gateway in 1972 was twenty-seven. Most were men, but there were a few women. Sutherlin's goal was to provide these people with more education and job skills because he believed life for those individuals seemed to somehow end once they finished high school. Sutherlin told the *Appeal-Democrat* in 1972 that "a lot of them went through the special education trip as students but returned home to—excuse the term—vegetate for a year or so before coming to us."

People who became part of Gateway were generally referred by state and area mental health clinics. Some were even referred to Gateway from the Sutter County Probation Department.

Gateway trainees were required to give five days a week and put in seven hours every day they were at the facility. Sutherlin would have the employees clock in and out so they had a better understanding of punctuality and responsibility. Education sessions were developed to build confidence in the trainees because many of them came from a world where they were told they could not do this or that because of their disabilities or mental illness. Those enrolled at Gateway were also provided with classes in personal hygiene and community awareness.

Sutherlin's time at Gateway came to an end in April of 1972 when he accepted a position in San Francisco to work for the Bay Area Rapid Transit System. They had developed a program to hire people with disabilities to perform janitorial services at their stations. Sutherlin was intrigued by the new program, which came with a higher salary.

By October of 1973, Gateway had a new director named Donald Garrett, who was described in an August 1975 *Time* article as "a jovial, bearded man who weighed a jovial three hundred pounds." He had previously served as the director of the Shasta County Opportunity Center and had twelve years of experience as a social worker in Southern and Northern California. Garrett had experience working with people with disabilities and those battling addiction. At the time Garrett was hired, Gateway was developing training programs for "the handicapped, retarded, drug rehabilitants, and alcoholics," according to a December 11, 1974, article in the *Appeal-Democrat*.

By the time Garrett was director, the average age of an individual enrolled at Gateway was thirty-five, and they had added a clerical work course to their workshops. Gateway had an annual budget of $250,000 and had expanded to multiple facilities in the Yuba City area. Gateway had been in existence for over four years and was providing resources and services to those in the community who needed a chance. Gateway was making the news for all the right reasons, but in February 1975, everything changed for the worse.

During the early morning hours of February 18, 1975, a fire damaged a Gateway facility on Franklin Avenue in Yuba City. The fire may have started in the warehouse section of the facility, and fire officials believed the fire had been going for at least an hour before someone contacted the fire department. Once the fire was out, officials determined that over $100,000 in damages was done to the Gateway portion of the facility along with some of their equipment, including cable from PG&E. It was not a complete loss as some equipment was spared and certain areas of the building were not damaged.

There were forty-seven individuals with Gateway who worked in the Franklin building at the time, and they were assigned to another facility by Garrett. A new facility would be required, and people waited for a response from the fire department regarding the cause of the fire that destroyed their Franklin building.

Things only escalated from that incident. A Molotov cocktail was thrown at a Gateway facility on Colusa Avenue in Yuba City, and a bomb threat was called in at another. An August 1975 *Time* article mentioned that Garrett pleaded publicly with the person responsible for the attacks. "If someone is doing this intentionally," he said, "I hope they will try to receive psychiatric help."

It was around 8:30 p.m. on April 6, 1975, when the body of Donald Garrett was found in his apartment face down on the ground. He had been set on fire in what was described as "a pool of flames." At the time, Garrett was living at the Sugar House Apartments in Yuba City, which was close to a police and fire station. Ten minutes after the horrific discovery, Garrett was pronounced dead. He was forty-three years old, recently divorced, and the father of two children. The day before, the Gateway staff had thrown him a birthday party.

There were "severe burns" on sixty percent of his body; investigators tried to figure out if it was murder or suicide. One of Garrett's neighbors reported seeing a flash of light in his apartment before his body was discovered. The April 7, 1975, article in the *Appeal-Democrat* regarding his death noted that there was "an odor of flammable liquid" in his apartment and investigators found the death to be "unusual." The *Sacramento Bee* reported on April 7, 1975, that a rag was found at the top of the stairs outside Garrett's apartment. The Yuba City Police Department, the Yuba City Fire Department, and the Coroner's Office from the Sutter County Sheriff's Department were on the scene.

Local photographers showed up as well, and the scene outside the apartment building where Garrett resided turned into a three-ring circus. Gern Nagler, a former professional football player from Marysville, arrived and went after a couple of photographers. The *Appeal-Democrat* reported that Nagler "forcibly removed" one of them from the apartment complex. One image in the April 7, 1975, edition of the *Appeal-Democrat* shows the covered body of Garrett being removed from his building. Nagler would then grab the camera of another photographer who was only eighteen years old. The photographer's mother would later tell the press that Nagler only damaged the lens of the camera.

If it was a murder, then answers were needed. Investigators knew that Garrett was going through a divorce, and there were rumors of a love triangle that included another staff member at the Gateway. Another rumor was that Garrett's love interest had a jealous friend. Despite the rumors, law enforcement was interested in investigating a possible link between the death of Garrett to the incidents at Gateway. However, law enforcement would have little to say due to an unofficial gag order from H. Ted Hansen, the District Attorney for Sutter County. Hansen stated to the *Appeal-Democrat*, "We know what happened, but we don't know if there was a crime at this point."

An autopsy was performed the next day, and fire was listed as the cause of death. "There was no evidence of any injury (other than fire-related) to the body," said Sutter County Sheriff's Captain Frank Harrison to a reporter from the *Appeal-Democrat*. The Department of Justice was called in to assist with reviewing evidence while the board of directors for Gateway called an emergency meeting for April 9, 1975, to discuss their plans for a new director and named Eldrid Barfield the interim director.

Barfield did not hold the position for long because in May 1975 Gateway hired Donald Larson, a thirty-seven-year-old who was the assistant director of a similar program in Eureka. Gateway staff welcomed Larson as the new director, and they threw him a small pool party in early June 1975 at the home of a Gateway staff member. Sometime around 9 or 10 p.m., people at the party smelled smoke and soon discovered two cars parked outside were on fire. Both cars belonged to Gateway employees; one of them belonged to Robert Pennock, a counselor and the basketball coach for the Gateway Gators.

Investigators determined quickly that the fires set to the two vehicles were the result of arson. The Sutter County Sheriff's Department would turn over the cars to the California Department of Justice for additional assistance in gathering evidence.

Staff at Gateway had named their nemesis "Weirdo the Fireball Freak." Larson told *Time*, "Weirdo the Fireball Freak is trying to dictate to the community 'Stay away from Gateway Center.' And we can't survive if people are afraid." Working at Gateway with the threats of arson and murder led to at least one staff member having a breakdown. That staff member told *Time*, "As long as Mr. Larsen [*sic*] hangs in there, I sure as hell can."

Weirdo the Fireball Freak struck again during the evening hours of July 7, 1975, when Don Larson's car was set on fire in the carport at his apartment complex. Yuba City Fire Chief William Burke told the *Appeal-Democrat*, "The fire did not start as the result of a defect or damage to the car—it had to be an incendiary device." The unofficial gag order from District Attorney Hansen had not been lifted, and Lt. Francis Adams of the Yuba City Police Department was quoted by the *Appeal-Democrat* on July 9, 1975 as saying, "Even if we did tie it into the other Gateway matters and the Garrett death, I wouldn't make any comment on it."

Larson told the *Appeal-Democrat* that he was not at all surprised by the incident because "it seems to be running in a series." The damaged car was not the only bad news for Larson from that event. Tenants at his apartment complex apparently became concerned for their own safety, so the building's owner sent Larson an eviction notice.

The attacks, six including Larson's car being set on fire, appeared to be on a nonstop course. Larson was even finding it difficult to fill an administrative assistant position at Gateway due to apprehension from potential employees to take the job. A female Gateway trainee answered the phone at one of the facilities at the time and was told by an unknown male caller that someone there was "going to be next." Newspapers compared the Gateway terror to that of the 1971 Juan Corona case. It wasn't the publicity they needed at the time.

A seventh fire-related incident occurred in a public parking area at the Sacramento Metropolitan Airport during the evening hours of July 25, 1975, when a Gateway staff member's car was set on fire. It started in their backseat area and it was discovered that gasoline had been poured over the floorboards, and a lit book of matches was dropped on top. The owner of the vehicle was the Gateway staff member who threw the welcoming party for Larson. They had stopped by the airport to meet a relative and parked their car with their windows rolled down. Witnesses saw the fire but did not see anyone in the car beforehand. The fire did not do a great deal of damage to the car, but it was yet another frustrating incident for those involved with Gateway.

The July 29, 1975, article from the *Appeal-Democrat* that reported the airport fire story mentioned that law enforcement in Sutter County had "at least one" suspect in the case, but no arrests were made at the time. The same article stated that Larson was beyond frustrated with the fires because the case wasn't even close to being solved, in his opinion. He was quoted by the *Sacramento Bee* in their July 13, 1975, article as saying, "I don't feel there's any physical threat to me personally. It's just a gut feeling."

It was August 1975 when the attacks ended. It appeared that Gateway staff and those who were part of the program were safe once again. This included Ted Weiher, Jack Madruga, and Jackie Huett. It may have been 1974 or 1975 when all three joined Gateway. Bill Sterling's arrival at Gateway is not known, but it was in 1976 or 1977 when Gary Mathias would join. It was Larson who recruited Huett due to their Eureka connection. Also, Larson was the one who reached out to the Mathias family to enroll Gary because they, too, had a Eureka connection.

Family members who were interviewed did recall the troubles at Gateway, but it did not deter the five from being part of the program. Also, the family members interviewed could not recall how the parents of the five felt about the attacks and the murder. It was something horrible and strange.

At some point, all five were part of the men's basketball team at Gateway, and they became the Gateway Gators. The five were not the only members of the team, but as a group, they spent time together and practiced regularly.

❧

Gateway closed for good during the 1990s, and its corporate archives are nowhere to be found. I was not successful in finding any memorabilia or photographs of people who were part of the program.

I was surprised how little the families recalled of the Gateway reign of terror. To some, it was not a big deal to the five or their families. Yes, there were issues with arson, but it did not seem like a deterrent. Perhaps the five and their families were not going to be terrorized by "Weirdo the Fireball Freak." Others did not know about the troubles, including the murder of Donald Garrett. What is even more frustrating is that his murder was never solved.

For all the good that Gateway provided for the community, their legacy included an unsolved murder and the disappearance of five members. Both were quickly forgotten, but the story of the five would be brought to the public.

CHAPTER EIGHT:
FEBRUARY 24, 1978

I live in the Midwest, and January and February are two dreadful months. We have days of constant overcast conditions mixed with bitterly cold weather and lake-effect snow. The cold and snow are one thing, but overcast days and overcast weeks are incredibly depressing. A lack of sunshine can lead to seasonal affective disorder, and it has happened to me. I recall one January when it was reported that we had less than twenty minutes of sunshine during a five-day period.

My January and February mindset is to zone out until the first of March. Things seem to turn around by then. We have more days of sunlight, we are teased with spring-like weather, and my mood improves.

I became more mindful during February when I researched the case of the Yuba County Five. There have been times when I text, email, or call my family contacts for help with quick questions. Sometimes they can turn into an hour-long phone call or a long text chain where we go off-topic and discuss family, the holidays, the weather, and tastes in music. But I learned early on in my work for this book to keep questions to myself during late February.

The five vanished on February 24, 1978, and I do my best to reach out and let some family members know I'm thinking about them that time of year. Nearly forty-five years after Ted Weiher, Jack Madruga, Bill Sterling, Jackie Huett, and Gary Mathias vanished, their families are still haunted by that day.

☙

By the end of February 1978, Bob Hamilton was in his eleventh season as head coach of the UC Davis Aggies men's basketball team. Described as a "towel-waving, hoarse-yelling tyrant" in a 1978 article, Hamilton had no issues with giving the officials or his own players an earful at the proverbial drop of a hat. The Aggies were part of the Far Western Conference in Division II athletics, and they had their sights on finishing the season with another conference championship. Under Hamilton, they had been sole or co-champions of the Far Western Conference the previous three seasons. The team even played in the Division II Men's Basketball tournament for two of those three seasons. In those two appearances, they had lost both first-round games.

The 1977–1978 season for the UC Davis Aggies was looking great by January 25, 1978, when they were ranked fifteenth in the Division II poll with a 13–5 record. Another Far Western Conference title seemed inevitable. The Aggies were 17–8 on that fateful February night. They needed a victory over the Chico State Wildcats that night to win or possibly tie for another conference championship. The two teams would meet that evening at 7:45 p.m. at Chico State.

☙

Ted Weiher, Jack Madruga, Bill Sterling, Jackie Huett, and Gary Mathias were fans of the UC Davis Aggies men's basketball team, and they were excited to cheer them on that Friday evening. Family members interviewed for this book could not recall what it was that attracted the five to the UC Davis basketball team. "I think it was just like one of the teams they decided to like," said Tom Huett, Jackie's brother. No one recalled which member of the group brought up the idea of attending the game, but all five decided to ride up together for a night out.

Maybe the five knew the game for UC Davis was important for their Division II championship dreams. That game may have also served as a spark of inspiration for their own tournament scheduled for the morning of Saturday, February 25, 1978, at Sierra College, a community college northeast of Sacramento. The Sacramento Valley-Motherlode Special Olympics Basketball Tournament would be their big event and they would represent Gateway as the Gateway Gators. That event was a step toward the 1978 California Special Olympics State Games scheduled for June 23rd to June 25th at UCLA.

Ted Weiher kept a personal diary. His last entry was on or before Friday, February 24, 1978, and it read:

We are no. 1
Our basketball tournament is Saturday
February 25 9:30
at Sierra College
in Sacramento

Gateway
Gators

According to a July 6, 1978, article by Cynthia Gorney for the *Washington Post*, the winning team from the Sacramento Valley-Motherlode Special Olympics Basketball Tournament would be awarded a weeklong trip to Los Angeles, including a visit to Disneyland. Their coach was Robert Pennock, who was one of the Gateway staff members to have their car set ablaze during the 1975 pool party for Donald Larson.

According to Gorney, Gary Mathias would continually tell Ida Klopf, "We've got a big game on Saturday. Don't you let me oversleep." Klopf would also mention this to the Yuba County Sheriff's Department because Mathias wanted to be woken up at 7 a.m. on the day of the tournament.

Excitement for the tournament even took hold of Ted Weiher, who had purchased some new white high-top sneakers but had scuffed them while trying them out. He had asked his mother, Imogene Weiher, to clean them up before the game. A few of the five had laid out their beige Gateway Gators uniforms in advance.

If they were to be ready for the big tournament on Saturday, then they needed to practice. It was common for the five to practice on Wednesday evenings at the Lincoln Elementary School in Yuba City. However, Bill Sterling had learned that the school had a function scheduled for the evening of February 22nd, so they had to find another place to practice. Juanita Sterling told the Yuba County Sheriff's Department that her son was "somewhat upset," but she advised Bill to call places to see if they could accommodate them. Juanita Sterling learned from her son that he had called around and that a school in Sacramento was available during the evening of Thursday, February 23rd.

Jack Madruga drove Bill Sterling, Ted Weiher, and Jackie Huett to Sacramento for basketball practice. It is not clear what time they left the Yuba City-Marysville area, but Jack Huett Sr. remembered that Jackie Huett arrived home before 10 p.m. on Thursday. Huett Sr. told the Yuba County Sheriff's Department that he advised Jackie before he left that he did not want his son going to "any of those X-rated movies in Sacramento." Jack Huett Sr. always told Jackie, "No booze, no cigarettes, no girls" before he went out with the five. Huett Sr. thought the trip to Sacramento for basketball seemed to be legitimate and did not suspect anything else from the group.

Juanita Sterling informed the Yuba County Sheriff's Department that Bill Sterling left without his equipment and was wearing street clothes.

Bill Sterling had already laid out his uniform and shoes for the big tournament. Also, Juanita Sterling was under the impression that Gary Mathias was going with them to Sacramento, but Ida Klopf informed the Yuba County Sheriff's Department that her son was at home that evening, and she recalled he went to bed early. It is uncertain if Mathias knew about the practice.

The morning of Friday, February 24, 1978, would be the last time that Melba Madruga saw her son, Jack, alive. It was around 9 a.m. when the two parted ways. Melba Madruga knew that Jack Madruga was going to stop by the unemployment office and then visit Bill Sterling at his house. From there, they would pick up the others and drive to Chico for the game. Jack Madruga told his mother he'd be home before midnight.

Juanita Sterling recalled Bill Sterling and Jack Madruga hanging out at the Sterling residence during the day of February 24th, and it was 6 p.m. when they decided to leave for Chico. One or both of Sterling's parents saw him at their Mico Gas Station on Colusa Avenue in Yuba City that evening. Madruga put $3 worth of gasoline in his 1969 Mercury Montego. Sterling was given his weekly allowance of $15 at that time and asked for an extra dollar because he owed Madruga for gas from the Sacramento trip the day before. Juanita Sterling was told by Bill that they were going to their last UC Davis game of the season because the remainder of their games would be "too far away."

Jack Madruga and Bill Sterling then drove east toward the Marysville-Linda-Olivehurst area to pick up the remaining three. Their first stop would be the Weiher house.

Imogene Weiher told investigators that Ted Weiher had been at work for most of the day doing his Gateway-related work for PG&E. She remembered it was 6 p.m. when her son arrived home from work. The low temperature for the Marysville area that evening was supposed to be fifty-four degrees with the possibility of foggy conditions, while Chico was to have a low of forty-eight degrees. Gorney's 1978 article for the *Washington Post* mentioned that Hazel Haight, Weiher's grandmother, asked him to wear a coat to the game. Weiher would reply, "Oh, Grandma, I won't need a coat."

Not long after Weiher had come home for the day, Gary Mathias arrived. Mathias had spent the day working with Bob Klopf at his place of business, and they arrived home sometime between 5 and 6 p.m. Ida and Bob Klopf decided to pick up chicken for dinner. Ida Klopf told investigators it took longer than usual to pick up the chicken, and when they returned home at 6:30 p.m., Gary was not home. Ida Klopf called Imogene Weiher to see if she had seen her son. Weiher told Klopf that Gary Mathias had stopped by the house to go with the others to the basketball game in Chico. It was the first time that Ida or Bob Klopf heard anything about a basketball game in Chico.

The last stop was the Huett home. Jack Huett Sr. told investigators that Jackie Huett left the house at 6 p.m. with the others for the game. Like the day before, Huett Sr. told his son, "No booze, no cigarettes, no girls." The last thing Huett Sr. remembered his son saying to him was, "Aw, come on, Dad! See you later."

The five were on the road in Madruga's Mercury Montego, and the trip from Huett's house to campus was an estimated one hour and six-minute drive. There are two highways running parallel from the Marysville-Yuba City area that would get the five to Chico. California Highway 70 runs out of the Marysville area to Chico, while California State Route 99 runs out of Yuba City to Chico. Both highways merge at a spot north of a town called Oroville, which is twenty-five minutes south of Chico. If they left around 6 p.m., then they would arrive in Chico a few minutes after 7 p.m. They would watch the game at the Art Acker Gymnasium at Chico State, where tipoff was scheduled for 7:45 p.m. Some reports have the men leaving Marysville around 6:30 p.m., which still would have had them making it to the game on time.

❧

Tom Huett recalled the feelings of his mom and the other mothers about the trip to Chico before their Saturday tournament. "I think it was one of the other moms that called my mom and said, 'They all got this thing tomorrow, but they want to go to Chico for a basketball game.' I know my mom and one of the other moms was apprehensive about letting them go but decided, 'OK.'"

Undersheriff Jack Beecham also remembered the parents talking about being hesitant about attending the game in Chico. "Some of the parents didn't want them to go." It was also Beecham's understanding that "they had made that drive quite a bit."

Family members interviewed were aware that the five had successfully traveled out of town together for UC Davis games or for their Gateway Gators games. "Yeah, they went to Sacramento a lot watching basketball games," said Tom Huett.

Dorothy Weiher-Dornan, Ted's sister, also remembered the five going to Sacramento for basketball games. "I know one time Jack Madruga got mad at them. He drove them—Jack was the driver—he drove them to Sacramento to a basketball game, and got mad at one of them, and left them there." Weiher-Dornan remembers Ted calling one of his brothers from Sacramento for a ride home.

☙

The Chico State University Wildcats men's basketball team was having a rough 1977–78 season under coach Pete Mathiesen. Their last game of the season was scheduled for that evening, and they had a 3–26 record, which was one of the worst seasons that anyone could recall at the time. They were not even competitive in their own conference, with a record of 1–11 in conference play. UC Davis was their opponent, and they had played at UC Davis in January, where they lost by thirty points. Chico State University was going to play a very motivated UC Davis that was hungry for a Far Western Conference title.

Chico State nearly pulled off a stunner on February 24, 1978, against UC Davis. Early in the game, Chico State jumped out to a 26–18 lead, but they watched it vanish quickly when UC Davis scored eleven unanswered points. By the end of the first half, UC Davis was up 52–44 against Chico

State. UC Davis started off the second half strong, but then Chico State rallied and found themselves with a 66–65 lead. Heartbreak only followed for Chico State because they went scoreless for nearly seven minutes.

The five were seated near the UC Davis section and were treated to a thrilling game where UC Davis ended up winning by a final score of 98–86.

UC Davis was still in the hunt for a conference title, while Chico State sank to a 3–27 record. Weiher, Madruga, Sterling, Huett, and Mathias were probably elated that their team won, and it is possible that they might have been a bit frustrated that UC Davis almost blew it against a struggling Chico State.

The game ended sometime before 10 p.m., and the five decided it was time to celebrate. They made their way to Behr's Market in Chico for snacks. Roughly eight minutes from the gymnasium, Behr's was a family-owned store. When the five arrived, it was closing time and Mary Davis was working.

Davis would later be in contact with investigators for the case. She remembered the five coming into the store at closing time. She recognized a photograph of Huett because he was the one that stood out the most—he stood quietly in a section of the store with his mouth open while the others went around and selected snacks. Davis could not recall the number of people in the group total, but she found it strange that men their age would buy "an abnormal amount of junk food," which included a Snickers bar, a Marathon bar, a Langendorf lemon pie, a Hostess cherry pie, a quart of milk, and one bottle of Pepsi. They paid for their food and left Behr's Market.

At this point, what the five did next is nothing more than speculation. They got into Madruga's car and took Highway 99 out of Chico. It would split northwest of Oroville, and there were two options to go home. If they continued on Highway 99, it would have sent them directly back to Yuba City to drop off Bill Sterling at his home on 90 Toledo Street. From there, Madruga would have gone east toward the Marysville area to drop off Ted Weiher, Jackie Huett, and Gary Mathias. The other highway,

California 70, would have led them directly back to the Marysville area. Both 99 and 70 run parallel to each other and would have brought the five back home safe and sound.

At some point, Madruga's car ended up in Oroville. Madruga then took the Oroville-Quincy Highway northeast into the Plumas National Forest. This was the wrong direction from home. The roads in the Plumas were not paved in spots, plus they were driving into the foothills of the Sierra Nevada, where they would encounter higher elevations and snow. Madruga then carefully drove up a dirt road near a place called Rogers Cow Camp. They would have driven an estimated one hour and fifteen minutes to get from Chico to the Rogers Cow Camp area. Madruga's Montego ended up being stuck at the snow line on that road. Weiher, Madruga, Sterling, Huett, and Mathias then exited the car. They were not alone. They encountered a person in their vehicle on the road. That person had suffered a heart attack and mistook the five for medical help. That person was the last to see the Yuba County Five alive.

ev)

Back in the Yuba City-Marysville area, the parents of the five were trying to figure out why their sons were not home from the game. Imogene Weiher was awakened with fear during the early hours of February 25, 1978, because Ted had not returned from Chico. Her fears grew following a phone call to Juanita Sterling, where she informed Imogene that Bill had not made it home either. Imogene asked her daughter-in-law, Nelda Weiher, for help.

"'We gotta go to Grandma's house because Uncle Ted didn't come back home, and we're worried,'" said Dallas Weiher Jr. when recalling what Nelda told him that morning. Weiher Jr. was eleven at the time and recalled the morning was filled with panic. He also remembered Nelda going to check with the Klopfs, and they informed her that Gary never came home. The Huett and the Madruga families would also notify the other families that Jackie and Jack didn't make it home.

Members of the Gateway Gators and coach Robert Pennock were supposed to meet at 8 a.m. at a Montgomery Ward department store in downtown Marysville that morning. From there, they were to take a bus to Rocklin for the tournament at Sierra College. Imogene Weiher sent Nelda Weiher downtown to see if the five had, for some reason, not come home but were at the store waiting on their coach and fellow players. When Nelda arrived at Montgomery Ward, the bus that was supposed to take the team to the tournament was gone.

Nelda knew Ted would not want to miss the game. She recalled he was at the State Special Olympics Event at UCLA the year before and was excited to meet Sally Struthers, an actress known for her work in the television series *All in the Family* and her charity work.

Nelda, like other families, began to realize that they had to get the word out about the missing five. Something was amiss that Saturday.

Sometime during the mid to late 1970s, Dorothy Weiher-Dornan married, started a family, and moved to Oregon. When asked when she first heard of Ted being missing, she said, "Probably the next day. I found out that he didn't come home." Weiher-Dornan decided to book an immediate flight with her children to California. Memories of this time are hard for Weiher-Dornan because she confessed, "I went crazy. I literally lost my mind over this."

Jack and Sara Huett were also worried about their son, Jackie. He had never been away from home overnight, and it was incredibly difficult for Sara, who was very close to her oldest child. Jack Sr. was working that morning and was in touch with Sara with updates. "It was hard to believe," said Huett Sr. in an interview. "I was workin' when we found out the next morning. The wife called me at the job and said, 'Them boys are missing.'"

Claudia Huett, their daughter-in-law, married into the family after the case but remembers talks with Sara about the investigation and Jackie being missing the next day. Claudia said that Sara realized that morning, "'Hey, he's not here. Why's he not home?'" Things were not making sense for Sara because she knew Jackie wouldn't miss his tournament, and his uniform was still at home. Sara even thought about their car breaking down and being stranded.

Tom Huett was not living at home at the time but was in the area. He remembers his mom asking, "'Have you seen your brother? Have you heard anything?' And I'm like, 'No. Why?' And I remember her saying, 'They didn't come home from the game last night.'"

Like Tom Huett, Mark Mathias was no longer living at home but was in touch with Bob and Ida Klopf. They asked him if he'd seen Gary, and he hadn't.

"I just know that Saturday I called Mom later that afternoon and asked her if Gary had fun," said Tammie Phillips when interviewed for the *Yuba County Five* podcast. She was unaware of the commotion and thought her brother was at the tournament in Rocklin. That is how she learned that her brother was missing.

Cathy Madruga was also out of town when her uncle, Jack Madruga, went missing. Living in Fresno at the time, Cathy recalls, "I got a phone call from a friend telling me about what happened to my uncle and friends." It was her plan at the time to stay for a week or two with Melba Madruga if needed and then return to Fresno.

Family members drove the highways from Marysville and Yuba City to Chico, looking for the five. Some believed that Madruga's Montego broke down, although some doubted they would have stayed with the car. "If they had a flat tire, they were very well capable of changing a tire," said Dallas Weiher Jr., who added, "Jack Madruga was very proud of his car from what I understand. I have a feeling [changing a tire] would have been in his skillset." Weiher Jr. also said the five walked everywhere around Marysville, Yuba City, and the surrounding communities, so they didn't need to stay with a car if it broke down. "They could have walked to Gridley if they were between Chico and Gridley. They could have flagged someone down or found a highway patrol officer." Weiher Jr. also believed they would eventually walk somewhere to call for help. As noted earlier, Imogene Weiher was under the impression Ted Weiher could only dial local numbers in the area code where he lived, and Jackie

Huett had something of an aversion to using telephones. It would have been Madruga, Sterling, or Mathias who would have made the call for assistance.

Some family members drove to Chico to look around with no success. "My dad, my brother, and I, we actually went out and drove in the car looking around in the area to see if we could find his car," said George Madruga, Jack Madruga's nephew, when interviewed for the *Yuba County Five* podcast. "We searched and made phone calls. It was a very rough time. Very tough."

Melba Madruga tried to report the five missing early on February 25th but was told to wait twenty-four hours before making a report. Tom Huett told the *Yuba County Five* podcast the frustration the families felt being told to wait. "They said they were all over eighteen, so you can't really report them missing until a certain amount of time."

Offense report #78-534 was created on February 25, 1978, when Melba Madruga called the Yuba County Sheriff's Department again at 8 p.m. Deputy Jim Harris and Reserve Deputy Jess Loftis were initially assigned to the case. Five adult men with disabilities were missing and had not been seen by their families since 6 p.m. on Friday.

Yuba County had descriptions of the men. Ted Weiher was a thirty-two-year-old male who was six feet in height and weighed two hundred pounds. He had brown hair and brown eyes. Weiher was last seen wearing a maroon and black velvet shirt with light blue corduroys. Jack Madruga was a thirty-year-old male who was five-foot-ten inches and weighed one hundred ninety pounds. He had brown hair and hazel eyes. Madruga was last seen wearing a white nylon jacket with plaid slacks. Bill Sterling was a twenty-nine-year-old male who was five-foot-ten inches and weighed one hundred sixty pounds. He had black hair and blue eyes. Sterling was last seen wearing a blue shirt with dark slacks, and he was wearing a leather jacket. Jackie Huett was a twenty-four-year-old male who was five-foot-nine inches and weighed one hundred sixty-five pounds. He had brown hair and green eyes. Huett was last seen wearing a light blue Levi's jacket, a blue pinstripe shirt, and dark blue pants. Gary Mathias was a twenty-five-year-old male who was five-feet-ten inches and weighed one hundred seventy pounds. He had brown hair and brown eyes. Mathias was last seen wearing blue jeans, tennis shoes, and a heavy tan corduroy jacket.

They were all traveling in a two-door 1969 Mercury Montego sedan that was white over light blue. The car's license plate was California XQG 831.

Melba Madruga told investigators that all five men were handicapped emotionally or physically. She also noted that they could function in a public environment, and the five were good at communicating their itineraries with family members. Melba also informed law enforcement that the five may have been carrying $10 to $15 each.

Since Bill Sterling lived in Yuba City in neighboring Sutter County, his parents called the Sutter County Sheriff's Department, and they completed a report for an overdue person. Someone had been in contact with Gateway, and they spoke with Caroline Stapleton. The families were told by Gateway that their sons did not attend the tournament that day. The Yuba County Sheriff's Department would be the main agency handling the case since four of the five lived in their jurisdiction. After Melba Madruga reported the men missing, the Yuba County Sheriff's Department put out an ATL (attempt to locate) for overdue persons. They would forward that information to neighboring Placer and Sutter Counties along with the Highway Patrol in Chico and Sacramento.

❦

Shannon McGarvey, the host of the *Yuba County Five* podcast, stated on an episode that the disappearance was out of character for Weiher, Madruga, Sterling, Huett, and Mathias. Some of the surviving family members have taken into consideration the possibility that Weiher, Madruga, Sterling, or Huett would be on the autism spectrum if diagnosed today. "Many people on the autism spectrum thrive on structure, routine, and predictability," said McGarvey. "Expectations are important. In this case, deviating from the expected routine of heading home after the game in Chico was likely to produce high levels of anxiety and would be avoided."

Weiher was set on being in bed at a certain time, and Madruga was set on going from point A to point B and would not tolerate back-seat drivers changing the course of his journey. Some of the men were not comfortable being in a location that was dark, which was the case for the Plumas. Also, they were known to avoid the cold and the snow.

Everything about this evening was incredibly out of character for the men. The Yuba County Sheriff's Department was on the case. What was, in their opinion, a group of missing adults would turn into an incredibly complex and frustrating investigation.

CHAPTER NINE:
THE YUBA COUNTY SHERIFF'S DEPARTMENT

"You're going to California to research this case, right?"

My wife asked me that question one day in 2020 as we were enjoying a beautiful day in the yard. I told her I wanted to go, but things were difficult with COVID and the California wildfires. We knew, however, that I'd get there eventually. It was May 18, 2021, when I landed in Sacramento. The next day, I traveled to the Yuba County Sheriff's Department to review the offense report.

I had reserved two days to do research at the Yuba County Sheriff's Department. A third day would be dedicated to going to the Plumas to explore. Detective Brian Bernardis and Community Service Officer Lyndsey Deveraux welcomed me and showed me around. Deveraux had digitized the file and had a computer set up on a large screen. There were rules. I was allowed to take notes. No pictures and no videos were allowed.

There was bottled water and a decent supply of coffee. I had packed a bunch of food so I could spend as much time as possible reviewing the files.

Before I started my research, Bernardis asked me if I was going to the Plumas, and I said yes. Bernardis and Deveraux offered to drive me up to the area so we could explore as a group. I thought it was a great idea since I was unfamiliar with the area.

They left me to go over everything on my own. As I reviewed the files, I saw the names of previous Yuba County Sheriff's Department employees. I had the opportunity to speak to a few people who investigated the case for the Yuba County Sheriff's Department before I traveled to California. They told me about their experiences and what was going on behind the scenes during the 1970s. Although four jurisdictions were involved in the investigation, none had their proverbial feet to the fire like the Yuba County Sheriff's Department. Not only were they busy with numerous cases, but there was drama within.

๛

Voters in Yuba County made their way to the polls on June 4, 1974, to vote for officials and propositions at the local and state levels. Gary Miller, the incumbent sheriff and coroner for Yuba County, was running for reelection but was up against three opponents. There was Thomas Miller Sr., an investigator from the Yuba County District Attorney's Office; Lloyd ("Pat") Finley, a deputy sergeant from the Yuba County Sheriff's Department; and James ("Jim") Grant, who was the police chief at Yuba College.

Gary Miller needed to secure a majority of votes that day to avoid a runoff election in November. Miller ended up with the most votes, but he did not have a majority. In second place was Jim Grant, and they would face off in November. However, there was a bigger problem in Yuba County during that time.

A new automated voting machine system would be used for that election, and it turned out to be a complete disaster. The equipment was not properly programmed prior to election day, and some of the results from the races were in doubt. It all stemmed from the machines misreading absentee ballot results, and that discovery was made late into the evening after the polls had closed. One of the races in doubt was for the Yuba County sheriff and coroner. County Clerk Karl Cozad, described as "exacerbated" in the *Appeal-Democrat*, had no choice but to do a complete recount of the election results.

Following the recount, Miller and Grant would still be in a runoff election for November, when Jim Grant would defeat incumbent Gary Miller in a close race. The front page of the Wednesday, November 6, 1974, *Appeal-Democrat* showed a victorious Grant flanked by his wife, Gerlinde, and his right-hand man from the runoff, Lloyd 'Pat' Finley. Yuba County had selected a thirty-two-year-old as sheriff, the youngest to be elected to the position.

Jim Grant was from Kannapolis, North Carolina. He served briefly in the Army and made his way to California. He was a deputy for the Yuba County Sheriff's Office for seven years, but in 1972 he was hired as the security chief at the Linda campus for Yuba College. A few years later, he decided to run for Sheriff of Yuba County.

Grant had won the election by campaigning door-to-door and promising people that there would be "major changes" at the Yuba County Sheriff's Department. One question for Grant would be the undersheriff position. While voters selected Grant, it was his responsibility to appoint the undersheriff. Grant was mum on the question following his election, but the presence of Pat Finley in his election photo seemed to answer the question.

Finley had been a problem for former Sheriff Gary Miller when he made it public that Miller gave preferential treatment to the son of a local judge following an arrest for drug possession. A grand jury reviewed the claims and found no wrongdoing, but it all played out weeks before the election. Despite this, one month following the election, Finley was named undersheriff.

જ઼

Avery Blankenship joined the Yuba County Sheriff's Department in February of 1959 and would be with the department until 1984. His family had moved from Oklahoma to California in 1937, and when interviewed for this book in 2020, he still had a twang in his voice. Blankenship would become a detective for the sheriff's department around 1967 or 1968, but in 1974 he became "the lead guy" for the detective unit. He would end up overseeing the detectives for the Yuba County Five case and had a front-row seat to the Jim Grant era.

Blankenship had been paired with Detective Dave McVeigh, and they would work as a detective duo for many years. Their biggest case at the time for Yuba County would be the murders of Doris Derryberry and Valerie Lane. It would be the case that would go cold that Blankenship absolutely wanted to see solved. "That one kind of stuck on me, you know, when you have a little twelve- and thirteen-year-old girl viciously murdered."

Another memory Blankenship has of his time at the Yuba County Sheriff's Department was his complete and total disdain for Undersheriff Pat Finley. Blankenship was probably not alone with his feelings, and it seemed to begin following the death of Lt. James Hawk, the deputy coroner for the Yuba County Sheriff's Department.

James Hawk spent eighteen years in law enforcement and died in September 1976 in an accident. When officers cleaned out Hawk's desk, Blankenship said Hawk's prized possession, an engraved Colt .45, was missing. It was later discovered that Finley had the gun and claimed he had it because Hawk owed him money from a loan. "That was bogus," said Blankenship, who added, "Jim Hawk had sufficient money, a new home, a property."

It was also discovered that Finley was taking items from the evidence room, like money and guns. "He had a problem of taking things that didn't belong to him," said Blankenship. Two jailers from the Yuba County

Jail reportedly witnessed Finley taking items from the evidence room and placing them in the trunk of his car. That incident put into motion an internal investigation regarding Finley's actions.

On March 21, 1977, Finley was confronted in his office by members of the Yuba County Sheriff's Department, including Blankenship and a Yuba County attorney. Blankenship remembered that Finley drew his revolver, and things got tense. "Yeah, the attorney didn't confront anybody," said Blankenship, who added with a laugh, "When the guns came out, [the attorney] took off down the hall at a fast clip, abandoning us and his post very quickly."

Finley turned the revolver on himself, and a standoff took place. It was an incredibly tense hour-long standoff, according to a March 22, 1977, article in the *Appeal-Democrat*. Blankenship was one of a few individuals involved in the standoff asking Finley to put the gun down. Finley agreed, called a lawyer, and was booked at the Yuba County Jail for charges of embezzlement and grand theft. A bail of $5,000 was set for Finley.

Meanwhile, other members of the Yuba County Sheriff's Department had a search warrant for the Finley residence, and they found cash, a portable television set, and a watch from the evidence room. Guns had been taken as well, including Hawk's gun. And all of this happened while Sheriff Jim Grant was out of state on his honeymoon. Grant took the next flight home and met with officers, including Blankenship, who briefed him on what had happened. Finley was relieved of duty by Grant.

Grant had been surprised by his own officers. He told the *Appeal-Democrat* that he knew nothing about the Finley investigation. Finley pleaded not guilty to the charges, and his lawyer told the press that the charges were nothing more than "a political maneuver."

This was not the first time Finley was in trouble as undersheriff of Yuba County. One year earlier, in April 1976, an anonymous letter claimed Finley had taken items from the evidence room and put them in his home. A grand jury decided not to bring charges against Finley because the claims were made in an anonymous letter and couldn't be substantiated according to a newspaper report. Finley was quoted in a 1976 *Appeal-Democrat* article saying those claims were "vicious lies."

The Yuba County Sheriff's Department needed a new undersheriff. Jim Grant would hire an outsider, Jack Beecham, in June 1977 for the position. "That's the only choice [Grant] made I remember that I really agreed with," said Blankenship.

Beecham was born in Riverside, California, in 1941 while his father was fighting in the European Theater. It was 1945 when Beecham's father returned home. "I thought I was in charge of the household," said Beecham with a laugh. A few years later, Beecham and his family moved to San Bernadino, and that's where he stayed through high school.

After graduation, Beecham worked in a furniture store and in construction. Both jobs allowed him to understand what it meant to really work. He had a passion for law enforcement, so in 1964, Beecham tested for a position and joined the Riverside Police Department. He began as a patrol officer and would spend the next decade building an impressive resume.

Beecham eventually became the SWAT sergeant in Riverside and then moved on as a training officer and juvenile bureau commander. Beecham would find the time to balance work and family life, plus he made the effort to earn a BA in criminal justice administration from UCLA then pursue an MA from USC. By the time he was thirty-two or thirty-three, Beecham was involved at the state level for standards and training for police officers. After four years on the job, Jim Grant reached out to him for the position in Marysville.

When Beecham was hired, he knew it was toward the end of Grant's term as an elected sheriff. "I knew he didn't have much of a chance of being reelected," said Beecham. Despite the negative press following the arrest of Pat Finley, the Yuba County Sheriff's Department vowed to right the ship and take on any challenges presented to them. The events of February 24, 1978, would test them more than they expected.

യ

Jack Beecham was the first member of law enforcement I contacted for an interview. He was less than thrilled with my call. "Why do you people keep calling me?" he said. His voice was deep with a bit of a scowl, and it sounded like he had zero tolerance for foolishness. My heart sank, but then he asked me about my interest in the story. I told him I was writing a book and wanted to get the story right, especially for the families. That seemed to more than satisfy him, and he gladly spent over an hour on the phone with me discussing the case. He agreed to another interview and then asked me if I do any gardening. I told him I wasn't a "green thumb," but he said that he'd send me a package of seeds for various vegetables.

When I first spoke to Beecham, I was under the impression that he was the only surviving investigator who worked on the case. He thought so as well. Months after my interview with Beecham, I was informed that Avery Blankenship, a detective for Yuba County at the time, was alive and well. Someone from Blankenship's family helped me get in touch with him for an interview.

Blankenship granted me a few interviews over the phone, and we have also texted. He splits his time between California and a place near the Gulf of Mexico. I was invited to his home when I was in Marysville to research the case. He showed me his grove of almonds or, as he refers to them, "al-mens." The trees had bloomed, and it was my first time in an almond grove. We sat inside a barn and discussed the Yuba County Five case on a cool but quiet May evening. Surprised is the best way to describe Blankenship's thoughts about the resurgence of the Yuba County Five case. Blankenship has theories about what happened, but he knew the clock was against them when they found the car four days after they went missing.

Somewhere in my research I also came across the name Larry McCormack, a former search and rescue officer for Yuba County. He worked on the case in its initial days, when the five were still missing. It was great finding another person from Yuba County. I found him on social media, and he agreed to an interview

PART II: THE INVESTIGATION

CHAPTER TEN:
FEBRUARY 25-28, 1978

My diet while reviewing the files at the Yuba County Sheriff's Department was almonds, granola bars, coffee, and water. I only took a break when I had to use the restroom. As I previously mentioned, the staff at the Sheriff's Department informed me that I could take notes, not take any pictures. I was also permitted to request copies of the original case files, but there was a good chance those would be redacted. If I wanted the complete case, then I needed to write down every bit of information until my mind turned into mush. It did on more than one occasion, but it is the price you pay when doing research.

At the time, I knew they had a few boxes of files for me to review, but I was not told that they had been digitized. It took forever and a day for some pages to load, and there were moments that I could only describe as "the glaze." Staring at a screen all day is not wonderful for your vision, and going eight hours nonstop may not have been my smartest decision. Walking around the conference room helped me get refocused.

I spent my evenings at an Airbnb reviewing the notes. I wanted to be sure I did not miss anything while writing down the information. It was a bit surprising to me that my handwriting was legible since I was writing at a near-frantic pace at times. There were also some phone calls and texts to the family members and my research associates those evenings. I asked if they recalled certain names or incidents. Something I may never know was what the families and investigators were experiencing the first four days.

↾

Ted Weiher, Jack Madruga, Bill Sterling, Jackie Huett, and Gary Mathias had been missing for twenty-four hours. The Yuba County Sheriff's Department began work on the case, and the families went back to their own searches. Photographs of the five were collected and a missing persons flier was created for distribution, especially to the media.

When I reached out to him, Avery Blankenship recalled his February 26, 1978, memories of hearing about five adult men who had been reported missing. "I was notified about the persistence of the (parents). I asked, 'What was so unusual about these young men—not necessarily young, from twenty-three to thirty-two or thirty-three years old—not to come home on a Saturday morning?'" Blankenship would be informed that four had been diagnosed with some sort of disability while one was schizophrenic. The local media was reporting on it as well, and Blankenship knew they had to "go full out" to try to figure out what happened to the five, more so than any other case he had worked on to date.

When I spoke to Larry McCormack, who was part of the search and rescue team for the Yuba County Sheriff's Department, he explained that he would also do regular patrol work, and he remembered one of the first times he was briefed on the men being missing. "There was a BOLO, be-on-the-lookout, type thing that was put out to patrol or put out to departments. All I knew about it when it first came out was that they disappeared from Chico. I'm like, 'What's that got to do with us?'" He was told that the men who went missing were from the Yuba County area. McCormack knew they would do what they could to locate the missing men since their descriptions were available, along with a description of Madruga's Mercury Montego.

Undersheriff Jack Beecham was the supervisor for Blankenship and officers like McCormack. When I spoke to him, he explained that a plan of action was put in place immediately. Their first task was to interview the families.

There would be different investigation areas of focus for the members of the Yuba County Sheriff's Department. Avery Blankenship oversaw the interviews with family and friends of the missing. Lt. Dennis Moore's group was responsible for reviewing the evidence, and they traced the activities the five made from Yuba City to Chico. Staff from the Yuba County Sheriff's Department involved in the case included David McVeigh, Bud Cozine, Jim Black, Harold Eastman, and Lance Ayers. Ranging in rank from deputy to sergeant, these men had many years of experience and were very capable. As the investigation evolved, Cozine and Ayers became key players. Blankenship remembered of Cozine, "He was the evidence guy, the evidence tech, would gather stuff, kept the evidence room, and would gather photos." Lance Ayers would probably put the most time into the case and end up as something of a last man standing in the Yuba County Sheriff's Department when it came to involvement in the investigation.

Ayers was an Air Force veteran hired by the Yuba County Sheriff's Department in 1971 as a deputy and was eventually promoted to sergeant. However, Ayers would be demoted by Jim Grant in June 1977 for a barroom incident involving Ayers and a local attorney. Ayers referred to the attorney as a "maggot" and a "scum." Plus, he allegedly said to the attorney, "Something is going to happen to you." Whatever caused the animosity or scuffle was not disclosed but is an example of Ayers' "maverick" ways.

"Lance was an interesting character, yes he was," said Blankenship, who added that, "Lance was a very sharp guy." Blankenship was impressed by Ayers's ability to remember people's faces but also stated he was "a tough guy to supervise." Blankenship shared that Ayers required his watchful eye at times.

Larry McCormack also remembered working with Ayers. "Lance and I went to high school together. We were very good friends for many years. He also served in Vietnam. He was in the Air Force, and I was a paratrooper [in the Army]. We gave each other a lot of shit, you know, about the different services."

✌

California radio and television stations covered the story of the missing men. In what detail is not known, but the story caught the media's attention quickly. Taped radio broadcasts about it likely do not exist, and only a few video clips from Channel 13 in Sacramento concerning the investigation are extant. As far as the story being reported by a newspaper, the *Appeal-Democrat* was first; on Monday, February 27, 1978, they ran a story about the missing men. Titled "Search on for Five Area Men," the paper stated that all five had not been seen by family since Friday evening.

Since the *Appeal-Democrat* was the newspaper for the Yuba City-Marysville area, it was the publication that covered the case more than any other newspaper. The *Sacramento Bee*, the *Chico Enterprise-Record*, the *Oroville Mercury-Register*, and the *Los Angeles Times* also covered the story but to a lesser extent.

Juanita Sterling, Bill's mother, did tell the *Appeal-Democrat* that the five had made previous trips without incident, and an explanation regarding their disappearance was nowhere to be found. She also told the *Appeal-Democrat* that all five men were in the car at the Mico station when they left for the basketball game on Friday. It wasn't unusual for Bill to go somewhere without telling his mother. If she became concerned, she could locate her son rather quickly once she contacted the parents of his friends. But this time that was not the case.

She would give a conflicting statement to another newspaper. In the case file from the Yuba County Sheriff's Department is an unknown February

27, 1978, newspaper clipping. Titled "Police Start Search for Missing S-Y Five," Juanita Sterling told the paper that Jack Madruga "never took Highway 70 before" during their trips to Chico. This statement was not included in any other newspapers or in any interviews with investigators.

Juanita Sterling brought pictures of the five to Chico State University during the weekend and showed them to people who worked at Acker Gymnasium. They did not remember any of the five from the game. Members of the cheerleading team for UC Davis were asked if they recalled seeing the men in the stands. The Chico Police and Chico State University police were asked to assist, and according to the *Appeal-Democrat*, they found no evidence of the car or the five attending the game.

Juanita Sterling had told her son during the evening hours on Thursday, February 23, 1978, that she did not want them to go to the Chico game on Friday because they came home late from basketball practice in Sacramento on Thursday. Bill Sterling would not listen to her case, and he did not budge. He informed his mother that they were going to the game on Friday at Chico State.

Other family members were equally frustrated and baffled by the disappearance. "We have no idea what happened: it's just a strange thing," said a member of the Weiher family who further stated, "[Ted] doesn't do things like that—overnight maybe, but not four days." The family member would also note that the five were "all good friends."

Sara Huett, Jackie's mother, told the *Appeal-Democrat* the families were "grasping for straws" because "they had never done this before."

The *Appeal-Democrat* ran a lengthier piece on February 28, 1978, regarding the missing men. It was featured on the front page and concluded on page twelve. Also, on page twelve was the story of a missing Massachusetts boy named Peter Gosselin. He had disappeared outside of his home in Uxbridge while playing in a blizzard. His family received assistance from local law enforcement and members of the community. They spent close to three weeks searching everywhere for Gosselin with no luck. A mail carrier later discovered Gosselin's body buried in a snowbank five feet from the front door of his family's home. It was a horrible and tragic accident. In retrospect, the incredibly heartbreaking story of Peter Gosselin would mirror that of the Yuba County Five.

⌒

Early articles written about the disappearance of the five stated that the men were "slightly retarded" and that would be a term used to describe the missing men from that point forward. The use of the word "retarded" may have been accepted by some during the time, and it may have been used to bring some urgency to the case. Also, it may have inadvertently done some damage as well. That word could have made some readers apathetic because they probably had the opinion that the five were lost due to their disabilities. Other articles would also use the terms "slightly disabled" or "handicapped."

A family member of the five told the *Oroville Mercury-Register* in a February 28, 1978, article that the men did a good job of handling themselves in normal circumstances, but once the situation turned stressful, they became nervous and childlike. Once investigators like Lance Ayers from the Yuba County Sheriff's Department had the chance to meet with the families, there were discussions about the men's abilities to handle situations under duress.

Imogene Weiher told investigators that her son was afraid of the dark but would fight back if scared or hurt by someone. In fact, Ted Weiher was involved in a few minor fights at Gateway and the Alta California Regional Center. An individual who worked at Alta said Weiher's skirmishes resulted from verbal situations or some sort of disagreement. Weiher was not viewed as the aggressor in those situations. The same individual said Weiher was well-liked by everyone at Alta.

Melba Madruga told investigators that Jack Madruga was not the strong leader type but wasn't really a follower. He was not afraid to express his opinions if somebody asked him to do something he did not want to do, but he would be submissive if someone threatened him with something like a gun. A doctor who had experience with Madruga said that he was a follower but felt he was easily persuaded to do things. Also, Jack Madruga was not fond of the dark as an adult. He also didn't like to use flashlights. Investigators asked Melba if she thought her son would ever pick up a hitchhiker. She said she didn't think he would, although if the hitchhiker was a woman, then he might.

Investigators were curious if the five had picked up a hitchhiker on their way home from Chico. It was theorized that a hitchhiker could have led them to the road in the Plumas, where they abandoned the Montego.

Jack Huett Sr. told investigators that Jackie Huett was a follower type with a nonviolent reputation. Family members recall Jackie Huett did not like fights and would walk away from arguments. Huett would shut down, and there were times when he would bite his hand but not break the skin, or yell into it in an act of frustration. However, if the Huett children ever had a major disagreement, Huett Sr. would have the kids put on boxing gloves and settle their differences. Jackie Huett was remembered by his brother Tom as someone who did not know his own strength.

The Yuba County Sheriff's Department spent Monday, February 27, and Tuesday, February 28, 1978, interviewing the family of the missing and gathering as much information as possible on the five. The media had reported the story by this time, and leads were coming regarding possible sightings.

"Detectives were searching every truck stop—everything—between Marysville and Chico," recalled Beecham. During a 2020 interview, he recalled interviewing the parents of the missing men. "The interviews with the parents in the beginning indicated that they suspected that Mathias had something to do with it." Beecham recalled that Bob Klopf seemed to agree that maybe something could have gone wrong with Mathias during the trip, so Beecham reviewed what they had on file for Mathias. "He had a propensity for violence," said Beecham, who added, "He was a pretty violent guy."

In some ways, Mathias was the new member of the group. He had known Ted Weiher the longest and Jackie Huett to a certain extent. No one could recall when Mathias met Jack Madruga and Bill Sterling. Mathias "did attach himself to that group, and the parents were very suspicious of him. Didn't like it because the four had been buddies for years," said Beecham.

↜

Not long after the five went missing, a $1,000 reward (roughly $4,542 when adjusted at the time of this publication) was offered for information regarding their disappearance. Family and friends had pooled finances, and the reward money would be given by them if they unanimously approved the validity of a claim. Two telephone numbers were provided by the Yuba County Sheriff's Department for people to provide information on sightings.

It was February 28th when the Sutter County Sheriff's Department was contacted by the Sacramento County Sheriff's Department concerning a sighting of the five. It was the understanding of Sutter County that Sacramento County mistakenly contacted their county, thinking the five resided in that county. Sutter County informed the Yuba County Sheriff's Department that a woman named Mrs. Baxter (pseudonym) called the Sacramento County Sheriff's Department with a possible sighting of the missing at a skating rink in Sacramento.

The sighting by Baxter was promising since the five loved roller skating. Baxter remembered the local television station had a news flash about the missing men. She saw one of the reports at home and possibly one on television at a skating rink. While she was there, she noticed six white males that she described as "possibly retarded." Baxter contacted law enforcement and informed them that she would be willing to help the family by reviewing photographs of the missing if they were interested. The Sacramento County Sheriff's Department checked the parking lot of the skating rink where they were allegedly seen, and there was no sign of Madruga's car.

Another possible sighting was called in on February 28th by a cashier at a convenience store near Marysville. The cashier was informed by a customer that a blue Mercury was parked at the Metro Airport parking lot in Sacramento with its lights on. The customer had seen the car during the morning hours of Sunday, February 26th, and airport security was contacted. An investigation of their inventory of cars at the airport showed the car was not there overnight.

A security guard saw six men matching the five's description at a Weinstock's department store in Sacramento.

Jack Madruga's sister discovered through the grapevine that Weiher, Sterling, and Huett would sometimes hang out in the foothills of the Sierra Nevada near Grass Valley. They would get beer and hang out in a wooded area and watch people with an acquaintance.

Another acquaintance of the five claimed they would go fishing with them in Gridley, a town south of Oroville. They enjoyed a spot off Highway 99, where a canal was located.

The sightings and leads all went nowhere, and the search for the five was incredibly frustrating for family, friends, and law enforcement. It was 7:28 p.m. on Tuesday, February 28, 1978, when a dispatcher from Butte County alerted the Yuba County Sheriff's Department that Madruga's car had been located on "the old Quincy Highway" and a search party was being organized.

Willard Burris was a U.S. Forest Service worker at the Plumas National Forest. On Monday, February 27, 1978, he made a discovery on an unpaved road near Rogers Cow Camp while marking timber. Burris would later tell a reporter, a 1969 Mercury Montego "was parked in the middle of the road. It looked like it had been stuck in the snow a couple of days."

Burris did not think much of the discovery at first since the area was used by people for snowmobiling or hiking during the winter. He would later find out that the car he saw in the Plumas National Forest was the car that belonged to the missing men from the Marysville-Yuba City area. He called during the Tuesday evening hours to report what he found.

Undersheriff Jack Beecham remembered hearing about the discovery of Madruga's car in the Plumas and described it as a "critical point." The Yuba County Sheriff's Department had been hoping for a break.

Rogers Cow Camp was located some forty-two hundred feet above sea level in the Plumas National Forest. To get there, one would take the Oroville-Quincy Highway from Oroville, which is located off Highway 70, which Madruga might have been driving on the night they vanished. However, Madruga would have had to have driven through the town of Oroville, crossed the Bidwell Bar Bridge at Lake Oroville, and driven the winding roads into the darkness of the forest to get to that location. Burris told reporters that the Montego was stuck in the middle of the road some one hundred yards away from where the road had to be closed due to the snow. Later, reports would claim the car was one hundred feet from the snow line. Regardless, all five men had ended up in the middle of nowhere. Reports from the time the story hit noted that tracks from the Montego reportedly went into the woods.

Burris's find was a major discovery in the case of the missing men. It was during the evening hours of February 28th that law enforcement members from Yuba and Butte Counties drove up to the Plumas National Forest to examine Madruga's Montego. Photographs were taken, and the car was examined. A milk carton, a Pepsi bottle, snack wrappers, and a newspaper were some of the items in the car when investigators examined it initially. A program from the basketball game was also in the car, and investigators noticed someone had written down scoring statistics. It would be reported that one of the windows was partially rolled down. The keys were not in the vehicle, but the car did start when investigators hot-wired it. The car had a quarter tank of gasoline. Those who went up to investigate noticed the car could be easily moved, and they noticed that there was not any damage to the undercarriage of the vehicle even though the road was described as "rutted."

Around the same time, a man named Joseph Schons came forward with an amazing story. He saw the five on the night of February 24th because he, too, was stuck on the same road. Schons's Volkswagen bug was also stuck in the snow, and when he tried pushing the car free, he suffered a heart attack. Schons said he noticed the Montego pull up the road sometime after 11 p.m. that evening. He called out for help, and the people in the car got out. They didn't help him, but instead, they went into the forest.

The good news for law enforcement was that they had a witness, and his name was Joseph Schons. The bad news for law enforcement was that they had a witness, and his name was Joseph Schons.

CHAPTER ELEVEN:
JOSEPH SCHONS

I've connected with a few people about the case of the Yuba County Five who wish to remain anonymous. Their information has been valuable, and they've been wonderful sources. When I was beginning my Yuba County Five research, I was introduced to someone who had knowledge of the story. They were curious to know what my intentions were in writing the book. Most importantly, they wanted to know if I had a theory or series of theories.

A great piece of advice they gave me was to look closer at Joseph Schons. At that time, I saw him as some poor guy with the worst luck possible. His car was stuck on the same road as Madruga's car, and he was suffering a heart attack. All he was doing was checking the cabins up there for a skiing trip. That is what I heard on the podcasts and YouTube videos. The contact told me in so many words that Schons's story was a bunch of baloney and to ignore what was being said online.

The more I researched, the more I questioned Schons. Looking at the file at the Yuba County Sheriff's Department gave me a chance to know more about the man. The five vanished in the middle of nowhere. What was Schons doing on that road? What are the odds?

સ્જ

As soon as the Yuba County Sheriff's Department learned about their witness, they gathered as much information as they could on the man named Joseph Harold Schons. He was in his mid-fifties, stood six-foot-one, and weighed two hundred pounds, with curly brown hair, glasses, and a big mustache. Schons lived in the Berry Creek area that was just outside the boundaries of the Plumas National Forest, some fourteen miles south of where the Mercury Montego was abandoned. He was more than likely the last person to see Ted Weiher, Jack Madruga, Bill Sterling, Jackie Huett, and Gary Mathias alive. Schons was on the same road near Rogers Cow Camp where Madruga's car got stuck in the snow, but he was parked ahead of them. It was an incredible story that Schons would tell of that night, but it must be taken into account that the most important details of this case relied upon the account of a man known for his drunkenness and dishonesty.

Schons was born in Kenmare, North Dakota, in 1921. He may have resided in the Kittson County area in Minnesota and the Madison County area of Montana during the 1930s. He served in the Navy during the late 1930s in San Diego and during World War II as a pharmacist mate third class. Schons was part of the Allied occupation of Iceland, and a record from 1942 stated that Schons was found drunk in his quarters, a violation of the Articles of War. In 1943, he was sent to the Pacific fleet, and by 1945 he was in Algeria. After the war ended, Schons lived in Minot, North Dakota, with his parents.

Marriage records from 1947 revealed that Schons was living in Detroit, Michigan when he married a woman named Alice Louberry. Schons may have moved to California in 1952, but definitely by 1955 Schons was in the Los Angeles area, and at some point, he would possibly be separated or divorced from Louberry. It was March 1, 1955, when Schons was either arrested or cited for driving drunk in Los Angeles. A pattern of public intoxication and drunken driving would develop.

By 1956, Schons was living in West Covina near Los Angeles and was employed by the Pacific Sun Supply Company. He would get in trouble with law enforcement in Burbank, California, in 1957 due to a June 28, 1956 theft. On that day, Schons convinced a neighbor to let him borrow their car so he could go to the courthouse in Burbank to pay a fine. Schons took the neighbor's car and stopped at his place of employment to speak with his supervisor. Schons convinced his supervisor to loan him $75 to pay the court fees, plus he was able to get his weekly pay in advance. The neighbor and the supervisor did not see Schons again.

Less than a month after Schons disappeared, his supervisor received a call from the Kelly Supply Company in Yuma, Arizona. A man named Joe Schons had put his name in for a job, and Schons put the supervisor's name down as a reference. Meanwhile, the neighbor had to contact their insurance company and law enforcement. The neighbor told investigators that they were in "a difficult situation" without their car, insurance would cover the stolen vehicle, but the neighbor wanted to press charges against Schons regarding the theft.

It wasn't until February 1957 that Schons finally surrendered to the Burbank Police Department concerning the theft. Schons was asked about the location of the car, and he told investigators that he had left it in Winterhaven, California, near the Arizona state line. Had Schons taken the car over state lines, then he would have violated the Dyer Act, which would make it a federal crime, and Schons would have been in serious trouble. Schons gave law enforcement the location of where he dumped the car, but the report from the Burbank Police, which was obtained by the Yuba County Sheriff's Department, noted that they did not believe the location that Schons gave was legit. In fact, the police believed Schons was lying about the location because he admitted to them that he journeyed as far east as New Jersey. Schons would post bail and be released. A court hearing was set for February 21, 1957, but the outcome was not reported in the papers, nor was it in his file.

Schons was arrested at least once following the car theft. On January 31, 1957, Schons was arrested in Minot, North Dakota, for being drunk and disorderly. It is possible that the arrest in Minot led to the return to Burbank so Schons could turn himself in to the Burbank Police Department.

Four months later, Schons was arrested in Burbank for being drunk in public. He would also have issues in 1958 with traffic warrants and misdemeanors in Delano and Los Angeles.

During the early 1960s, Schons was married to a woman named Rosenda Cecelia Gsell. She went by Cindy, and they were living in the Sacramento area. Cindy Gsell was from St. Joseph, Missouri. She was a stage actress and, at one time, was affiliated with the Carter Advertising Agency in Kansas City, Missouri. Schons had fathered children in his earlier marriage, and he also had children in his new marriage with Cindy Gsell.

Schons would be in trouble again in March 1960 when he was arrested in Sacramento following an auto accident for drunk driving and driving with a suspended license. Following the accident, he told police that he had been at a bar where he drank a highball and five beers. He was later sent to court, where he was given the choice to pay $250 in fines or spend five days in jail. However, the file from the Yuba County Sheriff's Department states that the case against Schons for that incident was dropped.

His next drunk driving arrest was in 1972 in San Bernadino, but records do not state if he paid a fine, spent time in jail, or had the charges dropped. In 1976, Schons had issues on two separate occasions with a store in Santa Ana, California. It was reported that Schons was under investigation for possible check forgery, but the case ended up being cleared. Within two years of that incident, Schons was living at two different locations, according to reports. He was living in the Sacramento area in Rancho Cordova, and he had a "summer place" in Berry Creek.

∽

"I was a pot smoker and I wanted to go live in the mountains," said Tom McGarry. He was a neighbor of the Schons family in Berry Creek from 1979 until the early 1980s. Although he was not living there when the Yuba County Five disappeared, McGarry was familiar with the Schons and their reputation for being unique and, at times, unruly neighbors. McGarry was born and raised out East and spent some time in the military. A bad knee saw him honorably discharged. At heart, McGarry was a survivalist and a hippie.

A cousin of McGarry's was living in Berry Creek with their spouse. Although he knew the cousin, they weren't close. McGarry wrote the cousin a letter and explained his intentions for going west to live in the mountains. The cousin and spouse were receptive and told McGarry he could live with them so he could learn how to live in the mountains. Something McGarry wasn't prepared for was the antics of his neighbor, Joseph Schons.

"He was one of the biggest bullshit artists in the world," said McGarry, who added, "Just to hear himself talk, he'd come up with these whoppers." One tall tale Schons loved to tell people was how he stormed the beaches of Guadalcanal in 1942, but Schons's military record with the Navy did not show any combat experience. Plus, he may have been stationed in Iceland at the time of the battle. McGarry said people up there wouldn't call out Schons on his stories; they would just let him ramble on until he ran out of steam.

McGarry, his cousin, and his cousin's spouse didn't want any trouble from anyone up in Berry Creek. They just wanted to be left alone. Somehow, they could not escape their neighbor. "Joe Schons, the guy, he was like an older guy. He was out of shape. He had a big potbelly, kind of longish grey hair, and a big grey mustache. He was a roly-poly, not a threatening guy in any kind of way," recalled McGarry. What McGarry and the rest of the people in Berry Creek knew for certain was that if Schons wasn't drunk, then he was lying through his teeth about something.

☙

When Madruga's car was discovered, Schons came forward as a witness. The Yuba County Sheriff's Department wanted to get in touch with him about the sighting on February 24th to see what he remembered. It was Thursday, March 2, 1978, when Undersheriff Jack Beecham interviewed Schons via telephone. Schons was recuperating at a hospital in Chico and gave information about the Friday night sighting to Beecham.

Schons said that at 6 p.m. on February 24th, he was eastbound in his Volkswagen bug on the Oroville-Quincy Highway going toward Bucks Lake. His car then became stuck on a road covered with snow and mud, so Schons decided to push his car free. Something felt wrong as he attempted to move the Volkswagen. Soon, it became apparent to Schons that he was suffering a heart attack. There was no choice but to get back in the car and rest.

Five to six hours after he got into the Volkswagen, Schons heard a whistling noise from behind his car. Thinking there was someone in the vicinity, Schons decided to yell and honk his car horn to get their attention. It did not work, so Schons emerged from his vehicle and began to look around. There was a bend in the road, and he saw headlights in the distance. Schons would estimate that the headlights were one city block away from his car. Schons told Beecham that he was in pain and experienced a "dreamlike impression" that he saw anywhere from two to twelve people, including a woman and her baby, in the distance. At that moment, Schons decided to yell for help. When that happened, Schons stated that the lights went off on the vehicle in the distance and the whistling noise came to an end. Highly annoyed at what had just happened, Schons got back into his Volkswagen to recuperate.

It was 4 a.m. on Saturday, February 25th, when Schons exited his vehicle and decided to walk down the road where he was stuck. He noticed the headlights that had turned off earlier were on again, so he walked in that direction. Once Schons made his way to the car, he saw it was Madruga's Mercury Montego, and it was abandoned. In Schons's opinion, the vehicle did not appear stuck, and if it was indeed stuck, then it would have been easy for the occupants to get it freed. The car was unlocked, so Schons decided to go in and get some rest but then decided against the idea. There was something about the contents of the car that Schons couldn't put his finger on, but he claimed there were baby clothes or toys in the car. Schons then made his way to Mountain House, a lodge with a restaurant/bar, some eight or nine miles down the road from where his car was abandoned. He claimed it was 9 a.m. when he walked into their establishment.

ↀ

Tom McGarry remembered the Mountain House fondly in an interview, and from what he remembered, it was an old stagecoach stop that may have been built in the 1840s for those traveling to Quincy, California. "Black Bart or some bandit hid up there. The place had a history, you know," said McGarry. By the late 1970s, Mountain House was something of a lodge with rooms to rent, plus there were five cottages adjacent to it that were rented out to what McGarry remembered as "various characters." Schons frequented the establishment, and so did McGarry, who recalled it was a place with a "hippie clique" and was the only place in the area that could serve as something like a hotel or motel.

The story of Schons having his car stuck in the snow and having a heart attack was nothing new to Tom McGarry. "Schons, the guy was always having a heart attack. He had angina or something. It was the excuse [he] used to get people to help him. We all, at one time or another, towed him out." McGarry recalled that Schons would spend his days getting drunk and driving his car around the area. "I towed him out of a ditch five or six times, and so did everyone else."

ↀ

When Schons returned home from Mountain House, he told his wife, Cindy Schons, a tale about a pickup truck at the scene as well that evening. Schons claimed he did not remember relaying this information to his wife, but Schons told Beecham about the truck because his wife had informed him that's what he told her. A hallucination was Schons's explanation of the truck, but he went on to add that his wife and a family friend got his Volkswagen unstuck the next day.

The Yuba County Sheriff's Department sent Detective Bud Cozine to interview Cindy Schons on March 7th to see what she remembered about February 24th and what happened to her husband that evening. At the time, Schons was at the Oroville Medical Center due to his heart attack. Hospital admission files for Joseph Schons were not included in the case file. When Cozine introduced himself to Cindy Schons, she told him she was getting ready to take her husband home. Detective Cozine convinced Cindy Schons to give her side of the story.

When asked about his memories of Cindy Schons, Tom McGarry said, "She was like a sourpuss brunette with pigtails. She looked like she ate something that didn't agree with her." During his time in Berry Creek, McGarry recalled the "toxicity" of Joe and Cindy Schons because he remembered the couple had a reputation for spreading malicious lies about the residents. When the residents tried to get to the bottom of the story, they found out it originated from Joe or Cindy Schons. "She was a real battle ax, you know, she was a trip."

When questioned by Cozine, Cindy Schons remembered arriving at the Berry Creek residence with her daughter around noon on Saturday, February 25th and finding Joseph Schons in bed. He informed Cindy and their daughter that his car was stuck up near Mountain House and that he was not feeling well. Cindy Schons took her daughter to Mountain House to see what she could do about retrieving the Volkswagen.

Irene Aycock, a proprietor at Mountain House, was given the full story by Schons and asked if they could get someone to help her get the car unstuck. The person was Henry Davis (pseudonym), and Davis decided to help Schons and her daughter. They made their way to where the Volkswagen was stuck. When asked to describe what the area looked like, Schons told Cozine that "Joe made quite a mess." According to Schons, there was vomit and feces near the car.

There was a Forest Service pickup truck parked up there as well, and Davis found a shovel in the bed to use to dig out the Volkswagen. Schons stated that with the help of her daughter and Davis, they moved her husband's car, which was some twenty to thirty feet from a Mercury Montego. Cindy Schons told Detective Cozine that she had written down the license plate of the Montego but had misplaced it by the time of their interview.

Cindy Schons attempted to start the Volkswagen by popping the clutch but soon learned the car was out of gas and the battery was dead. It was decided that Schons would go back on Sunday with an acquaintance to put gas in the car and jumpstart it. Sometime between 10 a.m. and noon on Sunday, February 26th, Cindy Schons returned with another person named Dennis Sanders (pseudonym), and they were able to get Schons's car out of the area. Cindy Schons then went to Mountain House to tell someone there that she had moved the car.

Once Cindy Schons told Cozine her story, he asked her to tell him what her husband had told her about his February 24th heart attack.

Joseph Schons told his wife he was up at the location where he became stuck to check the snow line. He then had a heart attack, became very ill, and decided to rest in his vehicle. Later, someone (or some people) was shining lights into his vehicle, and it woke him up. Schons claimed he waved his hands and told the people that he was sick, but they all just walked away. The next move for Joseph Schons, according to his wife, was to get out of the car and walk down the road toward a snowbank. Joseph Schons said that, from that point, he could see down the road toward the Montego, but there was another vehicle behind it, possibly a pickup truck. Cindy Schons said that her husband saw two figures near the Montego and two at the pickup. Although Joseph Schons told his wife the second vehicle was a pickup, he did not go into any detail about the vehicle. Also, Joseph Schons told his wife that the lights from the second vehicle were on, and it was hard to see the figures around the car because the lights shined off the snow. It was also noted by Cindy Schons that her husband kept talking about how bright the moon was that evening. Although the people from the car and truck wouldn't help Joseph Schons, he told his wife he was able to walk back down to Mountain House, where he found someone to drive him home.

Detective Cozine had finished up with Cindy Schons, but he decided to take the opportunity to interview Joseph Schons again. The second interview took place on March 7th at the Oroville Medical Center.

Joseph Schons told Detective Cozine that during the afternoon hours of February 24th, he was at his place in Berry Creek, which Schons described as "a vacation establishment." By 5 p.m., he had grown bored and decided to stop by the Brush Creek Bar to have a beer. From there, he went to Mountain House to have another beer. It was somewhere between 5:30 p.m. and 6 p.m. when Schons decided to leave to check the snow line. He knew his wife and daughter were going to come up from Rancho Cordova, so he drove up the Oroville-Quincy Highway to a spot where they could have fun in the snow. When Schons made his way up a road near Rogers Cow Camp, his car "bottomed out" because he lost traction and got stuck in the snow. This happened between 6 p.m. and 6:30 p.m., according to Schons. After thirty minutes of trying to get his car unstuck, he moved it twelve feet and then began to feel incredibly ill, and there were terrible pains in his chest. Schons began vomiting and claimed he was sweating profusely as well. He went back into the car, turned it on along with the headlights, and tried warming himself up.

Due to his illness, Schons claimed he left the car multiple times to vomit and defecate. Then Schons claimed that it was sometime around 11 p.m. or midnight when he heard a whistling sound that resembled a person calling for a dog. Also, lights from a flashlight were shone into his vehicle but the windows were fogged up and he could not make out the figure or figures outside his car. Schons claimed he rolled down a window in his car ever so slightly and told the person or persons outside the car that he was sick and in need of help. There was no response, and the person or people outside of his car walked down the road back toward Mountain House. Schons claimed that he tried calling them again to no avail. The only thing he could do was get out of the car and get help. Claiming it was a "laborious task," Schons crawled out of the car and made it to a snowbank.

From that point, Schons witnessed two vehicles in the distance. The first was a light-colored car that he immediately thought was a Ford but turned out to be Madruga's Montego. A rust-colored pickup truck was behind it at an angle with the lights on, and that made it hard for Schons to fully see the people walking around the Montego. What Schons witnessed next was that all the people got into the pickup truck and drove away.

The help Schons wanted had left, so he made the decision to get back in his Volkswagen, which he claimed was still running with the lights on, to get warm. Not long after he returned to the car, it ran out of gas. A few hours later, Schons was shivering in the cold and decided it was time to walk back to Mountain House. He did not immediately get out but spent the time "psyching himself up" for the long walk back to Mountain House. Two hours would pass when Schons finally emerged from the vehicle. It was Saturday, February 25th, at 4:00 a.m., when Schons decided to walk.

As he walked down the road, he made it to the Montego. Schons claimed he was able to open the driver's side door, and the dome light came on, showing him a bunch of items strewn about, which made him think of a child. Schons could not think of a reason why he thought of a child, but he just did.

Schons walked away from the Montego and made a difficult trek to Mountain House, an estimated eight miles away. Schons told Cozine that he would walk thirty to forty feet and then either collapse or lower himself to the road. It was 10 a.m. when Schons walked into Mountain House and requested a ride home. A man and his girlfriend offered him a ride, and Schons recalled he never thanked them for their hospitality. He would go immediately to bed. He next remembered that his wife and daughter arrived home at noon. They went off to try to get the car, but at 6 p.m. that evening, he was taken to the Oroville Medical Center, where he was admitted.

In the notes from the second interview with Joseph Schons, Detective Cozine noted a few things about Schons's demeanor. There was an attitude change with Schons when pressed for details. Cozine noted that Schons was redundant in those moments. Cozine noticed Schons would walk freely around his bed when describing the details, and sometimes he would sit on the edge of the bed. When Cozine inquired further about what Schons saw from the snowbank, Schons became very defensive. One moment that was particularly odd to Cozine was when Schons leaned back in his bed with both hands behind his head, saying, "I get the feeling you guys think I know something about these dudes."

Cozine then asked Schons about his time in the hospital, and Schons admitted that he was an emotional wreck during the first few days. Schons admitted that he was constantly crying and could not even communicate with his own wife due to his state. What may have triggered this reaction was Schons being asked by someone about the events of late Friday and early Saturday.

❧

The next step was to find those who interacted with Joseph and Cindy Schons from February 24th until February 26th to see what they could recall. Detective Cozine headed to Mountain House and interviewed anyone who saw the vehicles owned by Schons or Madruga.

Josephine Berman was the owner of Mountain House, and on March 8th, she agreed to an interview with Cozine. Berman remembered Joseph Schons coming into Mountain House around 5:30 p.m. on Friday, February 24th, and that he consumed three beers. They discussed dogs and them biting various people. Sometime between 5:30 p.m. and 6 p.m., Schons left Mountain House, and Berman saw him get into his Volkswagen. He decided to drive north toward the snow, which she found to be incredibly odd because people would get stuck up that way, and it wasn't a road where someone would run into someone else that time of day if stuck. Berman went back to work and told Cozine she did not recall if she saw Schons's vehicle the rest of the evening. However, Berman told Cozine that he should talk to Irene Aycock because she was the one who saw Schons at Mountain House on the 25th.

Irene Aycock was working at Mountain House that Saturday morning and witnessed Schons enter the building at 8:50 a.m. She said that Schons walked up to the bar and requested a glass of water and two Bufferin, an over-the-counter medication that is a combination of aspirin and an antacid. She then remembered that Schons put an elbow on the bar and placed his hand on his head. Aycock then told Cozine that Schons told her, "I should have done this two years ago." He then inquired if anyone could give him a ride home, and Aycock remembered that Schons was holding his head and his chest. Aycock noticed Dan Fink (pseudonym) was in the bar and asked him if he would give Schons a ride home. Fink was there with his girlfriend, Sandy Taylor (pseudonym).

Fink was interviewed as well and corroborated the statements made by Berman and Aycock, plus he also heard Schons say, "I should have done this two years ago." Fink and Taylor agreed to drive Schons back to his Berry Creek residence, and Fink told investigators that Schons was highly irritated with Fink's driving and was constantly telling him how to drive the car. While they were driving, Schons admitted that the reason he became stuck on the road was because another car tailgated him. A description of that car was never provided by Schons. Also, Schons complained that his physical stress was due to the car being stuck.

Berman, Aycock, Fink, and Taylor were asked if Schons ever said anything about suffering a heart attack. All four stated that Schons made no claims about suffering a heart attack, but Taylor heard Schons complain about chest pains. Aycock said Schons complained about chest pain when he put his hand on his chest. He did look tired to everyone, but they assumed it was because he had to walk eight or nine miles to Mountain House.

Berman and Aycock were asked about the presence of Cindy Schons at Mountain House on Saturday, February 25th. They said that Cindy Schons and her daughter showed up at 2 p.m. to retrieve the Volkswagen.

It did not seem like a good idea for Schons to go up to get the car with her daughter alone, so it was suggested that Henry Davis escort them. Berman and Aycock stated that Schons, her daughter, and Davis returned before dark, claiming they could not get the vehicle started. However, both told investigators that Cindy returned Sunday at noon with Dennis Sanders, and they returned with Joe Schons's Volkswagen some two hours later.

❧

The Yuba County Sheriff's Department would learn that on Saturday the 25th and Sunday the 26th, some other individuals had witnessed the Mercury Montego and the Volkswagen on the same road in the Plumas National Forest. Larry Nelson was discovered to be the person who owned the Forestry Service pickup truck that Cindy Schons and Henry Davis saw on Saturday.

Nelson, a resident of Berry Creek, was interviewed by Detective Cozine. He stated he drove up the Oroville-Quincy Highway on Saturday, February 25th, and made his way up a road near Rogers Cow Camp to do some cross-country skiing. It was 10 a.m. when Nelson noticed a Mercury Montego in the middle of it. He had a shovel and cleared a path around the Montego, which Nelson stated was sitting on top of five or six inches of snow. In Nelson's opinion, it would not have been hard to get the car unstuck, but he did see skid marks behind the rear tires. Spinning the tires would have caused that, according to Nelson. He then made his way to a bend and saw some forty to fifty feet ahead of him a Volkswagen that was also stuck in the snow. What he remembered about the Volkswagen was the rear trunk was open and he could see the engine. Nelson was under the impression someone had been working on the engine.

Cozine then asked Nelson if he noticed feces or vomit around the Volkswagen. Nelson saw what looked to him like a pile of "dog shit" but saw nothing in the way of vomit. Cozine asked Nelson if he could detect vomit by smell, and Nelson was certain he could. Nelson spent the rest of his time skiing and returned to the site after 2 p.m. but before it became dark. He did see that the Volkswagen had been moved closer toward the Montego, which he thought had been moved as well. When asked if he remembered anything about the Montego, Nelson claimed that he saw that the left rear window of the car was open.

Dennis Sanders, the second person to assist Cindy Schons, told Cozine that there were people playing in the snow on February 26th and there were four or five four-wheel drive vehicles in the area. When asked to describe one of the vehicles, Sanders recalled one was a light blue Ford Bronco. Cozine would find one of the individuals who was playing in the snow, but they did not remember seeing a light blue Ford Bronco.

People who were at the Rogers Cow Camp area between February 25th and February 26th were interviewed by the Yuba County Sheriff's Department. It is unknown if the people came forward or if a tip led investigators to the individuals. A woman from Gridley, California, was on that road on Sunday, February 26th, with her boyfriend and some of their friends. They took two to three four-wheel-drive vehicles on the same road where Schons's Volkswagen and Madruga's Mercury were stuck. One of the four-wheel-drive vehicles driven by the group became stuck near Schons's and Madruga's vehicles. They were able to get the vehicle unstuck and spent some time up that way having a picnic and playing in the snow. The woman stated that a light blue Bronco or Jeep came up the road and became stuck in the same area where their friend's car was stuck. They drove around that vehicle while it was still stuck and headed home. When asked about the Montego, the woman recalled that all the windows were rolled up and nothing looked unusual.

&

The Yuba County Sheriff's Department and the families had a location for the car, but they also had a witness in Schons. Finding Madruga's car in the Plumas National Forest was truly shocking and baffling for everyone. Finding out about Schons was a definite lead in the right direction, but Schons seemed more interested in telling a story about how he suffered a heart attack and how nobody helped.

The first newspaper Joseph Schons spoke to may have been the *Appeal-Democrat* either at the end of February or the beginning of March. His story that appeared in the article "Man May Have Seen Lost Five" ran on March 2, 1978, and was credited to reporter Milt Carland. Joseph Schons's stories differed from the Yuba County Sheriff's Department, and became a tangled mess in the papers.

Schons told the *Appeal-Democrat* that his car was stuck in the road, and he suffered a heart attack while trying to move his Volkswagen. It was around midnight when Schons heard two whistling noises, so he got out of his car, walked down the road toward a bend, and saw a vehicle. People were moving around it, and Schons called out to them for help. "I called out, and they moved away. I was very angry," said Schons to the press. When mysterious people refused to help, Schons went back into his car. When it ran out of gas at 4 a.m., he got out and walked down the road in search of assistance.

When he approached their car, Schons decided to shout to see if anyone was out in the wilderness, but he told the *Appeal-Democrat*, "Nothing stirred." Schons reported that he made it to Mountain House, where he informed the staff that a second car was stuck on the road. He also claimed that the staff at Mountain House failed to report the second car, but they were able to give him a ride directly to the hospital.

With his name available to the press, Schons would talk to other newspapers about his experiences during those late hours when the five disappeared.

A March 8th article for the *Oroville Mercury-Register* featured an interview with Schons following his release from the hospital. He did admit to drinking a few beers at Mountain House, but he told the reporter, "I just wanted to see the snow, and it carried me further than I wanted to go." The heart attack experienced by Schons was given a different spin. "I thought I was a goner, and I wanted it to be speedy."

All Schons could do was rest in his vehicle. "I just laid there for a while with my feet outside the car. I didn't have the strength to lift them inside," said Schons to the *Oroville Mercury-Register*. Following a period of rest, Schons brought his feet into the car, and he turned it on to stay warm. Schons said, next it was 10 p.m., and he was drenched with sweat when headlights appeared from behind his Volkswagen. "Help, I'm a sick man!" he called off into the distance, but there was no reply. Nothing. He then claimed that it was a few hours later when he heard whistling noises.

At that point, Schons had enough energy to get himself out of his vehicle, where he walked up to a small slope and saw the headlights of another vehicle off in the distance. A group of people was near that vehicle, and he believed there was a woman and a child among them. Schons would, at times, claim he saw anywhere from two to twelve people. "Help, I've had a heart attack! Please! Please!" Schons told the paper that nobody responded, and the lights of the vehicle turned off. He also stated there was a pickup truck behind the first vehicle.

"I thought they ran away from me," said Schons, who added, "I laid there in the snow and cried." All Schons could do was get back into his vehicle and rest more. He then told the story of the difficult walk to Mountain House, which lasted from 4 a.m. until 10 a.m. This story mentioned his trouble walking and him having to take various breaks. The March 8th article said Schons may have stopped "fifty to seventy-five times" to get a breather and his strength up. But in this article, there were some new bits of information.

Schons claimed that he got into Madruga's vehicle to rest in the front seat, but he told the *Appeal-Democrat* he only looked inside the vehicle. This time, he also told the press that he was "a rehabilitative therapist." Schons had a previous record of being employed as a salesperson in the stationery industry, and nothing showed he performed any therapy or counseling work in the state of California.

McGarry remembered that Schons always had "a flair for the dramatic." He did recall Schons telling people that he was a "drug and alcohol counselor," but McGarry never saw Schons go off to work. He was always hanging around Berry Creek and up to his usual shenanigans.

Schons was not done talking to the press. He was interviewed by the *Los Angeles Times* for a March 10, 1978, article. Schons claimed in that article his car became stuck in the snow because he was checking on his cabin. The residence in Berry Creek was supposed to be the family cabin, but he was fourteen miles north of said cabin. This was either a lie from Schons or a misunderstanding.

The same article has two vehicles pulling up some twenty feet behind his vehicle, which is not the city block he described earlier. Schons asked the people for help, and everyone drove away in a single vehicle. However, Schons would tell the *Los Angeles Times*, "I was half-conscious, not lucid, and in deep pain," when asked about the second vehicle. "Whether I half-saw or half-imagined the second vehicle, I just don't know," added Schons. He was certain he had seen Jack Madruga's Mercury Montego.

Schons would go on to tell the tale of his walk from his car to Mountain House. He would claim a manager there drove him home, which was not what witnesses at Mountain House told investigators. Schons then stated his wife drove him to a hospital. The *Los Angeles Times* article would have Schons stating his wife was the one who reminded him about seeing a pickup truck, but he had no idea why he mentioned it to her in the first place. That article may have been the last one that featured an actual interview with Schons.

☙

Avery Blankenship from the Yuba County Sheriff's Department was asked about the validity of Schons and his stories. Blankenship stated, "I don't think his story has any credibility whatsoever. This guy is bogus all the way around, in my view." Blankenship does not believe Schons had anything to do with the disappearance of the five but claims that Schons was "making stuff up as he went along."

Undersheriff Jack Beecham shared his thoughts on Schons and his story with the *Sacramento Bee* in a March 3, 1978, article. "His recollections are almost like a dream—he was a sick man. But he did recall some things that were substantiated." Beecham would also inform the *Sacramento Bee* that Schons's recollections had them investigating the possibility that the missing men were not in that location.

Tom McGarry never believed one word of Schons's account. "Who would misdirect the police in an important survival situation? People's lives were in danger. He just wanted to hear himself talk." McGarry isn't sure how much of Schons's story about the evening of February 24, 1978, is actually true, but he did have one thing to say about the incident: "The worst thing that could have happened to those guys was running into that idiot."

ⓔ✧っ

I believe 1971 was an amazing year for music. I'm not trying to digress, but *Who's Next* by The Who is packed with some amazing tunes. Pete Townshend's work included some classic tracks like "Baba O'Reilly" and "Won't Get Fooled Again." However, the standout track is "My Wife," which was written and sung by bassist John Entwistle.

"My Wife" is about a drunk who gets arrested, and quickly fears for his life. He's not afraid of the cops or time in jail. He worries about the wrath of his wife. When I hear that song, I think of Schons and his escapades in the Plumas. I see him stuck in a ditch after downing a few beers. He's waiting for someone to tow him out and thinking of one hell of a story to tell that person. In my mind, Schons must figure out what he will tell Cindy.

After reviewing the case files and newspaper articles, I have no idea what Joseph Schons saw the night the Yuba County Five went missing. His stories vary, which is infuriating. What's worse is that Schons was more interested in talking about his heart attack than the disappearance of Weiher, Madruga, Sterling, Huett, and Mathias.

If he saw the men vanish into the Plumas, then he should have known the five were doomed. Witnesses at Mountain House who saw Schons the next morning said he mentioned nothing of a heart attack. Schons did not even talk about his encounter with the five or Madruga's Montego. The ball was in his court, and he did nothing.

I still can't stop thinking about the odds. How did Schons end up on the same road in the middle of nowhere with Weiher, Madruga, Sterling,

Huett, and Mathias? The Plumas National Forest is just over one million acres of land. Known for its majestic beauty, it is also a place where others have vanished.

CHAPTER TWELVE:
THE PLUMAS

"The Plumas National Forest, it ain't no joke, man," said Tom McGarry during an interview about his time living there during the late 1970s and early 1980s. He has read articles and blogs about what people believe happened to the Yuba County Five up there, but in McGarry's opinion, they have no idea because they've never experienced it in person. "A lot of people don't understand how rugged that area is."

I saw it myself in 2021 when I first visited Marysville to research the case. Brian Bernardis and Lyndsey Deveraux from the Yuba County Sheriff's Department drove me up to the road where the Yuba County Five disappeared in the Plumas. We arrived sometime after 10 a.m., and it was obvious we were leaving the relatively flat area of Oroville for a more rugged and scenic area. The roads continuously wound their way into the foothills of the Sierra Nevada.

The temperature dropped the more we drove up. My ears popped a few times, and some snowflakes hit the windshield. It was late May, and the air was just above freezing. We stopped so I could get some pictures. I walked to the side of the road and looked down one incredible drop. The whole area was treacherous, and I was glad I didn't journey up there alone.

What I also noticed was the damage from the 2018 and 2020 wildfires. We passed by Berry Creek, and I saw the destruction to the forest and to homes. When I talked with McGarry, he said he had moved away from the Plumas years before but that he had reached out to his friends still out in the area, and learned that places like Mountain House were lost during one of the fires.

૭৩

The Forest Service is part of the United States Department of Agriculture. Founded in 1905 during the presidency of Teddy Roosevelt, the goal of the Forest Service was to provide quality water and timber to the people of the United States. Wildlife was provided some protection, and the forests also allowed recreational activities. The overall size of the national forests by 2022 was one hundred ninety-three million acres of land, and the Plumas National Forest made up some one million acres of that total.

Designated as a national forest in 1905, the Plumas National Forest is a mountainous region with the Cascades to the north and the Sierra Nevada to the south. Elevations range from three thousand to eight thousand feet, and recreational activities there include hiking, fishing, hunting, skiing, and snowmobiling. Visitors enjoy camping and they also have access to some twenty lakes.

"I bought a place in 1981 and lived on Four Trees Road, which is probably like, it was one road over from where the Yuba (County) guys ended up," said McGarry, who added, "I built a cabin up there and I lived up there for like a year. I'm very familiar with the area." McGarry recalled trips to an area known as Coyote Gap. The elevation, according to McGarry, was three thousand or four thousand feet. He lived up there, drove around up there, and had a bunch of adventures. He remembers taking walks and seeing mountains in the distance with some snow on them in June. "There were big timbers up there as well. They had one hundred fifty feet of sugar pines; they were logging old-growth timber out there."

ᜆ

While people enjoyed what the Plumas had to offer, there were those who went missing in the massive forest and the foothills.

It was January 1907 when Jacob Myers, an eighty-two-year-old man who lived in a cabin west of Quincy, California, in the Plumas National Forest in an area known as Hungarian Hill, went missing. Myers reportedly had lived in that area for forty years and was an immigrant from Switzerland. He was one of many who made their way to California to find their riches mining in the hills. Those who knew Myers said he lived a humble life alone. Myers was known to make weekly trips to Quincy, but when he didn't show up one week, someone went to check on him at his cabin. They were not able to find Myers there, but the individual checking on him reported the snow depth around his cabin was four or five feet deep. It was their conclusion that Myers may have fallen and was buried in the snow somewhere.

Attempts were made to locate Myers's body, and those searching theorized he may have wandered away from his cabin for some reason and died from exposure. As weeks passed with no news, a searcher found the remains of Myers near a group of trees some forty feet from his cabin. Some believed Myers was ill and left his cabin for some reason, became lost in the snow, and succumbed to the elements.

ᜆ

Royal Jones was a twenty-nine-year-old man from North Sacramento who went fishing at Grizzly Creek in the Plumas National Forest in May 1941.

He traveled with a friend, and they were possibly seven miles northwest of Rogers Cow Camp near the Feather River Highway. The two parted ways following a hike. Their plan was to have one person fish upstream and the other fish downstream. They were to meet at a designated spot at noon. Perhaps they wanted to compare notes on the best place to fish.

The friend made it to the designated spot and waited for Jones. He never showed. The friend searched for Jones and found his backpack along Grizzly Creek. The Forest Service was contacted, and a search began. Members of the search team said the task was difficult because the area along the river was rugged and steep.

It was theorized that Jones accidentally fell into Grizzly Creek and was carried by swift waters into the connecting Feather River. Another opinion was Jones was lost in the Plumas. The friend disagreed and told the press that Jones was familiar with the area and was an expert fisherman. Rangers from the Forest Service searched for Jones.

The Jones's body was discovered at the end of June 1941 in the Feather River. A positive identification was made because the clothing was a match. Some items he was carrying when he disappeared were found with the body. Sadly, the same fate was met by Gus Sholz of Feather Falls, California. One month following the discovery of Jones, Sholz fell into the rapid waters of Grizzly Creek and his body was discovered near the location where Royal Jones was found.

❧

There are twenty-six national parks and forests in California. Millions experience the majestic beauty and return yearly to hike, camp, fish, or ski. They experience the parks and forests without incident. Some are not as fortunate.

Weiher, Madruga, Sterling, Huett, and Mathias were unfortunate ones. Law enforcement had to battle the elements and difficult terrain to find the men. They vanished in the Plumas during the winter. Below-freezing temperatures, rain, and snow were constant.

By this point, the five had been missing for over seventy-two hours. Families and law enforcement wanted to find the five. They were willing to do whatever it took to find them alive.

CHAPTER THIRTEEN: EARLY MARCH 1978

Before I had access to the Yuba County Five case file, I had a PDF collection of newspaper clippings concerning the case and related topics. Those files came from the Sutter County Library, the Yuba County Library, and online newspaper databases. My newspaper collection was filed by topic and there was a folder for the investigation. It was not properly organized by month. I'm a Generation X slacker who turned it into an "I'll get to it later" project. Following an eternity of procrastination, I took the time and created monthly subfolders for the investigation.

When I reviewed all my March newspaper clippings, I noticed it was a time of hope and frustration. Hope came in the form of various sightings of the five in Northern California. Law enforcement made sure to follow up on every reported sighting by the public. The frustration was due to not knowing where the five were and how Madruga's car ended up in the

Plumas. Some were not even sure if the men were in the Plumas. Some were not even sure if the missing men were still alive.

cs

While the Yuba County Sheriff's Department attempted to find some truth in the accounts of Joe and Cindy Schons, they undertook a major search and rescue operation in the Plumas National Forest. It would be the responsibility of Butte County, which had already assisted Yuba County by gathering information in Chico, the largest city in their county. One newspaper article stated the location where the men went missing was "some of the roughest country in California." The five disappeared on February 24th, and the car was discovered and reported to law enforcement on February 28th, so they had to make up approximately four days of missed time. "We don't know what happened to them—we have a real mystery on our hands," said Yuba County Undersheriff Jack Beecham to the press.

There was nothing disclosed concerning the number of officers for the Butte County Sheriff's Department assigned to the case, but the main players were Undersheriff Dick Stenberg and Lt. Ken Mickelson. It was Mickelson who oversaw the search and rescue team for Butte County, which was considered the finest in Northern California. Both Stenberg and Mickelson reported to Butte County Sheriff Larry Gillick. When asked about the discovery of the car and what brought the men to that location, Gillick told the press in 1978, "We have no idea whatsoever."

A witness came forward to let investigators know he saw the five at the UC Davis game at Chico State. Bill Lee was the executive editor of the *Chico Enterprise-Record*. Lee was contacted by telephone by Jack Beecham, who wanted to know what Lee witnessed during the game. According to Lee, the game was sparsely attended, but he did see the UC Davis section of fans. Not that far away from the UC Davis section were Weiher, Madruga, Sterling, Huett, and Mathias. What stood out to Lee about the five was that they were more reserved in their cheering but were enjoying themselves. Weiher was the one in the group that stood out because he recognized Weiher's picture in the paper when the story broke about them being missing. Lee said the game ended around 9:50 p.m., and he did remember seeing the five at that time.

೧

Madruga's car was towed to Brower's Body Shop in Oroville by the Butte County Sheriff's Department for analysis. It would be examined on March 2nd, and a March 5th report provided their findings. Keys were made for the ignition and the glove box, but they opened it with the aid of a screwdriver. In the glove box were maps of Sacramento, Stockton, and San Francisco. Also in the glove box was an address book with the names of a few individuals, including Bill Sterling and Jackie Huett. An owner's manual, warranty documents, and a vehicle registration certificate were found in the glove box as well. A quarter tank of gasoline was noted. The back seats were removed, and scent dogs were brought in so they could smell those seats. A map of California found on the front seat, along with a sports-related newspaper. On the map were X markings at various locations and handwritten notes. The Butte County Sheriff's Department wanted to know more about who made the notes and markings.

There were stains on the driver's side sun visor. The Butte County Sheriff's Department removed the visor and used test strips on the stains. Results showed it was blood. They mailed the sun visor to Sacramento so the lab for the Department of Justice could further examine the stains. A few days after the visor arrived in Sacramento, the Department of Justice informed Butte County that it was not blood. The strips may have shown a false positive; it was believed that stains on the visor may have been a sauce from a fast-food restaurant.

Meanwhile, the search was underway in the Plumas National Forest. By March 1st, it was reported by the *Appeal-Democrat* that they had covered "five miles in diameter" from Madruga's car. It included searching cabins in the Merrimac's and Elk's Retreat areas, which were in the search zone.

The March 2, 1978, front page of the *Appeal-Democrat* showed an image of Sheriff Jim Grant standing on the road where the five went missing. Below is an image of Madruga's 1969 Mercury Montego. The paper reported that close to thirty-six individuals from three different counties were assisting with the search and rescue operation near Bucks Lake. Even some family members went up there to help in any way possible. If the information reported was correct, then Grant and the search team were nearly sixteen miles north of Rogers Cow Camp, where the car was discovered. That location would be an important one when discoveries were made in June of that same year.

Ken Mickelson from the Butte County Sheriff's Department and Sheriff Jim Grant were the search and rescue coordinators, according to the *Oroville Mercury-Register*. A four-wheel-drive ambulance from Oroville was called in case the missing men needed any kind of medical attention. The teams had begun searching the area near the abandoned car at 9:15 p.m. on February 28th, and on March 1st at 3:30 a.m., they halted their work. The team had access to a Sno-Cat, snowmobiles, and four-wheel-drive vehicles, and a helicopter from the California Highway Patrol was available for use.

An unidentified newspaper clipping in the case file explained the search. The teams were using a grid system to search the area. Five men were spread out about two hundred yards apart. Their goal was to walk to a certain point. They would retrace their steps so they did not miss anything on the initial sweep.

Footprints were discovered by Madruga's car, and they appeared to have been made by a group of individuals. The problem was the footprints were found in melted snow, so it was difficult for investigators to know if the footprints were going away or toward the vehicle. If they had been walking away from the Montego, then it would have been toward an area to the west known as French Creek Canyon. The area was a few miles west of their location and had a series of creeks, and the terrain would drop from thirty-two hundred feet to some twenty-four hundred feet. Butte County Undersheriff Richard Stenberg described the location as "the worst you could get into." However, Stenberg was a bit hopeful because there were some cabins in the area, and perhaps the five took refuge in one.

Early in the investigation, law enforcement told the press that they did not believe Madruga drove his car to that location by coincidence. "You just don't take that road by accident; that's just not the kind of mistake anyone could make," said Stenberg. The most pressing issue for the searchers was that the men had been exposed to the elements since the night they disappeared if they had not found shelter. "I just don't see how there can be much hope of finding them alive if they're in the area unless they holed up somewhere," said Stenberg to the press. What really puzzled him was that, between February 24th and March 1st, there were days when the weather had improved and the lost five could have attempted a walk down a road to seek assistance. "But people don't always act logically," added Stenberg.

A base camp was created in an area known as Merrimac, which was slightly north of the abandoned car. Another newspaper reported search and rescue workers were camped out near Mountain House, which is south of the area. Those who were involved in the search and rescue operation were affiliated with Butte County and reported to Ken Mickelson. He was forty-nine at the time and had seventeen years of experience. According to Mickelson, the search and rescue team comprised "working stiffs, doctors, farmers." He also stated they donated their time and materials.

Mickelson was concerned because the area they were searching was "rugged, bushy terrain." He added, "If they're down, they could be twenty feet away and not be seen. If they're holed up, there's a good chance they'll be okay." This quote was reported on March 4th, and another search and rescue team member claimed they had spent four days straight camped in the area looking for the missing men.

The areas they searched were not detailed on a map. Mickelson said they also checked an area known as the Feather River Canyon, which was west of the abandoned car.

A team of search dogs from El Dorado County, located near Sacramento, assisted with the rescue efforts at the time. Some volunteers went through the area on horseback. However, the weather made it incredibly difficult as heavy rain hit the region. The helicopter from the California Highway Patrol had to stop doing an aerial search because the heavy rain turned to hail at their altitude. When the helicopter resumed, it reportedly covered some fifty square miles. This information was included in a newspaper clipping from the case file. It was not attributed to a certain newspaper.

Some of the men in the helicopter were interviewed for the article. They stated that they could be in the air for fifteen minutes but had to land to refuel. Another issue was the temperatures during the day were warm, leading to steam coming off the ground, which made visibility from the helicopter very difficult.

✑

California was experiencing a heavy amount of precipitation from 1977 into 1978, and by February 1978, they had measured about twenty-two to twenty-six inches of seasonal rain in areas, which was above average. By March of 1978, the State of California had reported $20 million in damages from heavy rains and mudslides in Monterey County. Southern and Central California were declared federal disaster areas, with $45 million in aid needed. In the area where the five went missing, the National Weather Service said there was no precipitation reported there from February 23rd until the 26th, but the following day saw over half an inch of precipitation, which may have been snow at that altitude. If it had snowed, then it would have been heavy.

Also, those involved in the search were concerned about the below-freezing temperatures. They knew there were various cabins in the area where the men disappeared. Investigators hoped the men would find one and could keep themselves warm.

The search and rescue team for Butte County experienced snow, rain, mist, and sleet, which hampered their progress. One snowstorm in early March led to the search and rescue team being stuck up in the Plumas. A newspaper clipping in the case file said three men from the rescue team were hospitalized around March 10th due to a heart attack, exhaustion, and pneumonia respectively. A spokesperson said the men ended up leaving the hospital. They made full recoveries.

Also at this time, the Yuba County Sheriff's Department clarified that the situation of the missing men was in no way linked to the 1975 firebombings at the Gateway Projects. The *Sacramento Bee* allegedly had made a connection between the two, according to the *Oroville Mercury Press*, but Sheriff Jim Grant referred to it as "nonsense."

Yuba City's Police Chief, Robert Smith, commented on a possible Gateway connection to the disappearance. "I don't believe there is any connection at all," said Smith. Yuba City Police had investigated the 1975 death of Donald Garrett. The case was cold.

The Weiher, Madruga, Sterling, Huett, and Mathias families agreed that the five were capable of driving to Chico and returning home safely. Staff at the Gateway Projects stood by the families since they knew the five.

Jack Huett Sr. told the *Sacramento Bee* that "these boys are very impressionable." When the Yuba County Sheriff's Department spoke with families of the missing, they did note that their sons would comply if they felt threatened by an individual or a group. However, the mothers of Ted Weiher and Jack Madruga noted that their sons were afraid of the dark and were not fond of the cold and the snow. Jackie Huett had never spent the night away from home, and Bill Sterling was also not a fan of the outdoors.

Juanita Sterling was quoted in a March 2, 1978, *Sacramento Bee* article saying, "They'd never go out in the wilderness like that; they'd go to a pizza joint."

Another claim made in the same *Sacramento Bee* article came from Yuba County Undersheriff Jack Beecham. When questioned about the investigation of the five, Beecham said, "They enjoyed bowling, dancing, and skating, and at least one of them had been involved in a commune at one time." The case investigation files did not note any links between the five and communes in the area, but it was a theory a few had about the fate of the five.

A news station in Sacramento received a call from a viewer that the missing men could have joined the "Moonies," who were followers of the Unification Church founded in South Korea by Sun Myung Moon. There were Moonies living in Mendocino County, which is in the northwestern portion of the state. The Yuba County Sheriff's Department sent data to the Mendocino County Sheriff's Department just in case the claims were valid.

Another caller claimed the men joined a commune in Boulder Creek southwest of San Jose. The caller claimed all five were sent there by an unknown person. A package of information was sent to the Santa Cruz County Sheriff's Department in case the men were discovered in that area.

A woman named Naomi Brisker (pseudonym) contacted the Yuba County Sheriff's Department in early March concerning Gary Mathias. Brisker claimed to have known Mathias for several years. Mathias had reportedly told Brisker that he had many dreams where he and some others would simply disappear.

Brisker said Mathias spoke about UFOs and outer space. She was afraid of Mathias because she saw him as a violent man who hated women. Brisker told investigators that Mathias could seriously hurt men by punching and kicking them.

UFO sightings outside of Sacramento were reported in the March 2, 1978, edition of the *Placer Herald*. The article stated that there was a UFO sighting near Loomis, a community outside Sacramento, the night the men went missing.

❧

Snow played a major role in the search for the missing men. Two feet of snow fell in the Plumas National Forest between Thursday, March 2nd, and Friday, March 3rd, which resulted in a discussion of the halting of the rescue efforts during the weekend. Snow continued to fall in early March, and the Plumas were covered with six to eight feet of snow. Drifts were reported to be fifteen feet in depth.

The Plumas County Sherriff's Office sent deputies to Bucks Lake to check on a cabin that Bill Sterling had stayed in years before. Due to the location of the cabin, Plumas County was involved in the case, and they would aid in the search efforts.

The *Appeal-Democrat* reported on March 3rd that the location of the cabin in Bucks Lake was twenty miles away from the where the Montego was found. Families at the time told the press that they believed the men were in the car when it was abandoned. They believed they were the victims of foul play. The families also upped the reward money to $1,200 for any information that would lead to the discovery of the missing five.

☙

As Joseph Schons shared his story of the evening of February 24th, a woman would contact authorities to share a that she had seen the men at Mary's Country Store in Brownsville, California, which was nearly fifty miles south of the car. Law enforcement interviewed her.

She reported that it was the afternoon of Sunday, February 26th, and she was driving home from a ball game with her children when she decided to make a stop at Mary's Country Store. She parked next to what she described as a red 1953 or 1954 Chevy pickup truck with two men inside. One was seated in the middle, while the other was in the passenger seat. They both appeared to be "retarded" according to the witness, and they didn't say anything to her as she walked by the truck. She then noticed two other people at a phone booth near the store. She wasn't quite sure, but she was under the impression that one was a woman. One was on the phone and seemed to be the leader, while the other stood by nervously.

She then walked into Mary's Country Store and noticed a fifth person in one of the aisles. The best description she could provide is that this man may have worn glasses. She made a purchase, then exited the store and noticed the four again.

When interviewed by the Yuba County Sheriff's Department, the witness was shown all five images of the missing men. She was able to identify Weiher, Madruga, Sterling, and Huett as the men she saw outside of the store on the 26th of February. Before being shown images of the five, the witness did admit she had seen images of the men on television. She described Weiher as having shorter hair than he did in the provided image, and she felt Sterling had a rounder face than his provided image. When asked where the four were outside, she stated that Sterling and Weiher were in the truck while Huett was on the phone with Madruga near the booth. She remembered all five as looking dirty, with Weiher wearing a red and black checkered flannel shirt.

Five days after their interview with the Yuba County Sheriff's Department, the witness called and said she had seen the five on Saturday, February 25th, and not the 26th as she originally thought. When asked about this sighting, Undersheriff Jack Beecham told the press, "It's a very promising lead."

Next, the Yuba County Sheriff's Department got in contact with Carroll Waltz, who either worked at or owned Mary's Country Store. Waltz told authorities that Jackie Huett and Gary Mathias had been in his store on both Saturday, February 25th, and Sunday, February 26th, between noon and 1 p.m., buying burritos, chips, and milk. Waltz claimed he watched both Huett and Mathias eat the food outside his store. However, Waltz was not able to provide any details regarding the descriptions of the men or any information about the vehicle they used to get to the store. An all-points bulletin was put out to members of law enforcement in the area.

〇〇

Authorities had learned that Gary Mathias had friends some four miles north of Brownsville in Forbestown, California, so law enforcement contacted them and even searched some campgrounds in that area. None of the friends had seen or been in contact with Mathias or the others. To get to Forbestown, one would have to drive through Oroville. A road that led to the community was along the Oroville-Quincy Highway.

There were additional claims of people seeing the missing men during that time. One noticed five or six men acting "goofy" near the Marysville

Hotel on March 1st, while on March 2nd another reported seeing five or six men standing on the side of the road. The person who made this report was driving from Reno, Nevada, to Oroville on California Highway 70 when they noticed the men standing near a vehicle and looking at the canyon. The report at the Yuba County Sheriff's Department notes that this sighting was some fifteen miles from where Madruga's car was discovered.

One person contacted the Yuba County Sheriff's Department to report that an old friend named "Marvin" had returned to the area from "the coast." Marvin was reportedly a heavy drug user with a history of violence, plus the caller stated Marvin had a reputation for stealing automobiles. The name of a woman was given, and Yuba County was told to get in touch with her to find Marvin. Nothing else was noted in the file about this possible lead.

Another potential witness from the Sacramento area informed law enforcement in early March that she believed they saw the five young men at Longs Drug Store in the Bird Cage Mall on Thursday, February 23rd. The witness stated she was at Longs between 11 a.m. and noon when she spotted a young man at the register with his hand out, trying to buy cigarettes. The young man was in his early twenties, according to the witness, and she remembered the young man asked the clerk at the counter if they had enough money in their hand to buy the cigarettes. Also, the witness told the Yuba County Sheriff's Department that the five appeared to be "retarded" and they were being chaperoned by a nervous-looking older gentleman. The witness did see images of the missing men on television and was certain those were the people she saw at Longs. However, the witness did also acknowledge that there were homes for people with disabilities near the mall, but she was very certain she saw the missing five in line.

∽

Search efforts in the Plumas were hampered again on March 4th when more heavy snow fell on top of the two feet that had already fallen earlier in the week. It was reported that fifty deputies from Yuba, Butte, and Plumas Counties were involved in the search at this time.

Also, there were still doubts in Yuba and Butte Counties that the men were in the foothills of the Sierra Nevada in the Plumas. Butte County Undersheriff Dick Stenberg told the press in early March 1978 that there were "no clues" that showed the men were still up there. It was a possibility that they had walked down the Oroville-Quincy Highway back to Oroville to find assistance. Stenberg knew the five were excited about their Special Olympics event in Rocklin on Saturday the 25th and it would not have made any sense for them to go on "a side trip" on Friday night.

A person in Sacramento claimed to see the five at Sam's Hof Brau, a restaurant. The witness saw four men ordering food then go out to the parking lot to speak with another individual about driving to San Francisco. Two of the four men were identified by the witness. The Yuba County Sheriff's Department contacted the witness and Sgt. Jim Black noted the witness was somewhat "flaky."

There was a sighting reported in early March where the five were seen at the Thermaland Trading Post in Placer County, which goes northeast from Sacramento to Lake Tahoe. The person who reported the sighting knew Ted Weiher and Gary Mathias and was certain they were at Thermaland. Images of the five were shown to the proprietors, and they stated the five were never in their store.

⁊⁊

I took thirty-one pages of notes, front and back, while at the Yuba County Sheriff's Department. My plan was to write down everything in the file, and I didn't even come close. It was disappointing because there wasn't a guarantee that I could get copies of the case files. The Sheriff's Department allowed me to submit a records request, and it was approved. I was informed that the files would be redacted and to be patient.

It was time for me to leave Marysville, so I drove to Sacramento for what turned out to be one major headache of a flight home. I was supposed to fly from Sacramento to Chicago and then Chicago to Grand Rapids, Michigan. The plane I was to take to Chicago required maintenance and the delay meant I was going to miss my flight to Chicago. They booked me a flight from Sacramento to Denver. From there I would fly to Grand Rapids, Michigan. Portions of Colorado were under a tornado warning so our plane to Denver had to land at a small airfield in Western Colorado. We were stuck there for two hours. Then we got back on the plane and made it to Denver. Fortunately, I had enough time to catch my flight home to Grand Rapids.

Before I boarded the plane to Denver, I messaged Tom and Claudia Huett along with Dallas Weiher Jr. They were curious to know what I had discovered going through the files. I provided them with updates and asked if certain names rang a bell. They replied and shared some memories of the investigation, and a few photos of Jackie and Ted were sent to me. I shared with them some yearbook photos of the five that I had found at the library in Marysville.

I also made a last-minute phone call to Brian Bernardis at the Yuba County Sheriff's Department and thanked him for his time.

After boarding the plane, I opened my notebook and read over my notes. It was great having them for my research, but some things were infuriating and frustrating. The false sightings and the web of nonsense spun by Joseph and Cindy Schons gave me a headache. These events happened in early March 1978, but there was more. If law enforcement and the families thought they had experienced enough craziness, they were dead wrong.

CHAPTER FOURTEEN:
VISIONS AND CONSPIRACIES

I'm a huge football fan. Saturday and Sunday afternoons are spent watching my favorite teams winning big or snatching defeat from the jaws of victory. There is nothing better than watching a great game that ends with an amazing final play. One of my favorite plays is the Hail Mary pass. That's when the quarterback throws the football downfield with the hopes that a receiver makes an improbable catch in the end zone. When it works, they are a thing of beauty.

Then there is a proverbial Hail Mary pass we make in life. People take major risks with the hopes they make that magical catch. Sometimes it works, and other times it is a spectacular blunder.

When I was researching the Yuba County Five case, one of my earliest discoveries was that someone had contacted psychics to help figure out what happened to the five. I was surprised that this Hail Mary pass of a decision was made. What surprised me even more was the fact that the first psychic was contacted very early in the investigation. I was under the impression the psychics were brought in sometime in April or May as a last-ditch effort to find the five alive.

While looking through the files, I discovered that more than one psychic was involved. Some offered their services to law enforcement and others offered their services to various family members. It was not a popular decision, but psychics did speak with members of law enforcement and some family members.

There were others who offered their theories, and they were not psychics. They had some incredibly bizarre ideas about what happened to the five.

♋

With search efforts being hampered by winter storms and numerous witnesses coming forward, law enforcement was growing frustrated in their search for Weiher, Madruga, Sterling, Huett, and Mathias. Early in March 1978, a proposal was made, possibly by the Madruga family, to bring in a psychic to help with the case. Her name was Dr. Gloria Elizabeth Daniel. She claimed to have psychic powers, and she represented the Marysville branch of the Church of the Tzaddi.

Tzaddi was founded in 1958, and they are something of a metaphysical nondenominational church. The church's headquarters at the time were in Garden Grove near Los Angeles. Tzaddi claims to teach "how to combine your psychic and your spiritual selves and arrive at a better understanding of yourself."

Dr. Gloria Elizabeth Daniel and her husband, Dr. William O. Daniel, were available to help. Dr. William O. Daniel told the press in 1978 that his wife had "assisted many times" with missing persons and that "she is able, generally speaking, to receive something" to help with these cases. Dr. William O. Daniel stated that his wife did not volunteer her services, so there would be a fee for her to work on the case.

Imogene Weiher, Ted's mother, refused to take part in the meeting with the psychic. "My mother was the only one that would not call the psychic in," said Dorothy Weiher-Dornan, Ted's sister. "My mother was old-school religious, and we just figured it was the enemy." Some of the other family members met with Dr. Gloria Daniel on March 1ˢᵗ; the meeting was recorded by Sara Huett, Jackie's mother.

Daniel opened the meeting with a prayer and told those in attendance that she is not one to read the newspaper because she would "get feelings" from it, but she would enjoy "the funnies and Ann Landers." Her voice was raspy, and she spoke with an East Coast accent. A man appeared to her one morning and it was apparent in her vision that he had suffered "a massive heart attack" because he was pointing to his heart. According to Daniel, he showed her a man with "sandy" colored hair, and Daniel believed it to be Ted Weiher.

As the meeting went on, Daniel told those in attendance that Madruga's car was not driven to the Plumas by Madruga but by someone else. Daniel said it was "futile" searching that area. However, she wanted to know more about Schons's vehicle, and she also claimed to have a vision of a truck. Someone during the meeting informed Daniel that Schons claimed to see a woman and a baby, which led Daniel to tell those in attendance that she felt a woman's presence very strongly. She would go on to tell the families that she didn't want to give them "a false hope."

Daniel also had a vision of a young man in spirit. According to Daniel, he showed her the area, possibly where they went missing, and he was in "a state of shock" while acting erratically. The young man was crying because of something that happened, but not in that area. Daniels claimed to see a cabin, or what was left of one, in the woods to the east of where the car was found. The young man was repeating "March 15ᵗʰ" in the vision as well, and Daniel would state that it wasn't a good thing to happen to them.

The woman and the baby that Schons claimed to see were what Daniel thought led the five to their doom because she believed they helped the woman. One family member told Daniel that there were two other men involved, and Daniel informed them that she saw someone "in a western hat" with a connection to Nevada.

Although she claimed earlier that someone had driven Madruga's car to the Plumas, Daniel told the families that the five could have taken someone that way to drop them off. Daniel also believed the man who visited her and had the heart attack was Schons. What made Daniel believe it was Schons was because the man appeared to be sixty years old, in her opinion, and she *read* in the paper Schons was fifty-five, so she felt it had to be him because he looked older than his age.

She did tell the families a few times that the five were not in the area but somewhere else. Also, Daniel claimed that they would find them together, but she had a feeling that one of the men would be separated from the group. Daniel finally admitted to the families that she was reading the newspaper with the stories of the missing men, and she met with Sheriff Jim Grant beforehand to discuss the case. When she spoke with Grant, Daniel admitted on tape that she told him that the five would be found northeast of where the car was located in another state or outside the boundaries of a location.

There was, according to Daniel, a clue in the Montego that had not been found. She said it was shoved in the back seat and would be linked to the person they helped the night they went missing. It was also mentioned by Daniel that one of the five was crying that night and saying, "He's a bastard."

A happy ending was not promised by Daniel, and she informed the families she was trying to find a license plate number from a vision because she had luck with solving cases by finding license plate numbers in her visions. A "sandy-haired" young man kept appearing to her, along with the man who had suffered a heart attack. Turquoise jewelry and a man in a Western hat were part of her vision, and it was the man in the hat who was the "bastard" mentioned by the crying person. Physical harm had come to the five in some manner, but Daniel also stated that there was something she wanted to say but wouldn't put on tape. The tape recorder was shut off, and the session continued.

When the tape resumed, Daniel believed that the cause of their disappearance had something to do with what the five put in their stomachs after the basketball game. A discussion with family members, possibly between the Madrugas and Daniel, led to a theory that the crying person in Daniel's vision was Jack Madruga. His family stated that he became childlike in serious situations.

Mountain House was also connected somehow to Daniel and her visions. Also, she wanted the families to know that if the five were in the car and Schons called out to them for help, then they would have assisted him.

∽

When asked about working with Dr. Gloria Daniel, Undersheriff Jack Beecham told reporters in 1978, "We'd been doing everything she suggested right along anyway. She really wasn't much help." According to Beecham, Daniel told investigators to search other areas.

Beecham would later recall some of the visions that Daniel shared with investigators. "She saw two of the missing holding one another, freezing and crying." Another vision of Daniel's was some of the men were in green bags. According to Beecham, it was theorized by Lance Ayers that the two crying and holding each other might have been Jack Madruga and Bill Sterling.

Sheriff Jim Grant received multiple letters in the mail from people claiming they were able to assist. Undersheriff Jack Beecham recalled that psychics at the time had "come out of the woodwork" to help with the case. A psychic from San Francisco wrote to the Yuba County Sheriff's Department in early March and asked for photographs of the missing men. Sheriff Jim Grant obliged and received a letter from the psychic after he mailed them the requested images.

The psychic told Grant that Weiher, Madruga, Sterling, Huett, and Mathias never left Chico on February 24th. They stated that all five were dead as a result of hanging. A map of Chico and the vicinity was requested by the psychic, and he demanded that there were no markings on the map. At the end of the letter to Grant, the psychic clarified that everything they stated in the letter was nothing more than conjecture.

A resident of Santa Clara, California, reached out to Grant. The writer admitted that she had heard about the story on the radio in the beginning of March, but said they had not been reading the papers. However, something happened on March 15th when the person was cleaning windows for a psychic. The psychic told the writer that she should try locating the five. According to the letter, the writer did have some sort of psychic powers along with some sort of healing abilities that were not put into detail.

The writer went on to explain that she had experience in "telepathic contact" with close friends but not complete strangers. An attempt to contact the five telepathically was made, but there was no contact. Then, the writer decided to alleviate the worry of the families because she was certain the five had perished. She had some sort of vision that they were in a cabin at the end of February, and she was certain the five were the ones seen in Brownsville at Mary's Country Store. She was sure that one of the five was sick at the time.

Another vision appeared to the writer in the form of a reservoir or a water filtration plant. It was not completely clear as she saw a portion of the place, but she noted she saw green machinery, possibly pumps, with fast-flowing water. Also seen by the writer were various dishes and cups in a variety of colors. Those items could be in the cabin or in a museum near where they were located. Maybe they were close to a factory that made those items. The writer ended her letter by wishing Grant and everyone involved the best of luck. There was a possible follow-up letter that featured some drawings of what may have been the Oroville Dam and examples of the dishes and cups. The writing was barely legible and was something of a stream-of-consciousness style.

A letter of ramblings influenced by the Bible and *The 700 Club*, a televangelist show, was also received. The name of the writer and their address were not included, but the writer claimed that praying for so many minutes per day would lead to miracles. Examples of miracles were included when someone was put in a dire situation and they prayed for a miracle. Their miracles were granted, and all they had to do in Yuba County was pray for a miracle.

Families of the missing were also contacted by strangers about the case. Ida Klopf, Gary Mathias' mother, received a letter from a woman in Bakersfield, California, with some information about what might have happened to her son. The woman referred to Gary Mathias as "Jerry," and she asked Klopf to call her because Mathias might have been kidnapped due to "the National Conspiracy to gain an objective."

According to the woman, her husband was kidnapped in July 1976 and was held captive for a week. Those responsible for kidnapping her husband had reprogrammed him, and the result was that the man deserted his family and decided to live in Arizona. For some unknown reason, the wife could not "reach him mentally" because of the effects of mind control. The writer was upset over the situation because they thought that the United States Government believed in human rights. At the end of the letter, the woman told Klopf she would try to visit the area soon and would attempt to meet with Klopf. She knew the truth about why her husband was being held.

Lance Ayers, one of the lead investigators from the Yuba County Sheriff's Department, was assigned to follow up on that letter. He discovered after contacting the woman that she suffered from mental illness and was upset that her husband had walked out on her. She told Ayers that he would come back but was somehow hypnotized.

Sara Huett, Jackie's mother, was also contacted via a letter from a person attempting to help in the case. A woman from Oroville informed Huett that a psychic in Pennsylvania named Marianne Elko would be in contact with their family. Blessed with a "perception of ESP," Elko had aided the FBI, and the writer wanted the Huetts to know that she was praying for them. Huett also received a letter in the mail sometime during the week of March 3rd and the writer may have been Elko. The writer wanted her to know that glasses would be found, and they would be the clue that would lead investigators to the person responsible for the five's disappearance. The letter provided details about a Ford van that was blue with a scenic design on the back window along with a license plate that read EI or IE 3910. Also, the writer wanted Huett to know that two of the men were on a peninsula near a large body of water, and in parenthesis was written *Florida*. A possible suspect name was included, and it was "Crawmile or name similar."

"We got a lot of weird phone calls," said Dallas Weiher Sr. "One woman called me and said she was sitting on the pot one night, and she had a vision that there was somebody behind a log in the mountains. What would you say to somebody like that? 'Thanks, ma'am'?"

☙

Of all the people who wrote to the Yuba County Sheriff's Department, conjecturing what happened to the Yuba County Five, one truly stood out. Slater A. Judd Jr. from Burlingame, California, would frequently send letters from an area known as Little Wolf Creek in Mono County, California. Burlingame is a community south of San Francisco near San Mateo, while Mono County is located to the east near Stanislaus National Forest near the Nevada state line.

Slater A. Judd Jr. claimed he knew what had happened to Weiher, Madruga, Sterling, Huett, and Mathias because others had suffered the same fate. According to Judd Jr., a rogue group of ex-Marines with ties to the KKK were using a fleet of helicopters to hunt down and kidnap innocent people. They did the same thing to the five on February 24th because, according to Judd Jr., a squadron of rogue Marines in helicopters stopped the five in the Plumas National Forest, placed them in a helicopter, robbed them, and then threw all five out of the helicopter without parachutes.

The whistling noises heard by Schons were the helicopters because Judd Jr. had an experience once where helicopters landed some three hundred feet from his cabin, and they made a whistling noise as well. Judd Jr. was convinced this was the fate of the five and that it was a major conspiracy being covered up at all levels of government.

Not only did he write to the Yuba County Sheriff's Department, but he wrote to a television station in San Francisco to report his findings. The incidents, according to Judd Jr., could be traced back to 1973 in Modesto, California, when the infamous rogue helicopter crew landed in a parking lot and attempted to kidnap a man in a pickup truck. Also in the truck was a dog that reportedly jumped out and chased the ex-Marines back to their helicopter. They had no choice but to fire at the dog and take off. Judd Jr. stated in a letter that this incident was reported in the *Modesto Bee* newspaper.

Judd then claimed that a family "in the Northwest" disappeared when they were reportedly robbed by the same rogue helicopter crew. Judd Jr. noted that this incident was also reported in the media, and he stated that they knew the family had disappeared because the husband dropped his wallet on a rock by a stream when this happened.

Even Judd Jr. himself was apparently being harassed. He believed they were from a training center for the Marines near Bridgeport, California, in Mono County. The incidents occurred between 1975 and 1977 in Mono County and in Burlingame.

Judd Jr. had reported these activities to officials around February 15, 1978, and he believed that the Yuba County Five had been abducted by the helicopter crew during the evening of February 24, 1978, because of his letter. In his opinion, he believed that the poor and minorities were being targeted by this group because the rogue helicopter crew did not want them to find success from mining or prospecting.

Various newspaper clippings with his letters were included to prove the enemy was real. One clipping from a January 11, 1978, San Bruno *Recorder-Progress* was a story about two individuals who were robbed outside a liquor store in Burlingame. According to the article, the two were approached by a couple of robbers who drove up in a car; one robber got out and pointed a gun at them, demanding they hand over their money. Judd wrote notes on the clipping, claiming the robbers were part of the helicopter squadron, although the article only described the height of both robbers and nothing else.

Judd Jr. also sent an April 1, 1978, *San Francisco Chronicle* article about six white enlisted men at the Marine Corps Air Station in El Toro, California, being discharged for participating in a cross burning in a "secluded picnic" area. All six were arrested and the Marines and a spokesperson believed it was nothing more than an isolated incident.

Judd Jr.'s writing campaign included a letter sent to the FBI in April 1978 claiming the missing men from Yuba County had been kidnapped by the rogue crew. A copy of the letter was sent to Jim Grant for review.

સ

When he spoke with the *Oroville Mercury-Register* on March 9th, Undersheriff Jack Beecham said that the ground search in the Plumas National Forest was about ninety percent complete. Butte County Undersheriff Dick Stenberg told the same paper they were exploring all routes from Chico to the spot where the car was abandoned off the Oroville-Quincy Highway. "But what are we looking for?" he said when considering the possibilities.

Those involved in the search from Chico to where the car was abandoned were informed to "check anyplace someone might dump a body." Butte County Search and Rescue Captain James Doering told the *Oroville Mercury-Register*, "We are really grasping at straws at this point. We're trying to find out where the men are by finding out where they are not."

As days passed by in March, the Yuba County Sheriff's Department was following reported sightings in communities like Brownsville. They were chasing leads from psychics and looking into the claims of ex-Marine kidnappers and robbers using helicopters to terrorize the poor and minorities in California. Meanwhile, the Butte County Sheriff's Department continued work in the Plumas National Forest searching for the missing men. These events were regional news, but mid-March would see the story go national and people from all over would learn about the five. Once again, Yuba County was in the news, and it was for another tragedy.

CHAPTER FIFTEEN:
ATTENTION AND FRUSTRATION

I was fortunate to meet some other truly dedicated Yuba County Five researchers while working on this book. The first was author Drew Beeson. His book, *Out of Bounds: What Happened to the Yuba County Five?* was released in 2020. I had no idea another author was working on a book, but I quickly developed a great relationship with him. We have spent hours on the phone discussing aspects of the story and various scenarios. Beeson has also written books about the infamous D.B. Cooper skyjacking and the murders committed by the mysterious Zodiac killer. We are true crime brothers from different mothers.

The next person I met was Shannon McGarvey. She was the researcher and writer for Mopac Audio's *Yuba County Five* podcast. She also researched and wrote a podcast about the infamous Long Island Serial Killer. Like Beeson, McGarvey knew the Yuba County Five case well and was a great source of information. Mopac Audio had originally planned a documentary, but they turned their research into a podcast. They interviewed Jack Huett Sr. sometime in 2018 before he passed away.

What's great about Beeson and McGarvey is that they understand my frustration with certain aspects of the case. There have been times when I have called them to vent about a follow-up that was a complete dead end, or when a contact I needed to interview had a million telephone numbers listed and they were all disconnected. We have shared newspaper clippings related to our case research and audio recordings of various interviews and meetings. Most importantly, all three of us have developed relationships with the surviving family members of the five.

The Yuba County Five case still receives attention from true crime podcasters and YouTube creators. There are posts on Instagram and discussions on Reddit. *Auto/Biography: Cold Case*, a show on Motor Trend TV, aired an episode in January 2022 dedicated to the Yuba County Five. There is still interest because people want to know what happened to Ted Weiher, Jack Madruga, Bill Sterling, Jackie Huett, and Gary Mathias.

March 1978 was the beginning of national interest in the story. It turned out to be a blessing and a curse.

"This case is bizarre as hell," said Jack Beecham to the press in March. The story was no longer a California mystery. On Thursday, March 9, 1978, newspapers across the United States and in Canada began running the story about five "slightly retarded men." Sheriff Jim Grant and Undersheriff Jack Beecham were quoted in articles, and while Beecham told the press that their disappearance was totally out of character, he added, "In fact, as time goes on, it looks more like foul play" because Beecham believed "they were diverted to that road."

Hopes for finding Weiher, Madruga, Sterling, Huett, and Mathias were fading quickly. Beecham told the press that the area where they disappeared was difficult to search. "It's very heavily forested country, rough and mountainous and rocky. Some places, you can only get in on horseback." It was also reported that the families were concerned about the five being missing because they could not care for themselves when left alone over a long period of time. "It's hard to lose five people, that's for sure," said Beecham to the *Los Angeles Times*.

But some family members were holding on to hope. One of the mothers told the *Los Angeles Times*, "We definitely feel something has happened, but we also feel they are alive." Bob Klopf, Gary Mathias's stepfather, did not agree with the statement and believed all five were dead. The reward money for any tips leading to the discovery of the five went from $1,000 to $2,600 in mid-March. Adjusting for inflation, the $2,600 reward was equal to $11,000 at the time of this writing.

The article in the *Los Angeles Times* was written by Dave Smollar and titled "Missing 5: Foul Play Suspected." It was in the March 10, 1978, edition and featured an image of Imogene Weiher, Ted Weiher's mother, holding a missing persons flyer. Her expression was that of pain, sadness, and frustration. Next to her image was one of Carroll Waltz standing outside of Mary's Country Store in Brownsville. Waltz looked uneasy having his photo taken outside the store where the five were allegedly seen. The sighting had them in different clothing, in a different vehicle, with Jackie Huett using a public telephone.

Tom Huett, Jackie Huett's brother, told the *Los Angeles Times*, "He would just never use a phone, hated it. Ted [Weiher] always called my house as well as his own every time they went out bowling or to play basketball." Jackie Huett would only use a phone to speak with girlfriend Shirley Lancaster, according to Jack Huett Sr. If Jackie Huett was using the phone outside the store in Brownsville, then why did he not try to call his parents or Lancaster?

※

Imogene Weiher believed the five were being held prisoner in Brownsville. Others believed the five may have gone to Forbestown, a small community north of Brownsville. The Forbestown area, according to some locals, had a reputation for attracting young people, and there were communes in the area. It was also an area where an old friend of Gary Mathias lived. As noted previously, the friend was questioned by law enforcement, but they had not seen Mathias or the others.

Larry McCormack from the Yuba County Sheriff's Department was assigned to the areas near Brownsville and Forbestown. When asked what he did, he replied, "Searching roads and back roads. Going all over the place looking for any signs of this vehicle. Signs of this pickup truck. Signs of these guys. Just mainly back in those hills and logging roads and all the backwoods and stuff."

Bob Klopf wasn't sold on the Forbestown theory. "I think they're either in the [Oroville] lake or six feet under some brush somewhere. You have to think about that now."

Cathy Madruga, Jack Madruga's niece, decided to travel with her brother, George Madruga, and a family friend to Forbestown to investigate. "I went up to the [Forbestown] area, and don't ask me how I got the information, but I got the name of Mathias's friends that lived up there. I went up there searching. Me and George and my girlfriend from Fresno went with me. We had George sit in the car, and we told him, 'If we're not back in an hour, you go get help.'"

A feeling of regret came over Cathy Madruga as she made her way from the car. "We walked to the house; it was up in the mountains. We parked there, and it was all booby-trapped." She believed it was due to the growing of marijuana in the hills. Also, Cathy was familiar with the story of what Schons claimed he saw up there that night. "At this mobile home, what do I see? A baby, a baby carriage, a girl, a shed with a big padlock and chains across it." She thought the five were locked up and wanted to go up, but guys with rifles came out, and that scared off Cathy. They fled the scene and reported it to the sheriff's office. She was told by law enforcement, "'Oh, there's nothing up there. We looked on horseback.'" Cathy asked how they got up there if the area was booby-trapped, because it was difficult for her to get out of there because of all the traps. She regretted not going up to the four or five sheds and banging on them.

Meanwhile, William O. Daniel, Dr. Gloria Daniel's, was still speaking to the press by mid-March. He told the *Los Angeles Times*, "We aren't really working with the families, we are working with the sheriffs." However, when Dr. Gloria Daniel met with family members on March 1st, she had said that under no circumstances would she speak with the press. William O. Daniel stated that the discovery of the red pickup truck was something that Dr. Gloria Daniel had predicted before it made the papers.

Jack Beecham told the press that the truck had not been found. "We will not discount any information, but we will conduct our investigation based on logic."

As the case gained national attention, inaccuracies were being reported. Some papers listed all five as being over six feet tall and weighing over two hundred pounds because they were basketball players. Ted Weiher was the tallest of the group at six feet in height and was the heaviest, weighing over two hundred pounds. Some papers reported the men were on a team that played in Chico on February 25th and became lost on the ride home from their game. Ted Weiher would be listed as "Ted Weihel" in various articles.

An image of the five men appeared in the articles, showing individual headshots. From left to right it showed Jackie Huett, Bill Sterling, Jack Madruga, Ted Weiher, and Gary Mathias. Huett's and Sterling's images feature big smiles, while Madruga and Weiher have serious looks. The image of Mathias showed him in his Army uniform.

While information was going coast to coast, the Yuba County Sheriff's Department was working diligently to get answers. Bill Lee was the witness that put the five at the UC Davis game at Chico State. Mary Davis saw them at Behr's Market following the game, and to make sure she was a credible witness, the Yuba County Sheriff's Department conducted an exhaustive review of all grocery stores between Marysville and Chico, comparing the items found in the car against the stocked shelves of some thirty stores from Yuba City to Chico. Behr's Market sold all those items, and the story provided by Mary Davis was validated. There was still the uncertainty of Joseph Schons's story about the night of the 24th, and there was little to no credibility to the sighting in Brownsville at Mary's Country Store.

Frustration was growing with the investigation. Robert Pennock, the basketball coach for the Gateway Gators, had not reached out to anyone at the Yuba County Sheriff's Department regarding the missing men. Lance Ayers paid him a visit on March 9th after doing some investigative work to find out who the coach was for the team. Not only did Pennock fail to reach out to the Sheriff's Department, but he also made no attempt to contact the families, according to Ayers.

When Ayers met with Pennock, he wanted to know why Pennock made zero effort to contact law enforcement and the families. At the time, two weeks had passed since the five went missing, plus Pennock did not call the families on February 25th to inquire about them missing an important basketball tournament. According to Ayers's report, Pennock was nonchalant in his attitude and told Ayers, "I felt if you wanted to talk to me, that you would contact me." When further questioned about his silence following the disappearance of the five, Pennock stated that he hadn't "thought about it one way or another."

Pennock told Ayers that nobody from law enforcement had contacted him when the Gateway Projects faced issues with arson and the murder of Donald Garrett. It was Pennock's opinion that that's how law enforcement handled cases.

Although Pennock knew the five, he claimed he was not informed of their trip to Chico to watch a college basketball game. Players were to meet at the Montgomery Ward's parking lot the morning of the 25th to go to Sierra College, but Pennock was running late that morning and drove directly to Sierra, unaware that Weiher, Madruga, Sterling, Huett, and Mathias never showed up for the bus. Ayers was informed by Pennock that he was asked by Bill Sterling to suggest some places to practice in Sacramento on Thursday, February 23rd, but Pennock did not know if the five ever made it to Sacramento.

Ayers then asked Pennock to give his personal assessments of the five. Pennock said Ted Weiher was "quick-tempered" because he had been involved in a few altercations at Gateway. However, Weiher was not viewed as an aggressor. Gary Mathias was someone Pennock did not know all that well, but he viewed Mathias as "spacey" due to drug issues and believed that, at any moment, Mathias could "flip out." Pennock found Bill Sterling to be the most intelligent of the group, but Pennock saw him as "very lazy." Jack Madruga was seen as very quiet and reserved by Pennock, and he stated nothing about Jackie Huett.

☙

Candace Wagner (pseudonym) was a possible girlfriend of Ted Weiher's who was interviewed by Detective Cozine at a school in the Marysville and Yuba City area. The case notes did not state who Wagner was, but she was either a student or a member of the Gateway Projects. Although Wagner was interviewed, she did not provide any valuable information or possible leads, according to Cozine in his report. While Cozine was at the school, he met a teacher by the name of Joanne Martin.

Martin may have had some experience with students with disabilities. According to Martin, the five missing men had an impaired ability or limited "abstract reasoning ability" where they could function normally if given positive input and direction. Her belief was that the five would not "reason out an entire line of conduct from beginning to end." Cozine put in his report that he was told by Martin, "Collectively, they would probably reason the entire line one step at a time. The second step, being reasoned as they were doing the first step, or shortly after they completed the first step."

After sharing that information, Martin told Cozine that students with disabilities like the five were uninhibited in a sexual manner. Martin had experiences with these behaviors in class, and some students reportedly forced themselves on other people. Students often complained to her when this happened. While this was said in passing, it seemed to have stuck with Cozine and some other members of the Yuba County Sheriff's Department. A note was featured on one of the five's subject profiles stating that a statement from a parent should be double-checked due to the Martin's comment regarding sexual behaviors and people with intellectual disabilities.

Cozine then asked Martin to examine theories regarding the disappearance of Weiher, Madruga, Sterling, Huett, and Mathias. The first was that they went to the game in Chico, but some extraneous force was behind their disappearance. Another theory centered around the five losing themselves or breaking away from society for fun, but when they did so, they became confused and lost, and they abandoned their car.

Martin was not convinced by the theory that they would lose themselves and break away from society. The five, in her opinion, lacked the abstract reasoning ability to execute a plan of that nature. She also didn't believe that the five became completely lost in the middle of nowhere because they had experience driving to and from cities like Sacramento. Martin believed that the five were coerced by someone using extraneous force at the time or when they arrived at said location. Cozine also asked Martin if the men could have ended up in a commune, which were common in Northern California. Martin said it was possible and told Cozine that those environments were ideal for individuals with disabilities because they might find that lifestyle more enjoyable than their lives at home.

℘

The Yuba County Sheriff's Department was informed by another witness, Tanya Sermas (pseudonym) that an acquaintance told her that he had been in contact with the five since they had gone missing. In fact, the acquaintance knew the location of the cabin where they were staying. Sermas was told that the five would be found in Grass Valley, California, which was thirty-five miles east of Marysville.

Louis Rudolph (pseudonym) was the name of the acquaintance, and he had met with Sermas on the evening of March 7, 1978, at her residence. Rudolph had been talking about quitting his job, and she had asked Rudolph their thoughts on the missing men. According to Sermas, Rudolph admitted the men had been in contact with him, and he knew their location because one of the men called Rudolph at work. Rudolph claimed during the call that someone in the background said something to the effect of, "If you say something, we'll get in trouble."

Sermas was concerned that the missing men did not have food, but Rudolph assured her that there was plenty of food for the men. Rudolph said that the place was cold, but it was a cabin in Grass Valley that belonged to a father of one of the five. Rudolph told Sermas that all the men had grown tired of living in Marysville and wanted to get away from it all.

Bud Cozine from the Yuba County Sheriff's Department investigated Rudolph's claims. Cozine met with people at Rudolph's place of employment, and they were aware that Rudolph received calls at work. The coworkers were asked more about Rudolph, and they told Cozine that Rudolph had a reputation for exaggerating and fabricating stories. A coworker told Cozine they would speak with Rudolph about his claims. The coworker called Cozine back after speaking with Rudolph, who denied he was lying about the men. The coworker did not believe Rudolph due to his reputation.

⁊

At this time, additional cabins were being searched for the missing men. Two members of the Yuba County Sheriff's Department were sent to check cabins in Yuba County near a small unincorporated area known as Oregon House. It was twenty-eight miles east of Marysville, but the men were not found. A pile of baby clothes was discovered near a creek, but it was determined the items could have drifted there from another location.

A sighting of the five was reported in Los Angeles by a student at the University of Southern California (USC). The student claimed he was on a bus leaving the USC campus on March 9th when he saw the five on the bus. According to the witness, all five were dropped off at Hoover Street and Adams Avenue. The witness remembered that they were all laughing and joking around together as they exited the bus. They were confident it was the five because they had read about the missing men in the paper and saw stories about the search on television.

Another witness spoke with the Yuba County Sheriff's Department about someone they knew who owned a red pickup truck. The person who drove the truck was described as a "hippie," and they may have encountered the missing men.

One citizen admitted in mid-March that they had been listening to a police scanner on Tuesday, February 28th, and they recalled an animal control officer radioed in that a man had been "put out" of his car and was looking for "the Olympics." From what was reported, the animal control officer was not allowed to give the man a ride, and a vehicle was not available to pick up the man at the time. Also, the report did not state the city or county where this incident occurred.

Avery Blankenship and Lance Ayers met with a longtime friend of Gary Mathias's to see if he had anything to share. The friend told the investigators that Mathias would visit him frequently to drink a few beers, and February 23rd was the last time he saw Mathias, who talked about the basketball tournament at Sierra College and seemed very excited about playing.

The friend stated there would be times when Mathias seemed down and had an unpredictable vibe. Mathias, according to the friend, was a bit frustrated with his love life and had a very low opinion of women. On the other hand, the friend recalled Mathias having a love of children and enjoying the company of men. Blankenship and Ayers learned from the friend that Mathias was always a respectful guest and never got out of hand at his home. The friend had no theories as to why the five went missing and could not think of anyone who would want to harm Mathias.

On March 14, 1978, the Yuba County Sheriff's Department met with the Butte County Sheriff's Department to give them an update on their end of the investigation. Detective Captain Leroy Wood represented Butte County, and Detective Bud Cozine represented Yuba County. The sighting at Behr's Market had been confirmed. Other sighting claims were discussed, and information provided by Joanne Martin at the school was shared with Butte County.

On March 15, 1978, one day after the meeting, the Yuba County Sheriff's Department was contacted by Debbie Lynn Reese. A resident of the Marysville-Yuba City area, Reese wanted authorities to know that they had been the recipient of a bizarre phone call from an unknown male concerning the case. Reese did not know the voice of the caller, and she could not make out any background noises during the call. Also, there was no reason for anyone to call her about the missing men from the Yuba County area. When asked about the call, Reese told the Yuba County Sheriff's Department the following:

Debbie Lynn Reese: *Hello?*

Unknown Caller: *I know where the five missing men are.*

Reese told investigators that the caller ended the call with a sigh, and he was calm while speaking with her on the phone. Following the first call, she immediately contacted the authorities, who told her to call them back if she received another call from the unknown individual. Reese called back that same day, reporting another phone call from the same individual. She shared details of the second call. She recalled:

Debbie Lynn Reese: *Hello?*

Unknown Caller: *I had to hurt them.*

Debbie Lynn Reese: *Who?*

Unknown Caller: *You know who.*

Once again, Reese did not recognize the voice, nor did she hear anything in the background during their brief conversation. The second call ended with a sigh as well. Reese was advised by the Yuba County Sheriff's Department to record all calls if possible and to call them immediately if the unknown person contacted her again.

The next call to Reese occurred on March 16th and she contacted the authorities with details of that call:

Debbie Lynn Reese: *Hello?*

Unknown Caller: *I need help 'cause I hurt those guys bad!*

Debbie Lynn Reese: *Who did you hurt?*

Unknown Caller: *Don't play dumb with me!*

This call was different for Reese because the calm demeanor of the caller was gone. This time the caller was nervous and upset. Reese stated she could identify the caller's voice if she were to hear it "under different circumstances."

Reese called the Yuba County Sheriff's Department on March 17th following a fourth phone call. Reese provided the following:

Debbie Lynn Reese: *Hello?*

Unknown Caller: *Those five guys are all dead.*

Debbie Lynn Reese: *They're all dead?*

Unknown Caller: *They're all dead.*

There was no sigh to end the call as the caller simply hung up on Reese. The Yuba County Sheriff's Department requested a recording device for Reese in case she received another call. According to the case file, Debbie Lynn Reese never called back with any updates, and it is unknown if she was interviewed by the Sheriff's Department. Some were of the opinion it was a tall tale by Reese to collect the reward money or that she was the victim of a prank caller. However, Reese's number was unlisted, so the caller would have had to know her number. The calls were made over a series of days, which seems unlikely for a prank call.

❧

The *Appeal-Democrat* reported on March 9th that the ground search for Weiher, Madruga, Sterling, Huett, and Mathias would come to an end because investigators wanted to focus on the leads that were coming in from various citizens and supposed witnesses. Both Jim Grant and Jack Beecham were trying to figure out if foul play was involved. According to the article, if it was foul play, then it may have occurred in Butte County. Jim Grant promised another search via helicopter once the weather improved. In the meantime, forest rangers were informed about the missing men just in case any discoveries were made in the Plumas National Forest.

Another search effort was made in the Plumas National Forest in early March. They searched the area where the car went missing and even looked from Forbestown in Butte County to an area called LaPorte in Plumas County, which was twenty-seven miles northeast. A helicopter aided in that. They investigated the Brownsville area and places around Yuba County for the men but had no luck.

Also printed in that edition of the *Appeal-Democrat* was an article about Jim Grant filing paperwork for reelection. His term as the Sheriff-Coroner for Yuba County was coming to an end, but he was going to run for a second term. Four other people also filed as possible candidates. Grant had pulled off an upset victory back in 1974, and if he could solve the great mystery of the five missing men, he would likely win reelection.

The case and the election were not the only thing on Jim Grant's mind during this time. Lloyd "Pat" Finley would be heading to trial one year following his standoff and surrender at the Yuba County Sheriff's Department. Eight counts were brought against Finley, two felonies and six misdemeanors. Items taken from the evidence room by Finley and the theft of a pistol that belonged to a deceased member of the Yuba County Sheriff's Department did him in as undersheriff under Grant. Before the trial began, Grant sent a letter out to the community stating he stood behind his decision to fire Finley, which made Finley's legal team question the ability of their client to have a fair trial in Yuba County. They requested a dismissal but were denied.

Joseph Schons would also face something of a trial. He agreed to meet with the members of the missing men to discuss what happened on the night the five went missing. It was not reported where they met, the date of the meeting, and how many of the family members were in attendance. Also, it is uncertain if any member of the Yuba County Sheriff's Department or the Butte County Sheriff's Department was in attendance. Nelda Weiher, Imogene Weiher's daughter-in-law, recalled attending the meeting. An audio tape of the interview, recorded by Sara Huett, exists, but the audio is poor.

Family members pushed Schons for answers and he did his best to provide his memories of that fateful evening. Schons did discuss what was published in the press. He said there were "some long paragraphs of absolutely no basis of fact." When asked about his statement, he said the information about him was wrong. Schons wanted to give the families the truth.

He made a statement about "five boys charging into the night" into the snow and freezing temperatures. The cold was tough on Schons because he claimed that he was without heat in his own car for some four to five hours. Someone asked him about the amount of snow on the ground on February 24th and he replied, "Where I was, there was quite a bit." The snow was also described by Schons as a "solid pan," and that's how Schons's Volkswagen became stuck that evening. He then made some sort of statement about there being less snow, possibly a few inches, where the five became stuck in the Montego. Family members sounded dismissive, and one person yelled out, "There was four feet of snow!"

Schons said he thought he was going to die the night he was stuck, and he was upset when the men did not assist him. He then told the families he had no idea that the five had been diagnosed with disabilities. The other vehicle, the red pickup truck, was mentioned during the meeting, and Schons was also upset with the occupants of that vehicle because they, too, abandoned him on that road.

One family member, possibly Imogene Weiher, inquired when Schons first contacted the authorities. From what was audible from the recording, Schons may have put the blame on his wife, Cindy Schons. He made some sort of statement that was inaudible in parts where he said he instructed his wife to call the cops to find out more about the Montego.

Another attendee, possibly one of Jack Madruga's sisters, asked Schons why he was on that road in the first place. "Just horsing around," was Schons's reply. It was not his intention to be stuck on the road, but he was, and he told the attendees that he tried to push his car out but suffered a heart attack. Schons then said he got back into his car to stay warm, but the car ran out of gas at midnight.

Someone inquired when Schons saw the Montego. "Sometime between 11 p.m. and 12 a.m. I'd say 11:30 p.m.," replied Schons. He claimed he had heard whistling noises and stated that perhaps it was a couple of people who approached his car that night. Schons remembered they had flashlights, and they were shined in his window. The number of people that Schons saw that night was brought into question as well. Schons told the family members that he saw "two or three" people and the claims he saw five people that night were not true.

Schons was also asked if he saw a woman with a baby, plus someone wanted to know if any of the men he saw that night were wearing cowboy hats. Schons claimed that he never said he saw a woman with a baby, but he saw something that appeared to look like a woman holding something like a baby. However, Schons went on to explain that hours after first encountering the men, he walked down to Madruga's car. He claimed to see "a child's carrier" in the car. The man with the cowboy hat was something Dr. Gloria Daniel claimed to be part of her psychic vision. Schons told the family members that he did not see a man in a cowboy hat.

When asked about his heart attack, Schons stated that on Saturday, February 25th, at 6 p.m., he met with a doctor. He talked about his hospitalization and told those in attendance about his wife getting his car started and unstuck on Sunday. There were additional questions about him walking away from his own vehicle during the early hours on Saturday. Schons claimed he both walked and crawled in the snow to get from his car to Mountain House. While the audio on Sara Huett's tape was not entirely clear, there may have been a line of questioning from the family members where they asked Schons if he recalled the direction the five went after they abandoned the Montego. "They were there and then they were gone," said Schons with an agitated tone.

Tension began to rise when one person in attendance claimed they were told by a detective that Schons wouldn't answer any more questions about the case because a doctor feared it would be too stressful and the result could be another heart attack. Schons did not know anything about the statement and attempted to diffuse the situation.

As the meeting progressed, someone asked Schons if he was intoxicated that night and he denied it with a "No, ma'am." From what could be heard on the tape, there was a question about how much he drank that night, and Schons claimed to have had one beer. He then mentioned something about his beer consumption or his intoxication being documented.

By that point in the meeting, Schons had lied to the families at least twice about the evening of February 24th, first when he claimed he was at the snow line "horsing around" and then stating that he consumed one beer. Schons had previously claimed he was checking the snow line for a family trip, and other reports had him checking on a cabin in the area. During the questioning at the Mountain House, investigators were told that Schons had consumed more than one beer.

It was also discovered during this meeting with the families that Schons had hired a lawyer because he wanted "a retraction" in the paper. Schons may have been discussing an article in the *Appeal-Democrat*. His grievances with their article or articles are not known due to the condition of the audio.

∾

Lake Oroville's shorelines were searched on March 10th for the remains of the missing men, but there was nothing to report. Roadsides and culverts from Chico to where the car was abandoned were also checked for remains by Butte County, but nothing was found. There was another meeting between the Yuba County Sheriff's Department and the Butte County Sheriff's Department on March 13th to further discuss the direction of the case. Brush Creek, an area to the southwest of where the car was abandoned, was surveyed via helicopter on March 15th with no results. Foul play continued to be brought up as a possibility by law enforcement in the press, but there was nothing in the way of clues showing anything sinister had or had not occurred.

∾

When Mopac Audio interviewed Jack Huett before his death in 2018, they were given audio tapes by Tom and Claudia Huett. Sara Huett recorded meetings in 1978 with Dr. Gloria Daniel then Joseph Schons. There were some other tapes, including a meeting with Jim Grant. Mopac Audio converted them to digital files, and they did some editing work to improve the sound quality. Shannon McGarvey sent me links to the audio, and I was beyond excited to listen to the meetings.

The one I wanted to hear the most was that Schons meeting I just discussed. I wanted to hear his voice. I was curious to know if he was sympathetic or just there to hear himself deliver what Tom McGarry referred to as whoppers. The lies I heard Schons tell the families were infuriating, and at one point, I had to get up and walk away from my computer. The meeting with Schons was just part of the never-ending madness that was March 1978.

CHAPTER SIXTEEN:
LATE MARCH 1978

My commute to work is an hour and I have plenty of time to enjoy music or an audiobook. There are times when I just drive and think. The Yuba County Five case pops into my head and I go over theory after theory. I think about Madruga on the highway the night the five vanished. Why did he get off the highway and drive through Oroville to the Plumas? Researching this case has nearly sent me over the edge at times.

Nearly one month after the five disappeared, families and investigators were experiencing their own journey. There was frustration, anger, and sadness. Something had to give. Something. Anything.

છેડ

The search in the Plumas National Forest had come to a brief halt, and investigators were focusing their time on Jack Madruga's 1969 Mercury

Montego. When searched by investigators in Oroville, they found more than bottles and wrappers from items purchased at Behr's Market. Maps of Sacramento, Stockton, San Francisco, and a state map of California were found in the vehicle. One map was open and on the front seat, while the rest were neatly folded in the glovebox. The maps also had markings and handwritten data. They were believed to be the property of Jack Madruga, but it was soon discovered that the maps actually belonged to Bill Sterling.

Juanita Sterling, Bill's mother, informed investigators that the maps were her son's, so she was questioned again about them by Lance Ayers. From what Sterling remembered, they had belonged to her son for a while, and she also recalled the maps were old. According to Sterling, Bill had a love and appreciation for maps. He could read maps well, plus he would mark maps after watching a commercial on television that caught his attention. Ayers wanted to know more about the markings on the maps, but Sterling could only speculate why Bill had made certain markings and written down certain names and information.

The first map they discussed was the Sacramento map. Sterling was certain Bill had made the markings and notes. "Fun Masters" at 3026 Florin was the first item they reviewed. Fun Masters of Sacramento was a mini-golf facility that the five may have enjoyed visiting.

There was an "X" with a circle marked at 73rd Street and Marin Avenue, a circle at Abbey Road and Carlton Road, a circle near Perkins Golf Center at Florin Perkins Road and Folsom Boulevard, an "X" marked at Fulton Avenue and the Alta Arden Expressway, a circle at Sunrise Boulevard and Greenback Lane, an "X" with a circle was marked on Winding Way near American River College, and a circle at Florin Perkins Road/French Road and Florin Road. There was a note on the map at the William Land Regional Park with "200" noted on the map. Sterling was not certain why those areas were marked but surmised they were related to people Bill knew from the Gateway Projects or his bowling league.

I conducted a 2021 Google Maps examination of these locations and compared it against a 1975 Sacramento city directory to determine the importance of those markings to Bill Sterling. The Joseph Bonnheim

Elementary School, located in a residential neighborhood, was at the "X" marked at 73rd Street and Marin Avenue. This could have been the location of an event related to the Gateway Projects or a basketball game. The circle at Abbey Road and Carlton Road was for a Zion Temple Church Christ Holiness in 1975 and in 2021 was listed as Full Gospel Faith Assembly. Bill Sterling had been exploring churches to join during the 1970s and was involved in a Christian singles group, so the church may have been of interest for one of those reasons. The circle near Perkins Golf Center at Florin Perkins Road and Folsom Boulevard is, at the time of publication, the location of Cristo Rey High School, which was built twenty-eight years after the men went missing. A 1975 directory showed the Perkins Golf Center, a judo club, a restaurant, and apartments close to that area. The "X" marked at Fulton Avenue and the Alta Arden Expressway was for an intersection with various businesses and apartments. The circle at Sunrise Boulevard and Greenback Lane was a similar intersection with various businesses. The "X" with a circle that was marked on Winding Way near American River College could have been for the Seventh Day Adventist Church, an Episcopal church, or the Sacramento Union Academy that was in the area. Finally, the circle at Florin Perkins Road/French Road and Florin Road had various businesses and residences at the time the map was marked by Bill Sterling.

In the interview, Lance Ayers then asked Juanita Sterling for information about the San Francisco map. She remembered that Bill Sterling and his brother-in-law had visited the city years prior to watch the San Francisco Giants play baseball at Candlestick Park. She also said that Bill had not used the map in ages.

A state map of California was then reviewed, and Ayers noted there were markings on the map focused on the Los Angeles area with certain hospitals circled. Sterling thought they were of interest to her son because he had spent time in two state hospitals. She also theorized that people Bill knew from his time being institutionalized may have been moved to some hospitals in Los Angeles. Other California areas were circled on the map, like Napa, Sonoma, Penngrove, El Verano, Porterville, Costa

Mesa, and San Jose. The same map had "X" marks at Shaver Lake, Fresno, Hume, and Woodlake. Also on the map were handwritten notes of "tent, sleeping bag, ice chest swim trunks, etc." and Sterling determined they were connected to Bill's time with the local Christian singles group. They had made trips to locations such as Shaver Lake in Fresno County, but Sterling knew her son did not attend those trips because he was not a fan of the outdoors and camping.

There was no information about Ayers discussing the Stockton map with Sterling but, according to the report, it also had some areas marked, including the Stockton State Hospital. Other areas marked on the map included city hall and a place called Pixie Woods, which was a small amusement park for children of all ages.

The families of Ted Weiher, Jack Madruga, Jackie Huett, and Gary Mathias were made aware of the maps along with the writings and markings. None of the other families could comment on the writings or markings. Most importantly, they were not aware of the existence of the maps.

While the maps didn't shed any light on clues regarding the disappearance of the five, the Yuba County Sheriff's Department would be notified that the Butte County Sheriff's Department made a promising discovery on March 19th in the Plumas National Forest.

North of where the car was abandoned, four strips of gold-orange cloth were found by Butte County Search and Rescue Captain Jim Doering. The cloth was tied to trees in an area known as Soapstone Hill and was believed to mark a trail. The first and second pieces of cloth were found one-quarter mile before and after the Four Trees Road area. The third piece of cloth was discovered one and a half miles north of the Four Trees Road area, and the final piece was found some three miles past the road.

The location of Four Trees Road is four miles west of Rogers Cow Camp, while Grizzly Summit is nine miles north of Rogers Cow Camp. Grizzly Summit is one mile north of a spot known as the Daniel Zink Campground.

Also found by investigators were footprints that led into the canyon near Soapstone Hill. Ken Mickelson from the Butte County Sheriff's

Department said the footprints appeared to "wander" into the canyon. The report at the Yuba County Sheriff's Department stated the footprints were more "erratic" in nature. Mickelson believed the footprints were "real old" but wanted to investigate further. He would tell the press, "We don't know yet if the tracks have anything to do with the case."

The footprints led to some abandoned cabins that were searched but no evidence of the missing men was found. The footprints then led further toward the canyon. Deep snow proved an obstacle for search teams, but the terrain itself was described as "treacherous." Mickelson also told the press, "We can't even get in there with snowshoes or skis. It's too steep. If they went in there, they wouldn't come back out." The *Appeal-Democrat* reported on March 20th that a helicopter search was scheduled for that day, but it proved "fruitless" according to the Yuba County Sheriff's Department report. The search team saw the tracks and followed them but lost them at a certain point. Mickelson questioned if the tracks had any validity.

Undersheriff Jack Beecham theorized that the cloth could have been from the lining of a jacket. Bill Sterling had been wearing a leather jacket the night they disappeared, but a family spokesperson was not convinced the cloth was from Sterling's coat. Gary Mathias was also reportedly wearing a coat that night, and it was not reported if his family was contacted about the cloth.

Investigators believed they missed the cloth during the initial search of the area due to the snow depth at the time. The snow depth was roughly four to six feet deep when they first examined the vicinity, and enough snow had melted where it was down a foot or two when the gold cloth was discovered. Scent dogs were initially sent that way during the early part of the investigation, but they did not pick up on the scent of any of the men.

One day later, Butte County called off the search. Ken Mickelson stated, "Right now, we're out of leads."

Lance Ayers had a chance to review the cloth and said it looked weathered, but it also appeared not to have been exposed to the elements for a long period. Ayers stated they would follow up on tips that had been called in to the Yuba County Sheriff's Department. Within days of the discovery, the reward money rose to $3,500 (roughly $15,000 in 2022) for information on Weiher, Madruga, Sterling, Huett, and Mathias.

Sheriff Jim Grant, along with the family members, decided near the end of March to add the missing men to the *Sacramento Bee's* Secret Witness program. The program allowed people to provide tips on cases anonymously and it was cosponsored by groups such as the Northern California Grocers Association, the California Cattlemen's Association, and the Sacramento Society for the Prevention of Cruelty to Animals. The reward was up to $5,000; there were hopes that someone would come forward with a tip that would bring closure to the case. By that time, investigators and volunteers had spent thousands of hours of time investigating the five and searching the Plumas National Forest.

F. Melvyn Lawson, the chairman of the Secret Witness Rewards Committee, said, "We hope to get information which would result in the safe return of these men to their families." He went on to add, "But if they have been harmed, we would pay a suitable reward for information leading to the arrest and conviction of anyone who has victimized them."

Not long after the men were added to the Secret Witness program, a tip came in from a worker at a theater who claimed they saw Jack Madruga and Gary Mathias in their lobby on February 25th. According to the witness, Madruga and Mathias were not in line together, and that they'd had an incident with Mathias. The witness recalled that, as Mathias waited in line for a ticket, he told a worker at the theater there was a seating problem. When the worker told Mathias, "You sure are in a bad mood," Mathias replied to them, "Excuse me, but fuck you." The witness also remembered Madruga paid for his ticket in change but didn't provide the right amount when he tried to pay. Madruga ultimately paid the correct amount and then hung out in the lobby with Mathias eating popcorn.

Another person who contacted the Secret Witness believed that there was a possibility that the five abandoned the Montego and then got into another car. They stated they were a teacher and had students with disabilities in their classroom, and that those students enjoyed "playing games" because they were like children mentally. This witness recalled an incident, possibly near Sacramento, where they were driving and nearly collided with a light blue car with five men inside. The witness recalled a man in the backseat with glasses, but the same witness stated they looked over the pictures of the men in the *Sacramento Bee* and they "didn't ring a bell."

Sightings of Weiher, Madruga, Sterling, Huett, and Mathias continued to be reported to the Yuba County Sherriff's Office in late March. A man in Paradise, California, roughly twenty-one miles north of Oroville, claimed he played pool with two of the men at a pizza joint. The witness believed they were with a third man who stood by a jukebox. A few games of pool were played, and the three left the joint. A bartender there seemed relieved when the three left, according to the witness.

Lance Ayers reached out to the witness. He was shown images of the men, and the witness was certain the two men he played pool with were Gary Mathias and Jackie Huett. The witness could not describe the third man near the jukebox. However, the witness said Mathias was wearing a flowered shirt and glasses. Huett was described by the witness as having bushy brown hair and being shorter than Mathias.

Marianne Elko, a psychic, contacted Lance Ayers late in March. Although she lived near Pittsburgh, Pennsylvania, Elko was very familiar with the region. In 1973, she made headlines regarding her involvement in the case of Johnathan Goodier of Palermo, California. Goodier was a seventy-six-year-old man who had been reported missing. The Goodier's daughter knew about Elko's abilities and had telephoned her for help. Elko informed the daughter that Goodier was dead and that five teenagers were involved. Goodier's body was found days after the call, and those responsible were indeed five teenagers.

Goodier's daughter connected Lance Ayers with Marianne Elko. The daughter may have been the person who contacted Sara Huett earlier in the month. Ayers spoke with Elko over the phone and a report was created by the Yuba County Sheriff's Department. Elko told Ayers that a group of men followed Madruga and the others on the night they went missing.

She was not specific, but the incident may have started in Oroville. Elko theorized that the five grew nervous when they became aware that they were being followed. It caused Madruga to make some wrong turns, which led them to the road in the Plumas. Elko said the men were forced out of the car and placed in the back of a pickup truck and bound. The truck then drove northeast from the car. She also told Ayers that one of the men was dumped in a body of water.

Elko's claims of the five being driven northeast from the car were questioned by Ayers because the roads going that direction were impassable due to snowfall.

Ayers made a few interesting comments to Elko during the call. He informed Elko that while the Butte County Sheriff's Department had assisted with the search, they were "not much help anymore… they've done what they can do." Elko wanted to know if there was a connection between the disappearance of the five and the arson and murder at Gateway. Ayers told her there wasn't but admitted that law enforcement knew who killed the executive director, Donald Garrett. According to Ayers, Garrett had angered an individual and they had retaliated. Elko believed the five went missing because Gateway had "a horrible, negative manifestation of sin."

Additional psychics were contacted by the Yuba County Sheriff's Department in late March. They were provided a series of questions and asked to respond based on their visions. The investigators wanted to know the present locations of the bodies. They also wanted to know how they got to those locations and if any physical evidence would be found. There was also a question about Madruga's car and whether Madruga was the one that drove it the night they disappeared in the Plumas. Additional questions included whether the men were alive or if anyone in the group acted violently toward anyone. Dr. Gloria Daniel was one of the psychics contacted.

One psychic believed a green Chevy Blazer was the vehicle that followed the five to the road where the Montego was abandoned. They also believed something may have happened between the five and the driver of the Blazer at a four-way stop, possibly near a gas station. A cabin in the Plumas was where law enforcement would find the five.

Some of the psychics believed that Jackie Huett knew the woman with the baby. She was a decoy, according to the psychics. They also told law enforcement that all five were coerced in some way into cooperating. The psychics agreed that the five understood that their lives were in danger if they didn't cooperate.

Also, during this time, the Yuba County Sheriff's Department was contacted by Farren and Connie DeLozier about an incident a month prior to the disappearance of the five. Connie DeLozier was Jackie Huett's sister. The DeLoziers told investigators that they were attending a party at a friend's place when Gary Mathias showed up and struck Farren in the face. DeLozier responded by punching Mathias in the face repeatedly, until a bunch of people broke up the altercation. After this, Mathias immediately left the party.

Farren and Connie DeLozier were contacted by a mutual friend sometime in November or December 1977 about a similar situation that had occurred at another party. The mutual friend witnessed Gary Mathias getting into a fight at that party and also leaving when the fight was broken up by attendees. Mathias started to walk around the building where the party was taking place, looking through the windows. Some of the attendees decided to speak with Mathias about his behavior, but he told the attendees that he could not bother them since he already killed them. The Yuba County Sheriff's Department tried getting in touch with the mutual friend, but they were unsuccessful.

Another citizen came forward to the Yuba County Sheriff's Department to inform them that sometime in 1975 or 1976, he saw Ted Weiher hunting near Bucks Lake in the Plumas National Forest. He would go to that area to hunt and stay in a cabin owned by an elderly man. From what the witness remembered, he saw Weiher at the cabin with another man and a small boy. A few moments after seeing Weiher, he watched Weiher, the boy, and the man get into a pickup truck. He told investigators he was certain it was Weiher because he claimed he did not live far from the Weiher family in Olivehurst.

Imogene Weiher, Ted's mother, was interviewed about the sighting and told law enforcement that her son never went hunting and never owned a gun. "Ted might have gone camping with the family, but he never hunted," said Dallas Weiher Jr., who added, "I don't think they'd trust him with a gun without strict supervision." Weiher Jr. believed the witness was mistaken.

Easter was on March 26, 1978. When asked about his family celebrating without his uncle Ted, Dallas Weiher Jr. responded, "There was definitely a piece missing. We prayed for his safe return." He remembers the family celebration and the Pepsis stocked in the fridge at the Weiher household.

Shortly after Easter, Pat Finley was found guilty on two felony charges but was found not guilty on six misdemeanor charges. The *Appeal-Democrat* reported that Finley sat with his head in his hands as his family "sobbed quietly." He was later sentenced to eighteen months in the Sacramento County Jail and was given four years of probation. An agreement was made where Finley was housed at the jail but was free to leave on work furlough to do various jobs.

As March ended, search dogs from El Dorado County were requested for a second attempt at tracking the missing men. They had been unsuccessful the first time, but there was hope they could find something in the Soapstone Creek area after the discovery of the footprints.

⌘

When I was examining the files at the Yuba County Sheriff's Department, they showed me a copy of one of the maps that was in Madruga's Montego. It was a map of the Sacramento area. The Yuba County Sheriff's Department purchased a similar map and made the same markings on that one as the original. I spent some time reviewing the map and taking notes because I wanted to know why the markings were made. They gave me permission to take pictures since it was a copy.

Tom and Claudia Huett sent me images of Jack Huett Sr.'s map of the Plumas. He spent many days there in 1978 and had his own map with various markings. Rogers Cow Camp is marked and there are a series of concentric circles from that point. A line on the map goes from Rogers Cow Camp northeast to a spot known as the Little North Fork Campground. The line measures under three miles across the land. Markings in that area were done with a black pen or pencil. Markings north of there at the Daniel Zink Campground are in red.

I went online to search for road maps of California from the late 1970s. I found one and examined it to review the highways and roads near Oroville. Roads that went into the Plumas were not shown. This was interesting because a map was out in the car when the five vanished. I wondered if their map of California also did not show roads in the Plumas.

What the maps don't show are the dangers. While the story of the Yuba County Five has generated a great deal of interest, others have met a similar fate in the forests and parks of California.

CHAPTER SEVENTEEN:
THE DEAD AND THE LOST

When I taught history classes at a community college, I assigned excerpts of *Into the Wild* by Jon Krakauer. It is a 1996 book that examines the disappearance and tragic death of Christopher McCandless in the Alaskan wilderness. My reading assignment included a reaction paper. Most of my students enjoyed *Into the Wild*. Their reactions varied from sympathy to indifference. I thought about people reading the news in March 1978 about the five going missing. I wondered if they, too, were sympathetic or indifferent.

I was gathering newspaper data about the case and incidents involving missing persons in the Plumas. At one point, I decided to research a newspaper database to see if there were similar disappearances in the 1970s, especially in the national parks and forests in California. Why did they go missing? What was their fate?

Another thing that crossed my mind was people who went missing around the same time as the five. Did anyone vanish in Yuba, Sutter, or Butte Counties? What was their story?

❧

By the end of March 1978, the Yuba County Sheriff's Department had spent time investigating the case and providing search and rescue assistance to the Butte County Sheriff's Department. Data collected by the Yuba County Sheriff's Department showed that one hundred ninety-seven hours of overtime had been reported from February 25th through March 10th by their full-time staff. Posse and reserve units claimed two hundred forty-four hours of work to that point. By the end of March and into early April, there were fifty-seven hours of overtime spent on the investigation. Detective Lance Ayers accounted for most of those hours and was aided at times by Undersheriff Jack Beecham. Data was not available concerning the additional hours spent by the Butte County Sheriff's Department searching for the men in the Plumas National Forest.

Sutter County had some involvement in the case since Bill Sterling lived in Yuba City. While they did aid in the investigation, they were not as invested as Yuba or Butte Counties. A much bigger story had unfolded in Yuba City in 1978 and it had to do with the infamous serial killer Juan Corona.

Corona was found guilty in a 1972 trial, and in 1973, he was sentenced to life in prison. Months before his trial began, the California State Supreme Court had ended the death penalty in the state so that option was off the table. Not long afterward, Corona was repeatedly stabbed by another prisoner at the California Medical Facility, and it led to the loss of his left eye.

It was May 1977 when Corona made headlines again. A court of appeals ruled that Corona's first defense attorney's handling of the case was a "farce and a mockery." Corona's first attorney was apparently more interested in a book deal about Corona and was viewed as neglectful in the way he handled the Corona case.

A new trial was set for 1978, and there was a reported cost of $500,000 for the retrial in Sutter County. It was estimated that the retrial would last close to two years. Juan Corona had another chance in court.

ତ

Butte County had been dealing with another missing persons case since February 1978. Essie Hiett was forty-seven. She lived in Honcut, some fourteen miles south of Oroville, and she worked at the Card Room in Oroville as a dealer and hostess. It was sometime after 2 a.m. on February 13th when Hiett got into her 1975 Oldsmobile and left a place called Rusty Jack's Bar. Over an hour after she left the bar, Hiett's vehicle was found parked on the side of the road in the mud some one hundred sixty-five feet away from where it had crashed into a guard rail. Essie Hiett's car was close to her home, but she was nowhere to be found, and some of her clothing was at the scene. The pants belonging to Hiett were bloodied at the knee, and a shoe she had worn was discovered floating in a nearby pond.

At the time, LeRoy Wood of the Butte County Sheriff's Department said to the press, "It doesn't really make sense." The bloodied pants belonging to Hiett were found underneath one of the front wheels of her car. It was theorized that it was there for traction since her car was stuck in the mud. Wood found it odd that Hiett used her pants when she could have used a shirt or even a jacket.

Hiett was considered a good worker at the Card Room, and it was out of character for her to disappear. Her boss at the Card Room told a reporter, "She was just what you would call 'nice people.'" Those who knew her believed something sinister had occurred.

On March 14, 1978, Dave Smollar of the *Los Angeles Times* ran an article about the disappearances of Hiett and the Yuba County Five. They all disappeared in Butte County after they abandoned their vehicles. LeRoy Wood of the Butte County Sheriff's Department was quoted in the article but was mistakenly identified as LeRoy Moore. In the article,

Wood said, "We have nothing definite to connect the (Hiett) case to that of the five, but both happened, and we have a problem explaining them."

ℰℐℐ

On the same page as Smollar's article in the *Los Angeles Times* was another about the survival of Laurence Shannon from Grand Rapids, Michigan. Laurence and Emma Shannon were both in their eighties, and they had been married for fifty-two years. They made a cross-country trip from Michigan to California, where their daughter was living. Andy, the family's pet poodle, was along for the journey. The Shannons were driving through the High Sierra in Sequoia National Park east of Fresno when Laurence took a wrong turn on a back road, and they became stranded.

It was mid-February 1978, and the Shannons were lost in the middle of nowhere in the snow. They decided initially to stay in their motor home, but Laurence had plans to seek help. On the third day of being stranded, Emma Shannon stood up from a chair she was seated in, collapsed, and died. Laurence Shannon had no choice but to wrap his wife's body in a blanket and stay in the motor home with her body and Andy until help arrived.

Shannon told the press in 1978, "I did everything I could do to survive. I just figured I'd have to stay alive long enough to make sure Emma was buried properly." Instead of running his motor home to stay warm and wasting gas, Shannon layered himself in clothes and ate the food that was stocked in the vehicle. He Shannon ended up losing sixteen pounds. Andy kept Shannon company during the ordeal, and Shannon made sure the roof of the motor home was clear of snow in case an airplane or helicopter spotted them.

Almost a month after the Shannons' motor home became stranded, a man in a plane was flying over the area and spotted their vehicle. The authorities were alerted, and Shannon and Andy were rescued. Emma Shannon's body was flown out by a helicopter, and Laurence Shannon was reunited with his daughter.

The daughter believed that before her mother died her father was going to leave the vehicle to find help. There was a Boy Scout Camp in the area and Shannon would have tried reaching it, but his daughter thought he could have taken a wrong turn in the snow and died in the elements. "If my mother hadn't died, he would have tried to walk out of there," said Shannon's daughter in 1978. She also stated, "Even in death, my mother saved my father's life."

∽

It was December 1974 when Ray and Cindy DeCamp were camping in the Sierra Nevada, with their two-year-old daughter. They packed up and got into their truck. Somewhere near Rogers Cow Camp, their truck broke down.

It was snowing heavily at the time, so Ray DeCamp left his wife and daughter in the truck while h went to get help. He found a phone to call the Butte County Sheriff's Department. Ray DeCamp was gone for four hours, and it was a harrowing ordeal for Cindy and Victoria. A few attempts were made by Cindy to leave the truck with Victoria on foot, but the snow was relentless. She decided to keep herself and her child safe in the truck.

The family was rescued by Lt. Ken Mickelson and his staff from the Butte County Sheriff's Department. They assisted the family in finding a motel room to stay in temporarily while they recovered.

∽

Another compelling story of survival occurred three months before the five vanished when the Butte County Sheriff's Department was searching for two missing college students in the High Lakes area of the Lassen National Forest. Dennis Glover and Robert Dreher became lost in the snowy area on November 20, 1977. They were attending a fraternity function at a cabin at Philbrook Lake. A bonfire was dying down, and both Glover and Dreher volunteered to stay behind to make sure it went out properly.

Glover and Dreher got into a Volkswagen and decided to drive home. They became lost after a wrong turn somewhere near the Butte County line at Carr Mine. Then their car ran out of gas. The two decided to get out of the car and walk in the snow, hoping they would run into someone who could assist them. Help did not appear, so they walked into Plumas County where they discovered a cabin.

The pair decided not to stop and continued their walk through the snow. Dreher would later tell the press, "There were times that all I could think of was putting one foot in front of the other." He also remembered their clothes were soaking wet at times from walking in the snow. They decided to stop for the night and were somehow able to get a fire going. It was difficult for the two to rest or stay warm, so they decided to walk back toward the cabin, but they somehow walked past it and were lost again. Glover and Dreher found refuge under a rock overhang Monday evening. They decided to rest there, but dripping water from the overhang created puddles around the sleeping men.

Glover and Dreher had gone missing on a Sunday night and were reported missing sometime Tuesday by Glover's brother. The Butte County Sheriff's Department led the search and rescue operation. Searchers and rescue dogs made their way through two feet of snow in rugged locations to find the missing friends. An airplane was called in for the search, but the men were not spotted.

Butte County Undersheriff Richard Stenberg was asked by the press in 1977 if they thought of calling off the search following a few days of searching. "As long as there is a chance in a million, I don't know who wants to call it off. But so far, we've found absolutely no sign of them in there."

Hallucinations were haunting the two as they followed a creek bed that was near the cabin. Fortunately, they discovered it after what seemed like an eternity. "We hugged each other and started crying," said Dreher in a 1977 article.

The abandoned cabin provided little protection against the cold, and it was not stocked with any food. All they could find were a few teabags and a tiny bit of wine. However, the cabin had a box of matches for the two to use to start a fire to keep warm. There was also a twenty-foot-by-forty-foot barn, and Dreher had a plan. "I knew we were going to set that barn on fire."

Wood, paper from phone books, a mattress, and cardboard were placed in a corner of the barn and it was set ablaze on Friday, November 25th. The smoke from the fire caught the attention of a California Highway Patrol helicopter pilot, and the men were rescued. They were sent to a hospital where Glover spent roughly four hours while Dreher would stay longer to rest himself mentally and physically, plus some of his toes were badly frostbitten and needed treatment.

Lt. Ken Mickelson of the Butte County Sheriff's Department recalled that the rescue squad was "elated" when the two were found alive. Dreher and Glover had spent five days in the elements, and both men believed they covered thirty miles in knee-deep snow and subzero temperatures. "They had to be pretty sharp to keep going," said Mickelson.

Four months later, Mickelson and his Butte County search and rescue team were not having any luck finding Ted Weiher, Jack Madruga, Bill Sterling, Jackie Huett, and Gary Mathias. They also were not having any luck finding Essie Hiett. Perhaps April would bring better days and some news for the families.

CHAPTER EIGHTEEN:
APRIL AND MAY 1978

One of my initial thoughts about the Yuba County Five case was why didn't anyone contact the Federal Bureau of Investigation (FBI) to assist? By the end of March 1978, four jurisdictions had been working on the case and searching the Plumas. Weiher, Madruga, Sterling, Huett, and Mathias had not been found.

Some individuals interviewed for this book thought that someone from the Yuba County Sheriff's Department would reach out to the FBI for assistance. A few people I interviewed did not have a great deal of faith in Yuba County or Butte County at the time. "Back then, 'inept' is the best word I can think of," said someone who wished to remain anonymous.

Yuba County Sheriff Jim Grant was willing to hear what psychics had to say about the missing men early in the investigation. By April and

May 1978, Grant, along with other investigators, were willing to get any additional help from the public or another department.

❧

March 1978 ended with a rescue team searching a three-thousand-foot canyon at Soapstone Hill to find the missing five. They found nothing, while Sgt. Lance Ayers from the Yuba County Sheriff's Department was having little to no luck unearthing any new information. He even retraced the route they took from Chico to the Plumas National Forest. "I need to find these guys for their families' sake," said Ayers. "They need to know one way or another."

April saw little to no reporting on the case in local newspapers. The Secret Witness program still posted the men as missing in the *Sacramento Bee* with the promise of a $5,000 reward for information regarding their discovery. Families of the five signed and submitted a letter of gratitude to various newspapers in the Northern California area. In it, the families said the kindness of those helping and those who donated to the reward fund was beyond words. They also stated that God would help them find the five.

A husband and wife in Sacramento County reported to their local sheriff's department that they encountered a man walking in front of their home. He asked the couple if they knew the way to Yuba City, and they were somewhat suspicious since the man appeared to have some sort of disability. The Yuba County Sheriff's Department sent photos to the couple, but none of the images matched the man who had been in front of their home.

Rain and snow continued to be an issue in Northern California. Seasonal rainfall in the Marysville and Yuba City region hit eighty-six inches by April 6, 1978, which was twenty-five inches more than the previous season. Snow was still falling in the Sierra Nevada, and temperatures were below freezing at times. By the end of April, the snow level was reportedly at five thousand feet. Places like the Daniel Zink Campground in the Plumas were at that elevation.

℃⅋

In other news, David Berkowitz (aka the Son of Sam) was found competent to stand trial in the murder of Stacy Moskowitz. Berkowitz was accused of killing six and wounding seven. Also, Sacramento area law enforcement reported their 33rd rape case from the "East Area." A mysterious but frightening man had terrorized the area since June 1976. That individual would become known as the Golden State Killer. In San Francisco, the notorious Zodiac killer broke a fifty-one-month period of silence when he submitted a letter to the *San Francisco Chronicle*.

Crime in Yuba and Butte Counties did not slow down for investigators during the case of the missing five. Murder, Robbery, accidents, and other crimes still occurred, and they were investigated by both agencies. Avery Blankenship from the Yuba County Sheriff's Department stated in an interview that crime was so bad in Yuba County during the 1970s that their conviction rate was equal to Los Angeles County. He also mentioned that cities like Marysville struggled financially, and their local police departments were in danger of being cut entirely.

It was around May 11th when a man from Magalia, California, offered his help searching for the five men. He was a water witcher and claimed that he had found the bodies of the five in a boarded-up cabin by water witching. Also known as water dowsing, water witching is a practice where someone uses a forked stick or rod to detect underground water supplies or minerals. The forked stick or rod is to be held a certain way with the "butt end" pointed forty-five degrees skyward. When the person holding the forked stick or rod passes over something like an underground water supply, then the "butt end" would point down at the ground.

"I was up there in Butte County… and I got a call up to a site where we had some deputies, and we had a guy that was a water witcher," recalled Jack Beecham. "He had his witching stick, and he said he could detect bodies. We were desperate at the time. [The witcher] said, 'Those bodies are in this cabin.'" Beecham recalled the cabin was not that far from where the Montego had been abandoned. Beecham said that the witcher was walking around the cabin and pointing to it. Beecham reported that the witcher said, "'There's a body here, there's a body there.'" Beecham wasn't convinced the claims were factual, but he knew he could not leave a stone unturned in the investigation. Since the cabin was in in Butte County, Beecham spoke with Undersheriff Dick Stenberg to update them on the situation. Beecham recalled saying, "We got this little wacko," and explained the claims to Stenberg. Beecham and his deputies were given permission to "kick the door down" to the cabin to search for bodies. There were no bodies inside the cabin. Beecham remembered the witcher trying to explain his findings after they searched the cabin. "'Oh, this must be an Indian burial ground.'"

Investigators were also examining the Four Trees Road area again after a dog picked up on the scent of decay. Plumas County Undersheriff Dave Wingfield spoke to the press about the search. "The man heading the search party is convinced there is something in that snow." Searchers spent an estimated twelve hours in the area with no luck. Even a tractor was brought in to dig into snowdrifts that were fifteen feet deep to search for human or even animal remains. They found nothing. "Personally, I'd like to think they are not there," said Wingfield. At that point, investigators and searchers agreed that the snow would be melting soon and hopefully they would find something or someone.

Butte County Undersheriff Dick Stenberg was asked by the press in May about the earlier sighting in Brownsville of the five and the footprints that were discovered. "Right now, there is no credibility to anything," said Stenberg. "I would expect developments after June 1, when the snow melts."

❧

On May 4th, Yuba County Sheriff Jim Grant wrote to California Attorney General Evelle Younger to request assistance. Grant's letter mentioned that the families had requested assistance from the state. Jack Thompson, a special agent with the California Department of Justice, was sent to Yuba County to work with Jack Beecham and Lance Ayers.

Beecham told the *Appeal-Democrat* that Thompson would conduct "a total review of the case… to see if there's anything we missed and get a professional opinion from another source." Thompson arrived at the Yuba County Sheriff's Department on May 22nd. He wanted to see the road where Madruga's car had been abandoned. They found the road had been graveled and the snow had melted. They did not find anything while reviewing the road with Thompson.

Another plan was to get the phone records of the families to review. It was possible someone contacted the men, or the men contacted a possible person of interest before they vanished. Information about the phone records was not included in the file.

Thompson spent May 23rd reviewing records at the Yuba County Sheriff's Department. His goal was to reexamine the radio and patrol logs for the Oroville Police Department, the Butte County Sheriff's Department, and surrounding departments from the night of February 24th into the early hours of February 25th.

The Oroville Police Department received two calls after 1 a.m. from a bar in the Oroville area about a minor fight. Those who participated in the fight were asked to leave, and they did so before police arrived.

During his research, Thompson discovered there was an incident around 4:45 a.m. on February 25th. The Oroville Police questioned a man who was the owner of a red pickup truck. The driver was found parked at the intersection of Olive Highway and Oroville Dam Boulevard and was pulled over under suspicion of driving under the influence. When officers asked for his identification, the driver handed them a credit card instead of a driver's license. A sobriety test was administered, but the driver failed and was arrested.

The driver would be interviewed, and he admitted to attending a party during the late hours of Friday, February 24th, and stayed there until the early morning hours on Saturday. He drank five or six beers at the party, and he also agreed to drive a woman home. It was after he dropped the woman off at her residence that he was arrested for drunk driving.

Pictures of the missing men were shown to the employees at the bar in Oroville who had reported the fight, but those interviewed never saw the men in the bar.

❧

Although his name was not mentioned, a May 24th article in the *Sacramento Bee* stated that Jack Beecham was hoping that "a witness" would take a lie detector test to "clear up conflicts" in their story. This "witness" was Joseph Schons, who had given conflicting stories of the night of February 24th. Jack Thompson from the Department of Justice wanted a thorough investigation of Schons and his family. Butte County had also examined Schons and his family. Investigators had discovered that one of Schons's children was in their teens and had a disability. Records indicate that following some investigative work, there was no link between Schons's child and the missing men.

Information in the press about Joseph Schons following March 1978 was minimal. He did not speak to any other papers, nor is there any record of him speaking to a television or radio station about the case. However, there was an incident in Irvine, California, that may have kept him occupied at the time.

❧

Lion Country Safari was in Irvine, a community in Orange County. Harry Shuster was a South African developer who opened Lion Country Safari in 1970. It was a one-hundred-forty-acre zoo where people could drive around in their cars and experience an African safari in Southern California. There were reportedly some eight hundred African animals and birds, which included elephants, cheetahs, rhinoceros, and lions. Convertibles were not permitted to drive around the zoo for safety concerns. A riverboat cruise was also available for guests, and there were also various amusement park-type rides for people to enjoy.

Lion Country Safari experienced an after-hours incident during the Memorial Day weekend of 1978. A man in his early twenties named James Stanley Gibson walked into a building at Lion Country Safari where the cash from the daily sales was being held. Wearing a guard uniform, Gibson greeted Deborah Yarber (pseudonym), an employee working after hours, and immediately pointed his gun at her. When questioned by the police, Yarber recalled that Gibson would go from speaking in a calm voice to being incredibly angry in a matter of seconds. She was ordered to hand over the cash, and a little over $3,000 was given to Gibson to put into a bag. Once Gibson had the cash, he placed Yarber in the walk-in vault that was in the building and fled the scene.

Yarber was able to get out of the vault, and she alerted another employee at the facility that there had just been a robbery. A call was made to the police and a description of Gibson was given to law enforcement. Most importantly, a description of Gibson's getaway car was also provided. He was soon spotted driving on the highway near Irvine, and Gibson sped away when the police tried to pull him over. An off-duty officer somehow became involved in the chase and ended up assisting in pulling over Gibson's car. Guns were pointed at Gibson once the chase was over, and he called out, "I did it! I'm sorry!"

When the police searched Gibson's car, they found the money and a .22 caliber pistol. They took Gibson to the police station for questioning and examined his California driver's license. Records were checked; they found out that James Stanley Gibson was an alias. They pressed Gibson for his real name, and he admitted to them his real identity. James Stanley Gibson was Greg Malone (pseudonym).

Once his identity was discovered, Malone told the police, "I fucked up, and I'll have to pay," and added, "It's open and shut." Records show Malone was upset during questioning but calmed down once officers handed him a cup of hot cocoa. He told police that committing the robbery was like "jumping off the high dive for the first time." Malone told the police he had no choice but to go through with the robbery.

During his questioning by the police, Malone wrote a letter of apology to the victim. The police report noted that he was remorseful about what had happened. In his letter, Malone stated, "I just want to be loved. I just am having a difficult time learning how to do this. This robbery, I think, was sort of a cry for help." As the interview with Malone progressed, he admitted to conducting some additional minor robberies prior to the one at Lion Country Safari. When asked what he was going to do after the robbery, Malone admitted that he had planned to go to Colorado.

As the interview came to an end, there was paperwork to be filed. Malone was asked to write down the name of a contact, and Malone put down the name of Joseph Schons in Berry Creek, California. Joseph Schons and Greg Malone were family.

☙

Meanwhile, Yuba County Sheriff Jim Grant met with the families of the missing five men during this time. We do not know if he had met with the families as a group prior to this. The meeting was recorded by Sara Huett. The recording is difficult to understand at times due to poor tape quality, people talking over each other, a phone ringing, and a cuckoo clock making noise. However, it could be heard that there were a variety of topics covered that evening.

First, there was a discussion about using a private investigator. The tape began with comments by Jim Grant. He told the family members in attendance that he had complete faith in Lance Ayers. Grant stated that Ayers was "a fine man" with an excellent reputation. The meeting was then turned over to the private investigator, a man who was not mentioned by name on tape but had the opportunity to address the families.

The private investigator informed everyone that he was not a magician but would be willing to take on the case if a $500 retainer ($2,300 adjusted for the time of publication) was paid in advance. He was told by the Yuba County Sheriff's Department that he would have their cooperation, and he wanted the families to know that he had lived in the Yuba County area since the 1930s and knew it well.

It was the opinion of the private investigator that foul play was possible, but there was no supporting evidence. The total amount of money the five had on them that night was less than $100, according to the families. The private investigator told them that in his experience, criminals had done bad things to people for less money. There is a moment where the investigator talks about "adult desires" and how that could have been a factor in the men going up into the Plumas National Forest.

A man who was possibly Robert Klopf, Gary Mathias's stepfather, was at the meeting and was concerned about the search for his stepson. He told the private investigator, "At this point in time, Gary would not have any desires at all." The man said that without his regiment of Plixen, Stelazine, and Cogentin, Mathias "would not know who he was."

Ida Klopf, Mathias's mother, was at the meeting as well and added that when her son was not medicated, he would have conversations with someone not there. She added that in those situations, Mathias would speak in two different voices. There was a sense of urgency in her voice to find her son so he could resume his medication schedule.

The private investigator ended his pitch to the families and let them know that the ball was in their court. He was ready to take on the case if needed. The man left and Grant resumed the meeting.

Grant wanted the families to know that he respected the private investigator but believed he was not the right solution for this type of case. He wanted the families to understand that there was nobody overseeing the investigator, and he believed an unethical investigator would just take their money and sit at a desk all day. Grant also mentioned that the private investigator did not have access to the same resources, nor did they have the same training as him or members of his staff. It was their money and their decision, but he asked the families if they were happy with him and his staff, and if so they should continue working with Yuba County. There was a consensus in the audience to continue working with law enforcement and not hire the private investigator.

There was a discussion about Schons and whether his child, who was diagnosed with a disability, was in any way linked to the five. Grant said they investigated the family and discovered that Schons's child had suffered a head injury at a very young age, which resulted in his condition. They were not part of the Special Olympics, nor did they attend any educational programs or related events that the five attended. For some unknown reason, the child was not enrolled in Gateway or any similar agency.

Grant mentioned that they tried giving Schons a polygraph test but were denied by his doctor. The doctor did not want to put Schons in a situation that was overly stressful because it could trigger another heart attack.

Members of the families voiced their suspicions of Schons's stories. They wanted to know when he left his vehicle and walked to Mountain House. There were questions about why Schons went directly home and not to a hospital if he was having a heart attack. Grant stated that Schons did go home, and when his wife and daughter came home, they took him to a hospital in Chico. From what Grant was told, Schons was delirious in the hospital, and Cindy Schons told investigators that he was rambling incoherently for the first few days he was there.

There were questions from family members about the missing men being taken captive in the hills. One family member said that they thought the five were captured and were going to be used as "slave labor" for the gold mines. A few others were concerned they were being held by some sort of commune. Grant told the families that the communes do recruit people, but they had a reputation for making their new recruits call home for money. Also, Grant stated that the communes made members sell books and flowers in public areas. Grant was not convinced that the five were taken by a commune.

The meeting came to an end but family members still had questions and comments. They sounded frustrated and puzzled. One family member asked if the FBI could help, and they were informed about the process of bringing them on board, but Grant told them it was unlikely. Grant even made a comment during the meeting that he was not too pleased with the Butte County Sheriff's Department. He did not go into detail but said the

FBI was more reputable. As the meeting was ending, there was some sense of hope that answers would come sooner than later.

❧

Before I researched the case files, I did not know much about the involvement of the California Department of Justice in this investigation. After looking over the Department of Justice files at the Yuba County Sheriff's Department, I was surprised that it was late May 1978 when law enforcement learned of the bar fight in the Oroville area and the arrest of the drunk driver during the early hours of Saturday, February 25th. Did the Yuba County Sheriff's Department or Butte County Sheriff's Department have this information before May?

I contacted the California Department of Justice to request any additional Yuba County Five records and was informed they were not subject to release. I received the same response from Butte and Plumas Counties when requesting any additional case files regarding the missing men and their investigations. Also, all three departments believed if there were files to look at, then they would be with the Yuba County Sheriff's Department.

A clear answer was never given to me as to why records from the California Department of Justice, Butte County, and Plumas County were not releasable. My only theory was that since Gary Mathias was still considered a missing person, the files would be sealed until he or his remains were found. A couple of individuals interviewed for this book were under the impression Gary Mathias had been legally declared deceased. I did find some information online that showed the federal government had Mathias listed as deceased with February 24, 1978 as his date of death.

Jim Grant and Lance Ayers both expressed some disappointment in working with Butte County. Nothing was found on record or on any of the tapes concerning their opinions about Sutter County, Plumas County, or the California Department of Justice. I am curious to know what the

Yuba County Sheriff's Department thought about the other departments following the discoveries that June.

CHAPTER NINETEEN:
JUNE 1–5, 1978

June is another time during the year when I check on the family members of the five. It is another difficult time of year for them. I reach out via text or social media messaging to see how they are coping. Sometimes our discussions are brief; other times I listen to their sadness and frustration. A few times they will share some happy memories.

The discoveries of June 1978 were beyond heartbreaking. The locations of the remains would lead to more questions. A piece of the truth was found, but the entire truth was never discovered. Linking the events of February to June 1978 together is rather difficult. We know what happened but not why it happened.

や

Joseph Schons was still a person of interest to investigators, and they were hoping to hypnotize Schons so he could remember the evening of February 24th more clearly. A member of the Yuba County Sheriff's Department was trained in hypnosis. Jack Beecham told the press, "If we can obtain a medical release from Mr. Schons's doctor, we will hypnotize him and see if we can get further information." Not long after that statement, Beecham informed the press that hypnosis was not an option since Schons's doctors warned investigators that having Schons go back to the night of his heart attack could lead to another heart attack or worse. The Yuba County Sheriff's Department was warned that if he did suffer a heart attack, Schons's family could sue them and the doctor for a wrongful death.

The Southern California investigation involved Greg Malone because the Yuba County Sheriff's Office was made aware of his arrest, and his relation to Joseph Schons. Lance Ayers and Jack Thompson went to the Orange County Jail on June 2, 1978, to meet Malone and discuss Schons. Malone told Ayers and Thompson that the last time he was on Schons's property was two years earlier, but Malone admitted that he visited Schons in the hospital in March following his heart attack. Malone said that Schons told him about "five retarded men" who didn't help him when he had a heart attack. Schons said to Malone that the men ran into the forest and disappeared, which made Schons angry.

ං

The *Chico Enterprise-Record* ran a story about the five missing men on June 3, 1978, and stated that it had been 100 days since Ted Weiher, Jack Madruga, Bill Sterling, Jackie Huett, and Gary Mathias had vanished in the Plumas National Forest. The article noted that the Yuba County Sheriff's Department and the Butte County Sheriff's Department could not agree if the reason the men disappeared was because of simply getting lost or foul play. Lt. Ken Mickelson was head of the search and rescue team with Butte County, and he told the reporter for the story, "For whatever reason, they just went up there—for a lark or to take a shortcut or to see the country."

Mickelson theorized in the article for the *Chico Enterprise-Record* that, for some reason, they ended up stuck in the snow on the road and abandoned the car. From what Mickelson had learned from the investigation, some of the five were afraid of the dark and some of them became incredibly overwhelmed in stressful situations. Mickelson believed it was Schons yelling at them from the darkness that sent them over the edge and into the Plumas National Forest. Also, Mickelson stressed that the minute they ran into the forest, their lives were "measured in hours" due to hypothermia. He said the decline in their ability to reason, plus the below-freezing temperatures, probably killed all five in less than three hours. "I don't believe there was any foul play," said Mickelson.

Jack Beecham was not in agreement. In Beecham's opinion, it was "out of character" for them to be on that road, and there was no way the five men were going to miss an important Special Olympics basketball tournament. Foul play, either external or internal, was his theory, and the article stated some members of law enforcement believed it although they had "no concrete evidence."

The article mentioned that investigators had gone to Southern California to follow up on a lead. Beecham was mum on it but told the reporter, "At this point, we are no closer to finding them than we were then [when they vanished]."

The article also stated that investigators from the Yuba County Sheriff's Department believed that all five men were dead. Avery Blankenship, a member of the Yuba County Sheriff's Department, was one of those who believed that the five had perished. However, he theorized that the remains of the missing men would be discovered sometime later in the year when hunting season started.

On Sunday, June 4, 1978, Lorin Koch and his sixteen-year-old son Roger joined William Reamue for a motorcycle trip from Oroville to Quincy. They could have taken Highway 70, but they decided to take a more scenic route through the Plumas National Forest. Their plan was to travel on the Oroville-Quincy Highway, and once they hit Quincy, they would enjoy a cup of coffee. From there, they would take another scenic route back home.

"It was a very nice day. We started [our ride] pretty early. Probably 8:30 or 9 in the morning," said Roger Koch when interviewed for the *Yuba County Five* podcast. The three would encounter snow and fallen trees on roads as they made their way through the Plumas National Forest. "As we got up towards Quincy, okay, up around Bucks Lake, we're starting to see snowdrifts," said Koch. The three had been under the impression that snow would not be an issue since it was early June.

Koch told the *Yuba County Five* podcast that there was a section of road they encountered that had about four feet of snowdrifts. There was no way to get around it, so they had to navigate alternate routes. Their plans for an easy trip were erased. At one point, they passed some forest service trailers near the Daniel Zink Campground. As they rode on, they realized they were going to deal with more snow and more fallen trees. Someone in the group decided to go back to the Daniel Zink Campground area to see if anyone was around so they could ask for alternate directions.

Roughly twelve miles northeast of where Jack Madruga's car was abandoned was the Daniel Zink Campground. The twelve miles are measured along the roads that link both locations. If someone were to walk the distance "as the crow flies" along the rugged terrain from Rogers Cow Camp to Daniel Zink, then it would be five miles.

Lorin Koch, Roger Koch, and William Reamue found the Daniel Zink Campground deserted. There was a map at the campground they could review to figure out the best way to Quincy. All three men were met with a horrific smell. It was decomposition, it was pungent, and it seemed to be coming from two side-by-side forest service trailers measuring eight feet by thirty feet each. Roger Koch was the one who would follow the scent to the trailers, and that's when he noticed one of them had a broken window.

"That's when I jumped up and looked inside the trailer," said Koch for the *Yuba County Five* podcast. He was familiar with that style of trailer, but his experience was with the ones used for construction companies. Koch was surprised to encounter a dark but dirty trailer filled with bunk beds and dirty dishes. Due to the darkness, Koch reluctantly decided to get a better look inside. That's when he noticed a body.

"He was on the bottom bunk right next to the window. I could literally reach into the window and touch him," said Koch. It took him a few moments to process the situation.

William Reaume, interviewed by the press in 1978, recalled that Roger Koch told him and Lorin Koch, "There's a body in there." Thinking Koch was joking, Reaume went to get a look for himself. There was indeed a body on the bottom of a three-bunk-style bed, and it was badly decomposed. "It appeared he just laid down and went to sleep," said Reaume, who added, "He was covered with a sheet about up to his neck."

Roger Koch was shaken by the discovery and all three decided to get on their motorcycles and find somewhere in Oroville with a phone so they could call law enforcement. They rode to a Denny's restaurant and telephoned the Butte County Sheriff's Department at 9:45 p.m. that evening. Roger Koch recalled that they were met with skepticism from Butte County, but they eventually sent someone to the location to investigate. The three were able to meet up with the deputies so they could show them a map of where they could find the body.

The Daniel Zink Campground was not in Butte County but was in neighboring Plumas County. Butte County eventually sent someone to investigate the scene that night. It had taken law enforcement hours to get to the site due to some large trees blocking the road, but they did indeed find a body. The Yuba County Sheriff's Department was contacted, and they were to send people up to the location the next day.

On June 5, 1978, members of the Yuba, Butte, and Plumas County Sheriffs' Departments entered the trailer to examine the remains of a deceased Caucasian male lying on his back in a bed. Lance Ayers was one of the investigators in the trailer, At first glance, he did not recognize the man. The investigators noticed that the deceased was under eight sheets, and they decided to lift them up to review the body. Ayers took one look and realized the man was Ted Weiher because he was wearing the same clothes he wore when he went missing. What threw off Ayers at first was the massive weight loss, plus the fact that the deceased man had a full beard, and his hair was very curly and unkempt. When he went missing, Weiher was clean-shaven. Weiher's pants were now rolled up to his knees, and his hands were resting on his chest. They noticed that both of Weiher's feet were badly frostbitten, and he had lost three toes from his right foot and two from his left. There was a gangrenous infection that resulted in the veins in his legs being discolored. Investigators believed it was some sort of blood poisoning. They found identification on a table next to the bed where the body was located. A ring was also found on the table with the name TED engraved on it, plus a neck chain and a wristwatch. The ring and neck chain matched what Ted Weiher was wearing when he disappeared, but the wristwatch was later confirmed not to be Weiher's.

The items were gathered and were to be shown to the Weiher family for confirmation. Lance Ayers would give the items to Jerry Harrison of the Sutter County Sheriff's Department. Harrison was also the nephew of Ted Weiher.

Jerry Harrison's family was from Robert Weiher's first marriage, and he was younger than Weiher. "Probably five to seven years, but I'm not sure," recalled Harrison. The children of Robert Weiher's marriage to Imogene enjoyed spending time with Harrison. "We were, you know, like instead of aunt and uncle, we were all like cousins, if that makes any sense." Harrison joined the Sutter County Sheriff's Department around 1969 and assisted in exhuming bodies for the Juan Corona case. Harrison was not part of the initial group from Sutter County that went up to aid in the search for the missing. He was sent up once Weiher's body was discovered.

Pictures of Weiher's remains were taken by an investigator, and Harrison remembers someone had left out the negatives at Daniel Zink Campground. Harrison remembers seeing the negatives. "I don't know if I was one of the first, but I was there… back in those days, they took pictures… they left them laying there, so I looked through them and I could recognize Ted. I saw the negatives."

❧

The trailer was examined for clues by law enforcement, and they found a broken window on the north side of the trailer. The window had been broken from the outside, and they noticed that the door to the trailer was open. Empty C-ration cans were found outside the trailer window. C-rations were canned meals used by the military, which were to be eaten heated or straight out of the containers. Some would contain pork and beans or ham and beans, while others would have a fruit or dessert item. To open the C-rations, one would need to use a small military-style can opener called a P38, but the cans found on the site were presumed to be opened with a church key style can opener. Those are flat, with an opener on each end. One end would have a flat style opener used for opening beer bottles, while the other side would have a pointed opener that could puncture canned food or drinks. The pointed end could have been used methodically to open a canned item like a C-ration.

Several paperback books were found outside the back door of the trailer. A white bed sheet and a white sock were found thirty feet away from the trailer. There were more C-ration cans on the floor near the bed where Ted Weiher died, but only one of those cans was opened using a P38, while the others had been opened with the church key opener. There was a candle in the trailer that had been lit at some point, but no attempt was made to start any other type of fire.

Someone with a military background would have been able to use the P38 to open the cans. Both Jack Madruga and Gary Mathias had served in the Army and would have been familiar with using that opener. Jackie Huett was also familiar with a P38 can opener because his father, Jack Huett Sr., served in the military and showed his children how to use the can opener on hunting and camping trips.

❧

Jack Beecham was up there the day they found Weiher. "I looked into the back window of that trailer, and it was just a sack of clothing with his remains." Beecham remembered that the remains were not skeletal. "He just laid there and starved to death." Weiher's frostbitten feet stuck out to Beecham, and so did the open cans of food. It puzzled Beecham that someone was eating food while Weiher seemed to have died from starvation. He also wanted to know what happened to Weiher's shoes.

Had Jack Madruga, Bill Sterling, Jackie Huett, or Gary Mathias been in the trailer with Ted Weiher? The tennis shoes that Gary Mathias was wearing when he disappeared were found in the trailer, while the leather suede shoes that Weiher was wearing when he went missing were nowhere to be found. Ida and Robert Klopf would later positively identify the shoes as Mathias's.

C-ration cans, various pieces of paper, and some pieces of cardboard were gathered by investigators and given to Special Agent Jack Thompson to send to Sacramento for their lab to review for any prints. Weiher's body was transported to Quincy, the county seat for Plumas, for an autopsy.

The neighboring Forest Service trailer was examined, and it appeared to have been ransacked. Forest Service employees also reviewed the trailer and could not say if anything had been stolen or moved from one trailer to another. There was also a discovery in the trailers of dehydrated food, which was not touched.

Another discovery was made a half mile to the northeast of the trailers. Some blankets and a flashlight were found along the roadway. Forest Service employees identified them as their property, which would have been in the trailer.

Jerry Harrison believed Weiher put those items outside the trailer for someone like Bill Sterling. "My opinion, and I may be all wrong, but I found… I walked around the area and, quite a ways off from the trailer, found blankets laying, and it's my opinion that Ted got blankets out of that thing and tried to head back to try and find him." He believed Weiher went out to look for one of the remaining four, couldn't locate him, but left everything out there just in case.

The news of the discovery of Weiher's remains needed to be told to the Weiher family. Perhaps the first person in the family to receive the news besides Harrison was Nelda Weiher, the sister-in-law who had assisted Imogene Weiher during these turbulent times. When they told Nelda Weiher that Ted's body had been found, she requested an ambulance be available for Imogene Weiher and Hazel Haight, Ted's grandmother, just in case.

Dallas Weiher Sr. and Perry Weiher, Ted's brothers, were in Texas packing melons at the time Ted's body was discovered by authorities. When they found out the news, the melon-packing coworkers chipped in so they could purchase flights home to be with their family.

As the news of Ted Weiher's discovery made its way to his family, investigators inspected the two trailers for additional clues. There was a tool shed that had been pried open and someone had used a bar or another tool to break the lock. There was another shed with a generator inside, but the lock to that shed was not breached. Marks on the lock for that shed showed someone tried to use a file to cut the lock, though. Investigators were not sure if the men were the ones responsible.

In the trailer where they found Weiher were a couple of coal oil heating stoves; there were no clues showing that they had been used. Some heating cans were discovered with the C-rations. Those cans were filled with cooking fuel that could be lit to heat food, but they could have provided some warmth in the trailer as well. They, too, were not used by the men. Matchbooks were also discovered unused. As investigators examined the trailer and the area outside the trailer, they noticed that no attempt was made to start a fire to keep warm or to signal searchers.

Tammie Phillips, Gary Mathias's sister, remembered going to the Daniel Zink Campground after she heard the news that Ted Weiher's remains had been found. "I was there the next morning after he was found," said Phillips. "I went directly into that trailer. Nothing was isolated from the public there." The sights and smells of that trailer stayed with Phillips for decades. She is frustrated by some of the things that have been reported. "They didn't tell you that GI rations were outside by a trash can. Just that there were some in the trailer." Another discovery that Phillips remembers is handwritten notes on a memo pad. She looked over those notes and knew they were written by Gary Mathias. She believes Mathias was there with Weiher and Huett. Phillips also believes her brother decided to go out for help.

☙

I have looked over a few maps of the Plumas National Forest from the 1970s. The Daniel Zink Campground is a marked location in Plumas County. One of the biggest questions I have had during my research is if anyone ever searched that area, especially the trailers, during the hunt for the missing men.

Dorothy Weiher-Dornan, Ted Weiher's sister, was one of the first people I interviewed for this book. One question I had for her was if the Weiher family was ever provided an explanation for why the Daniel Zink Campground was never searched. Weiher-Dornan shared some memories she had of what was explained to her about the search. "The forest rangers told the Sheriff [in] Oroville that they would go [check] because they had just closed the trailer where Ted was found," said Weiher-Dornan. "And they asked the sheriff if they could go up there… and he said, 'Nah, they're retarded, they would have never made it up there.'"

Weiher-Dornan believes if they had checked the trailers at the Daniel Zink Campground, they might have found Ted Weiher and Jackie Huett alive. She also believes they may have found Gary Mathias as well because it is her opinion that Mathias broke into the trailer and opened the food. Ted Weiher would not have done that, in her opinion. Weiher-Dornan remembers Ted not taking tips at his one job because it was stealing. This would have been a similar situation.

She is beyond puzzled as to why her brother deserted a car in the Plumas National Forest and went to the trailer at the Daniel Zink Campground. "Ted hated the snow. He did not like to be cold," said Weiher-Dornan.

An unidentified newspaper clipping in the case file from March 1978 quotes Plumas County Sergeant Doug McAllister. He told a reporter that they had "looked in every feasible place."

Another person interviewed for this book claimed that they were told the Daniel Zink area was to be searched by two individuals. From what the person was told, the two had been drinking and never made it to the Daniel Zink Campground due to a massive hangover. It's hard to separate fact from fiction in events as traumatic as the search for the Yuba County Five.

The reality is that Weiher had been found. Investigators and searchers were preparing themselves for more discoveries. Also, the families of the remaining four were on edge. Deep down, they knew the Yuba County Sheriff's Department would be in contact and the news would be devastating.

CHAPTER TWENTY: JUNE 6–10, 1978

I rarely remember my dreams as I get older, but I have these recurring dreams where I show up to a college class and it is finals week. For some reason I have not been attending classes and need to study for the final. I am not prepared, and it is pure panic. Another dream is I own a house and decide to walk into an area of the home I have never seen before.

My wife remembers her dreams perfectly because I act foolishly. I have no idea why my actions are nothing but absolute buffoonery in her dreams.

There is one dream that I remember vividly, however. It happened not long after my youngest child was born. I was in a random room and there was a telephone ringing. It was one of those old, corded phones that was used years ago. I remember picking up the phone and it was my grandmother from my mom's side of the family. She asked how the baby was doing and she asked about my wife. I had a moment of clarity in my dream while talking to her on the phone. I said, "Grandma, you died," and I heard her hang up. I woke up after that.

I have no idea what happens in the afterlife, but I thought about that dream while working on this chapter.

☙

It was 10 a.m. on June 6, 1978, when the remains of Jack Madruga and Bill Sterling were discovered in the Granite Basin area some three miles down the road from the U.S. Forest Service Trailer on the Daniel Zink Campground. An estimated group of forty people were searching the area following the discovery of Ted Weiher's body, and some of the searchers apparently had followed a trail of blankets from the trailer to where they found the two men.

Madruga was found on the northeast side of a roadway near a stream. He was badly decomposed, was clutching a watch, and his remains appeared to have been picked at by animals. Lance Ayers from the Yuba County Sheriff's Department was the one who would identify Madruga based on the clothing he was wearing the night he went missing, along with some personal items. While searching his remains, investigators discovered the keys to his 1969 Mercury Montego.

Sterling was found across the road in a southwest line from Madruga in an embankment. Animals had scattered his remains over an area measuring fifty square yards. Dennis Forcino from the Plumas County Sheriff's Department identified Sterling based on the clothing he was wearing the night he went missing, along with some personal items, including his wallet. Inside were pictures of his sisters, Deana and Debbie, along with his Social Security card.

Both Madruga and Sterling were also tentatively identified by Butte County Undersheriff Richard Stenberg. He, too, was able to match the clothing with the missing men and would tell a reporter from the *San Francisco Chronicle* that he believed the two died from exposure. The remains of both men were sent to Quincy for autopsies.

When talking to the press about the discovery of the three, Stenberg stated that no person involved in the search was informed of the existence of the trailers. The Sheriffs' Departments for Butte, Yuba, and Plumas Counties all stated that the Forest Service never informed them that there were trailers at the Daniel Zink Campground. All three jurisdictions claimed they found out about the trailers when Ted Weiher's body was discovered. "We guessed wrong… but our conscious [*sic*] is clear," said Stenberg to the *Chico Enterprise-Record*. He also stated, "We exhausted every possibility. We'll just have to live with it." The *Modesto Bee* did speak with Stenberg about the trailers, and he told them, "We didn't get up that far. We believed they were coming out and heading down the mountains." In the same article, Stenberg told them that the trailer was out of the search area.

Stenberg was amazed that Weiher, Madruga, and Sterling made it to the trailer and the surrounding area because it was a rugged fifteen-mile walk along the roads, while traveling "as the crow flies" along the terrain was a nearly impossible five- to seven-mile walk in areas that ranged from three thousand to five thousand feet above sea level. It was reported by the *Chico Enterprise-Record* that on the night the men went missing, there was an estimated four to eight feet of snow on the ground. There were other reports that claimed the snow could have been ten feet deep. Adding in the below-freezing temperatures and limited visibility at night made this discovery more bizarre. Stenberg knew from investigating the trailer that there was plenty of fuel and food to keep Weiher and anyone else who made it there with him warm and well fed. "[Weiher] could have survived for a month if he had all his faculties when he reached the trailer," said Stenberg. Stenberg's initial opinion was that Weiher was the one who broke the window and entered the trailer.

Ken Mickelson, who ran the search and rescue unit for Butte County, was astounded that the men made it as far as they did. "Experienced men who knew what they were doing would've had a hard time making it here under the conditions," said Mickelson. What really puzzled him was how they made the trek wearing tennis shoes. Meanwhile, Jackie Huett and Gary Mathias were still missing. Mickelson had little hope of finding them alive. "We're going to be lucky to find them," said Mickelson. "We almost have to stumble on them."

The lack of information about the trailers was echoed by Mickelson to the press. He told the *Chico Enterprise-Record* that, to his knowledge, on February 23, 1978, members of the Forest Service had visited the trailers. If search and rescue teams had known about them, then they would have found a way to them. "We did everything we could. I'm sorry we were not able to find them." Mickelson, like Stenberg, wanted the families and the readers to know that they were not negligent in their duties.

A June 9, 1978, article in the *Appeal-Democrat* reported that Royal Mannion, a District Ranger in Oroville, was aware that two Forest Service employees pointed out to Mickelson the trailers near the Daniel Zink Campground. The two employees said they pointed them out along with other trailers in the area on Mickelson's map. According to the article, Mickelson told the two that he would "pass it along" to the Plumas County Sheriff since the Daniel Zink Campground was in Plumas County. Mannion told the *Appeal-Democrat* that search and rescue operations in the Plumas are the responsibility of the Sheriff's Department. "Our responsibility is to give them the service they ask for," said Mannion.

Dennis Forcino tried to make sense of how the men went from the car to the trailer because a road did not directly connect the two locations. According to Forcino, it was unbelievable that they made it to the trailer. "If you don't know where it was at, it would be one [chance] in 1,000 of finding that place."

An image that appeared in a June 7, 1978, edition of the *Sacramento Bee* showed Jim Sterling, Bill Sterling's father, sitting on the side of the road in the Plumas National Forest following the discovery of his son's remains. It appeared that Jim Sterling was completely inconsolable while a friend sat next to him, providing support. Jim Sterling had gone up to the Daniel Zink Campground area with three family members following the discovery of Ted Weiher. Bill Sterling's brother, David Sterling, stayed back in Yuba City to help run the family business.

Deana Mote, Bill Sterling's sister, spoke to the *Appeal-Democrat* on June 7, 1978, and told them, "I feel relieved. By this time, I have accepted the fact that they might not be alive when they are found, but it's a relief to know something." Mote also told the press that her mother, Juanita Sterling, had been dealing with the ordeal as best as she could. The mothers had been in contact with each other at times, and that provided some solace. Mote commented on the area where the men were discovered. "I feel if they had searched this area earlier, they would have found Ted alive."

Bill Sterling had visited that area in the past. Mote brought it up in her interview with the *Appeal-Democrat* and said, "He hated it." Like investigators, Mote was surprised that Weiher did not use a stove in the trailer for warmth. "Ted [Weiher] by himself may have known how to light a stove in the trailer… he probably was too scared. He didn't know what would happen to him."

"We still have no idea what those men were doing here," said Yuba County Undersheriff Jack Beecham. A discovery of a cigarette lighter was made near a snow line, and Beecham knew that it might have been Gary Mathias's since he was believed to be the only member of the group that smoked. Ted Weiher and Jackie Huett would smoke occasionally, according to an interview.

The search would continue for Jackie Huett and Gary Mathias.

The discovery of Jack Madruga's body was something that Cathy Madruga, his niece, knew was coming. She was living with Melba Madruga and was doing everything possible to help her during this difficult time. "I don't want to sound corny. I do believe in the afterlife; I believe in this stuff, and the night before they found my uncle, I had an experience. I slept in Doc's room, and I was in bed, and I heard someone crying, a man crying. I thought, 'What the hell am I hearing?' and there was the sound of pages being rustled."

She then felt a weight on the side of the bed as if someone was sitting down. Her sheet tightened up, and she decided to address the presence in the room. "I went, 'Oh my God,' and I set up and said, 'Doc, it's okay, you're home now.' I don't know why it scared me, but it did. I said, 'You can have your room.'"

Making good on her promise, Cathy grabbed a pillow and a blanket. She walked to Melba Madruga's room and slept on the floor. Later that same night, she would have a dream that has never left her memory. "[Melba] and I were sitting in the front room, it was lunchtime, and I had just fixed her lunch. She was in one chair, and I was in another," said Cathy Madruga. "There were windows behind us, and we heard a car pull up, and I turned around and looked, and it was the Sheriff's Department. I had a can of Coors Light Beer in my hand, and I never drank beer out of a can at that time. I remember this like it was yesterday, and it was the sheriff coming to tell us that they found Doc."

The dream woke her up, and it also woke up Melba Madruga, who was puzzled as to why her granddaughter was sleeping on the floor in her room. Cathy didn't want to bring up the encounter in her uncle's bed because the family was brought up in a strict household "the Portuguese way." Melba convinced Cathy to tell her what had happened during the night. Once the stories were told, Melba told Cathy, "You shouldn't have been scared. Doc would never hurt you."

It was lunchtime on June 6th when Cathy made Melba a fried ham and cheese sandwich. Cathy popped open a can of beer, which she did only because of the dream, and then she saw the Yuba County Sheriff's Department pull up in front of the residence. Melba noticed something was wrong and asked Cathy if it was the Sheriff's Department. All Cathy could do was nod to confirm, and Melba began crying. It was one of the few times that Cathy Madruga saw her grandmother cry.

c⁄ɔ

Jack Huett Sr., the father of Jackie Huett, was up at the Daniel Zink Campground. He was there with one of his other sons, Tom Huett, and a cousin, Floyd Huett Jr. Back at home was Sara Huett, Jackie Huett's mother, and she spoke briefly to the *Appeal-Democrat*. She too was puzzled why nobody mentioned the existence of those cabins during the early days of the investigation. "I just wish they searched that area earlier," said Sara Huett. According to her, she recalled Jack Huett Sr. was on the road leading to the Daniel Zink Campground in late February when the Montego was discovered. He had gone up that way to do his own searching but did not have knowledge of the trailers or the road that would have led him to the campground. She recalled that Jack Huett Sr. took a different road to search.

A June 6, 1978, article in the *Los Angeles Times* mentioned that the men were searching for a cabin in Bucks Lake near the Daniel Zink Campground because a friend lived in the area. "That's the only way we can figure out why they were on that road," said Yuba County Sheriff Jim Grant. "That road leads to nowhere in the winter." This was the first mention of the men traveling that way to get to Bucks Lake. Previous theories had included a shortcut through Oroville to get to Forbestown, which is over a two-hour drive from Bucks Lake.

∽

Meanwhile, voters in Yuba County headed out to the polls on June 6, and one of the offices up for reelection was Sheriff-Coroner for Yuba County. Jim Grant was on the ballot, and he was not running unopposed. When the polls closed and the votes were counted, the people of Yuba County cast the most votes for Robert Day, a longtime employee of the Yuba County Sheriff's Department and a former undersheriff. He did not have enough votes to secure the position, so a November runoff election was scheduled. Day's opponent would be Jack Miller. Jim Grant ended up in third place in total votes, and it was loud and clear that he was no longer viewed by the public as the right person for the position. His legacy would be one term.

Plumas County Assistant Sheriff Dave Wingfield made a statement in the *Los Angeles Times* on June 7, 1978, that the autopsy of Ted Weiher was completed and the cause of death for Weiher was pulmonary congestion due to exposure. Signs of foul play were not discovered, and that threw a proverbial wrench into the Yuba County Sheriff's Department's theory.

❧

Jack Huett Sr. searched the Daniel Zink Campground area for the remains of his son following the news that Weiher's body had been discovered. Lance Ayers had advised Jack Huett Sr. not to travel to the Plumas National Forest to assist with the search for remains. Ayers's pleas for him to stay home fell on deaf ears because Huett Sr. was not going to sit back and wait.

Tom Huett remembered that his dad went up to the Plumas any chance he had to search for Jackie. Huett Sr. was employed at the time with a local plumbing company, and they told Huett Sr. to take time off work to search for his son. The company even paid Huett Sr.'s salary while he was away.

Lance Ayers had spent a great deal of time up in the Plumas area as a representative of the Yuba County Sheriff's Department, and he had built a relationship with Huett Sr. Ayers respected Huett Sr.'s dedication. Claudia Huett, Jack and Sarah's daughter-in-law, had many conversations with Jackie's parents about the investigation. Huett Sr. told her about his time in the Plumas with Lance Ayers. "I don't know much about Jack Beecham, but I know that Jack Huett Sr. spoke highly, could never say anything negative ever, about Lance. He looked up every piece of evidence he could find. Any small lead, he'd follow through."

Ayers also had Huett Sr.'s back during a few tense confrontations with other members of law enforcement and the search parties. One issue involved the Butte or Plumas County Sheriff's Department taking offense to Huett Sr. carrying a pistol while he searched the Plumas for his son. Officers wanted him to hand over the pistol to them, but that wasn't going to fly with Huett Sr., who responded, "This is my country. I'm in charge here. I don't give a fuck who you are." Ayers walked into that heated argument and told his fellow members of law enforcement that it wasn't an issue if Huett Sr. was carrying his pistol because he was looking for his son. They never bothered Huett Sr. about his pistol after that incident.

That wasn't the only incident that Huett Sr. had up in the Plumas. He told Mopac Audio circa 2018 that he discovered some members of the search party in the Plumas at a campfire having a little party and they were drinking beer. Huett Sr. was driving his truck along a road and saw the festivities. He could not believe what he saw, so he backed up his truck to get another look. If the search was going to be done right, then Huett Sr. would be the one to do the job. It was an urgent situation, and he had no time for incompetence. Huett Sr. shared his anger about that incident with Claudia Huett years later. Claudia remembered how hurt and angry he was over it all. She said the people were "basically partying it up instead of looking for his son."

Huett Sr. recalled something that happened on June 6th when he was taking a break and having a sandwich along a creek. There was a certain noise that got his attention. "Here come this guy up above walking through beating the living shit out of his dog. He was with four or five dogs and he's beating the shit out of his dog, and I said 'Hey, what the hell you doing?'" The man explained to Huett Sr. that the dog had a deer bone and would not let it go. Huett thought nothing of it at the time and went back to eating his sandwich.

The next day, Huett Sr. returned to search for his son. It was a quarter mile from the trailers where Huett Sr. made the discovery of Jackie Huett's remains. "I was the first one to spot it. When I seen that bone, naturally you're going to look at it, to see if it's a deer bone or a human. Anybody could tell it was a leg bone from here down the hip because the ball joint was still there and then I got twenty feet away and I found his pants with a billfold in it."

Huett Sr. then found the jacket that Jackie Huett was wearing the night he disappeared. He picked it up off the ground and that is when something fell out of the jacket. It was a spine. The rest of Jackie Huett's remains were scattered over an area northwest of the trailers. Searchers continued looking for other remains and they would eventually locate Huett's skull some one hundred yards away.

A volunteer with tracking dogs from Quincy, possibly the person Huett Sr. saw the day before, spoke to the press about the discovery of

Jackie Huett's remains. "We were driving down [a] road and [a dog] hit on the scent from the back of the pickup."

Reporters had been in the area since investigators announced Weiher's discovery. One reporter had an encounter with Huett Sr. after he found Jackie Huett's remains. Huett Sr. knew he would be taking pictures and told the reporter not to take any, but the report informed him that he would regardless of Huett Sr.'s wishes. Jack Huett Sr. recalled this interaction with the reporter for Mopac Audio. "I said, 'You take a picture of this, and I'll bust every damn camera you have.'" The reporter told Huett Sr. he would do what they could, but made no promises. Huett Sr. was worried that the news of his son's discovery was going to be broadcast on television and the radio. He knew Sara Huett would hear the news, and Huett Sr. remembered that she had become almost "unglued" over everything because Jackie was their firstborn. Huett Sr. called his wife to tell her the news. The day had been hard, and Huett Sr. decided to smoke a cigarette, which was the first one he had smoked since going cold turkey a few years earlier. He ended up smoking two packs of cigarettes that day. It would take Jack Huett Sr. another ten years to quit smoking again.

When Huett Sr. returned home around 5:30 p.m., he found Sara Huett passed out. Attempts to wake her up were futile. He had a hunch something was terribly wrong, so he called poison control. "They said, 'Well, if you get… if you can get her up and walk her, [then] walk her until she can't no more and call us,'" said Huett Sr. He followed the directions from poison control and ended up walking with his wife until 10:30 p.m. or 11 p.m. that night. "And then, I found a note that she wrote to me. She just can't take it anymore and I still don't know what she took, but she had to go to the doctor the next day and they… I forget what it was that they said they thought she took." Jackie Huett was the firstborn child of the family, and Huett Sr. believed the discovery of their son's remains sent Sara over the edge.

෨

It was an incredibly difficult time for the Weiher family as well. Dallas Weiher Jr. recalled it was a relief that his father was home from Texas. "I wouldn't have to be the man of the house," he said. However, the return wasn't easy for his father. "Seeing your daddy cry is not something you see a lot as a kid but seeing him cry showed me how much he loved his little brother."

The autopsy of Ted Weiher was performed by a Dr. Liptrap in Plumas County, and on June 6th or 7th, Lance Ayers met with the doctor to review the results. Weiher's cause of death was ruled to be exposure to the elements and pulmonary edema, which is the buildup of fluid in the lungs. Causes of this condition are linked to heart problems, trauma to the chest wall, and traveling at high elevations. The Daniel Zink Campground was located at five thousand feet above sea level, and it might have been the culprit since Weiher's autopsy report did not mention any trauma to his chest wall. Also, Weiher's family did not know if he had an existing heart condition.

Weiher was discovered lying on his back, and that worsens pulmonary edema because it makes breathing more difficult. The time he spent in the trailer must have been an incredibly painful and traumatic experience for Weiher. Also, sepsis may have occurred, which caused his veins to be discolored. Sepsis is a condition when the body's ability to fight infections turns on itself, creating a deadly situation where the organs fail or act abnormally. If not treated by a doctor, then the result is death. Weiher's feet had frostbite, and walking must have been agonizing. Had the trailer been on the radar of searchers, there was the possibility that Weiher could have been rescued and treated at a hospital.

Liptrap was asked by Ayers if he could determine when Weiher died. It was Liptrap's opinion that Weiher may have died shortly after being exposed to the elements, but Ayers questioned the opinion because Weiher was clean-shaven when he disappeared. This shocked Liptrap because Weiher had a full beard when he was discovered, so Liptrap requested a portion of Weiher's cheek and beard to be sent to him for further analysis.

During the meeting, Liptrap updated Ayers on the results of the autopsies he completed for Madruga and Sterling. From what Liptrap had of the remains, he could not determine the cause of death due to the extent of their decomposition, but from what he had examined, he did not see any evidence of foul play. Jack Madruga's lower teeth and Bill Sterling's upper teeth were given to Ayers so he could have the dentists of the victims review them for confirmation. Jackie Huett's skull would also be given to Ayers to send to Huett's dentist for examination. Huett's dentist examined his skull and positively identified Huett based on his dental records. A few days later, Sterling's dentist informed investigators that based on what he was given, he would state the remains were Sterling's, but the statement came with reservations. Sterling's dentist said that Sterling had extensive dental work over the years. Investigators found Sterling's identification with the remains, so they were very positive that it was Sterling.

Meanwhile, the search for the remains of Gary Mathias was still underway in the Plumas National Forest. The other four families had now written obituaries and made funeral arrangements for their sons. Ted Weiher was buried on June 8th at Sierra View Memorial Park, Jack Madruga was buried on June 9th at Browns Valley Cemetery, Bill Sterling was also buried on June 9th at Sutter Cemetery, and Jackie Huett was buried on June 11th at Sierra View Memorial Park.

A Northern California television station filmed some of the funerals. Weiher's video is brief but shows the funeral service at Sierra View Memorial Park in Olivehurst. A man plays an acoustic guitar, and a group of people is singing the old spiritual 'When the Roll is Called Up Yonder.' Imogene Weiher spoke to the press after her son's funeral and said, "Ted was a very loving person."

"There were thousands of people at Ted's [funeral]," said Dorothy Weiher-Dornan. She remembered the crowd at Sierra View Memorial Park in Olivehurst. For some reason, and she can't recall why, Weiher-Dornan and Imogene Weiher were advised not to attend the funerals for the others. Weiher-Dornan believes that attending the other funerals would have put an incredible emotional and physical toll on her and her mother.

Weiher-Dornan also remembers a call from someone in the Kennedy family. Eunice Kennedy Shriver was the founder of the Special Olympics and was the sister of President John F. Kennedy and Senator Robert Kennedy. Weiher-Dornan does not remember who called, but they gave their condolences to the Weiher family.

I watched the video of Madruga's funeral next. It showed an American flag draped over the coffin, which is typical for those who served in the military. The view is from the back of the church or chapel. People are seated in pews and music can be heard.

Bill Sterling's funeral was outdoors at Sutter Cemetery in Yuba City. The video shows a minister standing next to Sterling's coffin, reading from notes while holding a Bible. There are random shots of people in attendance. Jim and Juanita Sterling are seated next to each other, and Jim Sterling is inconsolable.

Video does not exist of the funeral of Jackie Huett. However, there is video of an interview with Jack Huett Sr. in the Plumas National Forest. The video is dated June 8th or 9th, 1978, so Huett Sr. may have been interviewed immediately following the discovery of his son's remains. Huett Sr. is equally devastated and furious in the interview. His words are meant for someone in law enforcement, but that someone is not mentioned. Huett Sr. said the investigation was wrongly handled by someone, possibly the Sheriff for Butte or Plumas County. He was mad because the person blamed the men's intellectual disabilities for being lost.

☙

I grew up in the Catholic church and was a server for our local parish. The server is nothing more than a fancy title for an altar boy. There were times when I was assigned to work funeral Masses. One I recall was the funeral for a child who died unexpectedly. I had been a server at funerals before, but not for someone so young. The sadness in the church that day was overwhelming.

I remembered that funeral while watching the video clips of the funerals of Jack Madruga, Ted Weiher, and Bill Sterling. The Sterling family's very personal moment for their son was being recorded by the media. There were numerous people crying. After watching the clip, I understand why the Sterling family has remained out of the spotlight.

Claudia Huett sent me images of the program for Jackie Huett's funeral as well as pictures of letters from various agencies expressing their condolences. The Alta Regional Center said that Jackie was "a perfect gentleman" and loved by their staff. The Sacramento Valley Mother Lode Special Olympics sent a letter as well. They mentioned that donations were being made on Jackie Huett's behalf by various people in the community. Jim and Juanita Sterling were one of the donors. During the most difficult of times, the families of the five were there for each other.

Included in the letters that Claudia Huett has on file for Jackie is a receipt from the Yuba County Sheriff's Department. Personal items found with Jackie's remains were given to the Huett family. A comb, a wallet, a set of keys, and an ID bracelet were some of those and were listed individually on a receipt.

Some of the family members told me that although they had the remains and some personal belongings of their loved ones, they didn't have the answers. In June 1978, the Mathias family wanted answers as well, but they also were still hoping to hear something about the whereabouts of Gary Mathias.

CHAPTER TWENTY-ONE: JUNE 11–30, 1978

I have been asked a few times if the story of Gary Mathias will ever be complete. It is a rather difficult question to answer. My hope is that his remains are found while his siblings are still alive. That is the proper closure for them. In my opinion, Mathias was in the trailer with Weiher and simply walked into the Plumas to try to find help. We have no idea where he went and where his remains are today.

June 1978 was one incredibly frustrating month for the families and law enforcement. The second week was full of discoveries. Difficult news was shared with the families, and a community mourned. The rest of the month was dedicated to Mathias. He had to be somewhere in the vicinity of the other remains. He had to be. There was no way they could give up at this point.

❧

Jackie Huett's services were scheduled for June 11th at Hutchinson's Colonial Chapel, and he was to be cremated at Sierra View Memorial Park. The Gateway Projects decided to cancel all services and events on June 13th in remembrance of the five. A request had been submitted to Beale Air Force Base that an aerial reconnaissance mission be conducted over the Plumas to assist in the search for Mathias. Also on June 13th, a lieutenant from Beale Air Force Base informed the Yuba County Sheriff's Office that the request was denied. The main reason was it would be impossible for aerial reconnaissance to spot a body or any type of human remains. Meanwhile, some thirty-five searchers were looking for the remains of Gary Mathias in the Plumas National Forest.

While investigators were still searching for the remains of Gary Mathias, newspapers across the United States and Canada reported on the fate of the five missing men. The news of their disappearance had been reported across the nation and beyond early in March, but starting June 13th and 14th, some of those newspapers updated readers with news of the deaths of Ted Weiher, Jack Madruga, Bill Sterling, and Jackie Huett. A few examples of the headlines were "Why Did Men Walk to Their Deaths in Snow?", "Police Discover Four Snowbound Bodies," and "Final Journey of Five Leaves a Mystery."

They all wanted to know what happened to the "five slightly retarded men" in Northern California. The stories had a quote from Melba Madruga, the mother of Jack Madruga. She told the press, "We know there's more to it than what's been said."

One newspaper interviewed Undersheriff Jack Beecham. Beecham said he believed the reason the five ended up in the Plumas was because Gary Mathias wanted to visit friends in Forbestown, a small community thirty miles east of Oroville. If this was the case, then Beecham believed they somehow got lost because they did not turn right onto Forbestown Road in Oroville. "The turnoff can be missed easily," he said. "There is a tendency for people to keep going, the 'around-the-corner' syndrome."

The people in Forbestown who knew Mathias had not seen him in ages. It would not have made sense for Mathias to visit these friends the night before a major basketball game. Also, Madruga was the driver, and he had a reputation for driving where he wanted to go, no questions asked. Weiher was someone who wanted to be in bed at a certain time, so this shortcut would not have sat well with him.

"Maybe they were just feeling good and wanted to take a ride," said Ken Mickelson to the *Oroville Mercury-Register*. As coordinator for the Butte County Search and Rescue Team, he believed the five exited the highway in Oroville to take a circuitous route to Marysville. They were to go through Forbestown and then head south. Mickelson believed that "they thought they were going the right direction and just kept on going."

℘

Searchers were focused on looking for Mathias in the Granite Basin and Bucks Lake area since that was where they found Weiher, Madruga, Sterling, and Huett. A cigarette lighter was discovered in the area, and Mathias was a smoker. It was a long shot connecting the two, and investigators believed it could have been left there months or years before the men went missing. Most importantly, the shoes Mathias was wearing the night he disappeared were found in the trailer. The area was still difficult to investigate in spots because snow was melting. One searcher told the *Chico Enterprise-Record*, "There is so much snow if you get above the basin, it may be a waiting game. We can't seem to find anything." Steps were retraced to make sure the remains were not missed the first time due to the snow.

Another problem was the ground brush. "The ground brush is so thick you can hardly see anything," said an investigator who added, "We're even looking in the trees."

Meanwhile, Lance Ayers was still trying to figure out what led the five off the highway into the Plumas. He claimed to have numerous theories, but supporting evidence was nonexistent. "I don't have five leading theories," said Ayers. "We're looking into many theories. We're doing that because the one we don't look at will be the one."

Something that baffled the investigators was the fact that the five took a straight path up the road into the Plumas. Dave Wingfield from the Plumas County Sheriff's Department told the press, "Most people go downhill when they're lost. Or they go in circles. Not a straight line like this." Had they walked south down the road, they would have come across Mountain House.

It was reported by the *Oroville Mercury-Register* on June 15th that the Yuba, Butte, and Plumas County Sheriff's Departments met in Oroville with the California Department of Justice to "pool information." After the meeting, a reporter asked Butte County Undersheriff Dick Stenberg for an update. "We still don't have any idea [as to why the men went to that area]," said Stenberg. He did admit to the press that, "We kicked around a few ideas and came up with a few possibilities, nothing definite, nothing releasable." He also informed the press that the search would go on until they exhausted all possibilities.

A day after the meeting in Oroville, it was reported by the *Appeal-Democrat* that investigators wanted to interview Joseph Schons again to see if he could provide any new information about what he had witnessed in the Plumas. Dennis Forcino from the Plumas County Sheriff's Department wanted answers because he wanted to know if Schons was telling the truth about the pickup truck, the woman with the baby, the other people, and the whistling noises.

Family members were aware of the theory of the impromptu trip to Forbestown to visit Mathias's friends, but it didn't make sense to them that a group of men who lived their lives on a rigid schedule would make a spontaneous decision to make that trip. The missed exit to Forbestown was one theory for law enforcement, but it didn't make sense to Cathy Madruga. It didn't explain why they kept driving into the Plumas following the missed turn. "If [Jack Madruga] did [miss a turn], then he had enough goddamn sense to turn around and go down the hill. It made it sound like they were all dimwits, and that's not the case."

Imogene Weiher had the same opinion when she was interviewed by the press. "Jack Madruga would have never driven his car up there. They wouldn't have gone up there, got scared, and just run off." In Imogene Weiher's opinion, the men were probably enticed to that area.

Debbie Sterling, Bill Sterling's sister, knew Jack Madruga and believed he was forced to drive up the road where his Montego was abandoned. The road where they abandoned the car near Rogers Cow Camp was not paved, was rutted, and was snow-covered in areas. It was not an easy drive, and Debbie Sterling knew that Madruga hated the idea of damaging his car, even the underbody. She recalled a time when Jack Madruga refused to drive Jackie Huett home because the road where he lived was in poor condition.

"I don't know if we'll ever know what happened, but they didn't get lost," said Juanita Sterling to the press. There was no convincing Juanita Sterling that the five decided to make the drive into the Plumas on their own. "They'll never make me believe they just drove up there, never. They could read road maps and signs." She also believed that they could have worked together to get Madruga's car unstuck and returned home. In her opinion, the men were forced from the car and were instructed not to come back. Sterling's theory was that the five tried getting back to the main road but became lost in the Plumas.

☙

The *Los Angeles Times* ran an article by Cathleen Decker on June 19th titled "Mystery of 5 Men Lost in Sierra Deepens," and it featured an interview with Melba Madruga. When asked about the disappearance and deaths of the five, Madruga responded, "Things aren't right." Madruga also said, "They [the investigators] want to say they [the men] got stuck, walked out like a bunch of idiots, and froze to death." When investigators found Madruga's car, a window was partially rolled down, and she told Decker that her son would never walk away from his vehicle with a window down. Jack Madruga was very particular about his car. Melba Madruga also stated that her son avoided driving his car on poor roads because he did not want his vehicle damaged.

She was frustrated like many of the parents and siblings of the five because there was no reason for her son to drive into the complete darkness of the Plumas on a cold February night. Again, she knew most of the people in the car did not care for the snow, the dark, or the outdoors. Additionally, the game on Saturday in Rocklin was of the utmost importance.

In the same article for the *Los Angeles Times*, Lance Ayers was interviewed and was asked about the Montego. Ayers was impressed that someone got the car up the road because it was in poor condition, and it would have done damage to the underbody if the driver was a bit careless. "I suspect someone who knew the road drove it up," said Ayers. "But we're in the rather peculiar position that anything is possible because we know so little."

As mentioned in previous articles, the assumption was that the men did not walk in circles once they left the car. Ayers was under the impression they walked over nineteen miles uphill in a straight line. According to the article, a Sno-Cat operated by a Forest Service employee had plowed a path from the car to the Daniel Zink Campground area. The operator of the Sno-Cat made that trip to clear off snow from the roof of the trailer to avoid collapse. It was reported that the Forest Service employee completed the work on February 23rd, and they never returned after that.

"People often get the 'around-the-corner' syndrome," said Ayers. It was the same theory shared by Beecham to the press. The men, according to Ayers, were possibly under the impression the path going up the hill would lead somewhere and that somewhere was right around the corner.

Ayers theorized the men all walked that road together, but either Sterling or Madruga became exhausted or succumbed to hypothermia and decided to rest on the ground. He believed, due to their friendship, that Sterling or Madruga would not leave the other behind while Weiher, Huett, and Mathias made it to the cabin. The damage to Weiher's feet from the frostbite would have made it too painful for Weiher to do much walking, and Ayers believed that either Huett or Mathias assisted Weiher in the trailer.

☙

On June 19, 1978, investigators postponed the search for Gary Mathias. They told reporters that they had been searching the Daniel Zink area since they were alerted about the discovery of Ted Weiher's remains. There was hope that the remaining snowdrifts would melt, and it would be easier for investigators to search for Gary Mathias later in the season. An article from the *Oroville Mercury-Register* stated the drifts were four to six feet in height. "Every cabin, every hole in the ground, anywhere a person could possibly be has been checked," said Plumas County Deputy Rod Day. Although they said that the search was postponed, it was essentially over. The main report with the Yuba County Sheriff's Department does not provide an explanation regarding that decision.

A Northern California newspaper reported an update on the search for Gary Mathias on August 3, 1978. Dave Wingfield, Plumas County Assistant Sheriff, stated, "Nothing is being done from a practical standpoint as we don't have the manpower or volunteers to continue." He did state that Dennis Forcino from the Plumas County Sheriff's Department was going up to the Plumas on his own to search areas for clues or a body.

Captain Leroy Wood from the Butte County Sheriff's Department informed the press that his jurisdiction was no longer involved in the search for Mathias and that they had no plans for resuming it in the near future.

Jack Beecham was also interviewed, and he stated, "Leads and information flow has pretty much stopped." In Beecham's opinion, it was unlikely that Mathias was alive because, as he informed the reporter, John Thompson from the California Department of Justice had been in touch with hospitals and mental institutions to see if Mathias was in their care. Nothing turned up. Beecham was convinced that Mathias fell through a snowdrift into a thick patch of manzanita and died. Manzanita is an evergreen shrub with dense foliage found in California.

Beecham told the press that they had followed every lead, and the case was still open despite the fact the search had been called off. Beecham told a reporter in late June 1978 that the Yuba County Sheriff's Department had spent nearly twelve hundred hours investigating, which did not include some two hundred to two hundred fifty hours of his own time doing additional investigative work. Members of the Yuba County Search and Rescue team, along with volunteers, spent two hundred forty-four hours searching the Plumas National Forest in areas that were situated in Butte and Plumas counties.

Leroy Wood told the press that Butte County's Search and Rescue Team alone had over seven thousand hours of time searching the Plumas. He also stated that most of the people who helped were volunteers, and Wood would not send up any more people to search until they received "further information." There was a hope among the departments that, at some point, a "wayward deer hunter" would stumble upon the remains of Gary Mathias.

❧

While researching this book, a fellow Yuba County Five researcher told me that Gary Mathias liked the song "Lido Shuffle" by Boz Scaggs. I checked with Tammie Phillips, Gary's sister, to see if it was true. She said she owned the album *Silk Degrees*, which features the song, and they would listen to it together. I used to play "Lido Shuffle" for my youngest when they were one or two, and they would bop along. It was a song we would listen to at night before I got them ready for bed. It was good to know Gary enjoyed it, too.

Gary Mathias also loved the music of Creedence Clearwater Revival (CCR) and The Rolling Stones. Tammie Phillips has some pictures of Gary with his own band, The 5th Shade, along with his old record collection. I asked her what albums he owned, and she said she'd find time to look them over when she had the chance. I never heard back from her on this, and I didn't want to press her.

I was careful in asking about the halting of the search for her brother. It is still difficult for the family to discuss, and there is plenty of anger and sadness about how the search was abruptly called off. All that was left was the story staying in the spotlight.

CHAPTER TWENTY-TWO:
JULY to DECEMBER 1978

While I was gathering information for this book, the Yuba County Library announced that their newspaper collection had been digitized. Yuba County newspapers from 1850 to the present were scanned, and the text in those publications was now searchable. There were other newspaper collections from California that had been digitized, but I focused on the *Appeal-Democrat* because they reported on the case more than any other newspaper.

The main reporter for the Yuba County Five case was Milt Carland. A Minnesota native, Carland made his way to the *Appeal-Democrat* in 1961 and covered law enforcement and local government. "Marysville suited Milt, a bright, iconoclastic guy," said Mike Geniella, a former reporter for the *Appeal-Democrat*. Carland was a mentor for Geniella, who remembered, "[Carland] worked the morning shift, covering the police beat mainly. Then he was done for the day and headed for his favorite watering holes."

Carland also loved classical music and Japanese novels. "Milt helped me understand the importance of clarity and facts in news reporting," said Geniella. "He instructed me, by example, in how to cover City Hall and county government."

The disappearance of the Yuba County Five was one of the biggest stories in Yuba County that Carland covered. He reported on the case from beginning to end. For many years, those articles were only available if requested from the archives or from people who clipped them at the time but now his articles are now available for researchers via the Yuba County Library digital collection. Carland passed away in 1999. It would have been interesting to hear his recollections.

Another reporter who covered the story is Cynthia Gorney, and she was the first person I interviewed for this book. Her article for the *Washington Post* is considered by Yuba County Five researchers to be the starting point for understanding this mystery. I was pleased she agreed to an interview. She had not forgotten about the five and their case.

Cathleen Decker's June 19, 1978, article for the *Los Angeles Times* titled "Mystery of 5 Men Lost in the Sierra Deepens" was the first major piece about the case written for a national newspaper. The Thursday, July 6, 1978, edition of the *Washington Post* ran a story about the disappearance of Ted Weiher, Jack Madruga, Bill Sterling, Jackie Huett, and Gary Mathias on page B1 of the "Style" section and was written by reporter Cynthia Gorney. "The Feather River Mystery: A Mountain Road, Deserted Car and Five Who Never Came Back" was the most in-depth article written about the Yuba County Five at the time.

A picture of Imogene Weiher was featured in the article, and she was holding a picture of her son. Weiher appeared to be completely defeated and overwhelmed with life. Gorney's article captured the anger and bewilderment not only from the families but from law enforcement as well.

Cynthia Gorney grew up in California, and in 1975, she joined the *Washington Post*. When the Yuba County Five disappeared, Gorney was working in their Western Bureau Office in the San Francisco area. "I was doing a variety of pieces from around the West, and I do not remember how that story came to my attention," said Gorney. "I'm sure it was through… most of the stuff I got back then for the *Post* came as a result of me seeing something short and attention-getting in a local daily paper or a wire service clip and thinking that might make an interesting story for a national audience and going and plowing in more deeply. I'm ninety-nine percent sure that was the case there." When asked about her memories of discovering the story, Gorney said, "It was a really creepy story, and I was quite distressed by it."

She would spend one to two weeks in the Yuba County area knocking on doors and interviewing family and law enforcement for the story. People were willing to talk with Gorney, and she believed the reason was she worked for the *Washington Post*. It was not a local newspaper, and any dirty laundry would not be on the doorstep of friends or neighbors.

"I'm a pretty dogged reporter," Gorney shared. "I didn't have any special connections or clever ways of getting to people than just calling and saying, 'I'd really like to hear your story.' I don't remember how I got to all the families." Gorney believed another reason people were willing to talk with her was because she was a female reporter. "Sometimes people are more comfortable talking about really emotional things with a female reporter, and I just don't know if that was the case."

The Yuba County Sheriff's Department was willing to speak, and Gorney was able to interview members of their staff, including Lance Ayers. "They were frustrated, and exhausted, and sad. It was helpful for them just to talk to an outsider to say, 'This makes us crazy because we don't understand it.'"

The *Feather River Mystery* article provided a slight glimpse into the mind of Lance Ayers. He was, after all, the one who spent the most time on the investigation from the Yuba County Sheriff's Department. Ayers told Gorney in the article that he dreamed about the five one night and awoke from the dream with his arms outstretched as if he were to embrace the five lost men. "You do a lot of headshaking… and a lot of drinking," said Ayers in the article. It also mentioned Ayers working with the psychics and how one of them provided Ayers with an Oroville address of 4723 and 4753 because it was a house where the missing men were murdered. Ayers told Gorney in the article that he spent two days driving around Oroville looking for an address that did not exist.

John Thompson from the California Department of Justice was also interviewed. He, too, was completely baffled by the situation, and described it as "bizarre." According to Thompson, there were no explanations, but there were "a thousand leads."

Gorney also gained access to Gary Mathias's family. Newspaper articles from Yuba City, Oroville, and Sacramento seldom featured a quote from anyone from Mathias's family. Bob and Ida Klopf were interviewed for Gorney's article, and she spoke with them either during the week of or the week after the remains of Weiher, Madruga, Sterling, and Huett were discovered. Both were experiencing a great deal of sorrow. The Klopfs admitted they were done talking to the press, and they had turned off their television set weeks earlier because they didn't want to hear about the discovery of their son's remains that way.

Bob Klopf wanted to know why they had not been able to find Gary Mathias. Klopf told Gorney that Mathias had not "gone haywire" in two years. Klopf had spent time in the Plumas assisting with the search efforts to find Mathias's remains. What Klopf wanted to find was Mathias's glasses because he thought animals wouldn't have wanted to eat them. It was his opinion that the glasses would be near the remains of his stepson.

What puzzled Klopf the most was the fact that Mathias or the others who were in the cabin did not start a fire to alert searchers. "All those paperbacks and they didn't even build a lousy fire. I can't understand why they didn't do that unless they were afraid," said Klopf in the interview. Klopf just could not understand what Mathias was afraid of up in the mountains. It must have been something or someone.

Cynthia Gorney was interviewed by Mopac Audio for the *Yuba County Five* podcast series. She shared her thoughts concerning the fate of the five. "As a parent, there's only one thing I can imagine worse than losing your child, and that's not knowing how you lost your child. Not ever knowing what happened. I cannot fathom that horror."

The mystery of the Yuba County Five haunts her to this very day. She also told the *Yuba County Five* podcast, "I remember thinking so much when I was reporting it about the darkness of when they disappeared. How it's the middle of the night when their parents start realizing something's wrong. How dark it must have been in that cabin. The moon. Grief. Fury at the mystery of it and darkness."

A couple of weeks after Gorney's article was published, the opening ceremonies for the Special Olympics State Games were held at UCLA in Los Angeles. During the event, there was a brief tribute, and the names of Ted Weiher, Jack Madruga, Bill Sterling, Jackie Huett, and Gary Mathias were read. The participants and guests observed a moment of silent prayer. Had the five won their event in Rocklin on Saturday, February 25th, they would have been in attendance.

Dallas Weiher Jr. had joined a little league team that summer: the Angels. He had celebrated his birthday while his uncle Ted was a missing person. Then, grief from his uncle's death was everywhere. Weiher Jr. enjoyed the opportunity to play baseball as an escape from all the world's problems. There were times when his father, Dallas Weiher Sr., would catch his games, but it just wasn't the same without his uncle Ted in the stands cheering him on.

As summer faded away, the fall brought some news regarding the search for Gary Mathias. Brad Bollinger, a reporter for the *Chico Enterprise-Record*, wrote an article for the October 14th edition titled "Family Still Searches for Lost Man." According to his article, it had been two hundred thirty-six days since Gary Mathias had disappeared, but his family was not finished looking for him in the Plumas National Forest. Lance Ayers was interviewed for the article. By then he had left the detective's division and returned to being a patrolman. He told Bollinger that he hoped some news about Mathias would occur during deer hunting season. Ayers believed hunters would stumble across Mathias's remains or find something that belonged to him.

Bob and Ida Klopf were also interviewed, and they told Bollinger they had made numerous trips to the Plumas during the summer to look for Mathias. "We've gone down every nook and cranny and canyon, and there are no clues," said Ida Klopf. "The very idea of not knowing something for sure keeps us going up there." At the time, they had planned for one more trip before the winter snows arrived. Ida Klopf told Bollinger, "Every time I hear of an unidentified body, I get on the phone. If someone could just prove to me that he is dead, I think I could accept it."

Three days before the story in the *Chico Enterprise-Record*, an article in the *Reno Gazette-Journal* reported a series of accidents from the previous evening. At 10:10 p.m., somewhere outside Reno, Nevada, on US Route 395 near Parr Boulevard, a pickup truck overturned. The driver of the vehicle was unharmed, and he told troopers that his truck crashed when it avoided colliding with another vehicle. The driver's name was Joseph Schons, he had minor injuries, and he resided in Berry Creek, California.

☙

On November 29, 1978, Melba Gail Madruga, the mother of Jack Madruga, died. She was seventy years old and was buried at Browns Valley Cemetery near her son. Her health had been in decline since June when Jack Madruga's remains were found.

Christmas was celebrated by the families, and it was perhaps another difficult day for them, knowing someone who was a son, brother, or uncle would not be there. As 1978 came to a close, the *Appeal-Democrat* decided to review the top stories of the year for their December 30th edition. The disappearance and search for Ted Weiher, Jack Madruga, Bill Sterling, Jackie Huett, and Gary Mathias was the second top story of the year. The reversal of the Juan Corona conviction was the main story, according to the *Appeal-Democrat*.

It was somewhat surprising that the disappearance of the five was not the top story of 1978 for the *Appeal-Democrat*. The news about the Corona verdict shocked California. However, Corona would have his second trial in 1982 and be found guilty. The story of the five would make it into 1979 with some articles and a chilling discovery. After that, it would begin to slowly fade into Northern California folklore.

PART III: LOST AND FOUND

CHAPTER TWENTY-THREE:
1979–2016

From 1980 until 2017, there was a thirty-seven-year dark period for the Yuba County Five case. I have reviewed newspaper articles and documents from the Yuba County Sheriff's Department from this time and mostly they deal with Gary Mathias since his remains were never found. Law enforcement believed they had gone above and beyond the call of duty in the investigation and search and rescue operation. In their opinion, the case was closed because five men got lost one night and four were found dead. The fifth one was in the Plumas somewhere, and their remains would be found at some point. Possibly.

The families were not satisfied. They knew something had gone horribly wrong on February 24, 1978, and since there were no clues or leads, law enforcement was no longer motivated to investigate. For a while, it turned out to be the families' battle and their battle alone. Some of the family members I interviewed experienced various ups and downs over the years. Even in the gloomiest of times, they knew not to give up. Some were determined to find answers by any means possible.

At times, there would be brief glimmers of hope. There were other moments where it seemed that Gary Mathias could be alive. Then the Yuba County Five story became dormant. However, changes in technology allowed the case to be known to a new audience, and their interest could not be stopped.

∾

A letter to the editor from the families of the Yuba County Five was printed in the February 24, 1979, edition of the *Appeal-Democrat*, one year following the disappearance of Ted Weiher, Jack Madruga, Bill Sterling, Jackie Huett, and Gary Mathias. Titled "Still One Missing, Still A Reward," the letter was a special "thank you" to the community for all the time they had put into the investigation and the search. They also expressed their gratitude to those who sent their sympathies. The families wanted the community to remember that Gary Mathias was never found, a reward was still available, and that there were numerous questions that needed answers.

The families wanted to know if someone had chased the five into the Plumas. And if so, why? They asked who was in the pickup that Schons allegedly saw that night. Also, they wanted to know why the cabin where Ted Weiher was found was never searched in March. The letter implied that Butte County knew about the trailer but never took the advice of the Forest Service to inspect it in the months before Weiher's body was discovered. The families said they were experiencing bitterness, bewilderment, and anger.

The same letter was submitted to the *Oroville Mercury-Register* and was featured in the February 26, 1979, "Letters to the Editor" section, and titled "A Reminder of Tragedy." It was perhaps a last-ditch effort by the families to have someone come forward with any helpful leads about what happened to the five. The families wanted the readers to know the reward money was still available to anyone who had any information about their disappearance. The money, according to the letter, would stay in the bank until all five were accounted for.

Other newspapers also recalled the disappearance of the men. The January 7, 1979, edition of the *Daily News* in New York City ran "Mystery of the Sierra Nevada" by Anthony Burton. It provided an overview of the case. Burton only had a quote from Lance Ayers concerning the investigation. We do not know if Burton reached out to the families or other members of law enforcement for the article.

Eleven days after that article ran, the *Daily News* printed a letter from a reader in their "Voice of the People" section. A man named Stanley Fisher wanted law enforcement in California to know that they should have contacted psychic Jane Roberts. She reportedly had a connection to a spirit named "Seth," and Fisher wanted Roberts to be the one to help because Seth could get information from the other side. It is difficult to determine if Fisher was a fan or critic of Roberts.

The *Chico Enterprise-Record* ran an article on February 24, 1979, titled "One Year Ago, 5 Men Disappeared into the Hills" by Roger Aylworth. Like Burton's article, Lance Ayers was interviewed. As Beecham had stated previously, Ayers was of the opinion that the reason the men got lost was Gary Mathias wanted to visit friends in Forbestown, but they drove past a right turn in Oroville leading to Forbestown that was easy to miss if one did not pay close attention while driving. Ayers told Aylworth that Mathias had frequently visited the Forbestown friends, although they informed law enforcement that they had not seen Mathias in ages. Additionally, the article stated that the road where they missed the turn to Forbestown had been fixed after the five vanished. It was originally a "Y" style intersection, but they made it a "T" style intersection so the turn was easier to notice.

Ken Mickelson of the Butte County Sheriff's Department was also interviewed for Aylworth's article. He too thought that Madruga had missed the "Y" style intersection and just kept driving. "It has nothing to do with mental retardation or anything else," said Mickelson. "It's a natural reaction to keep going if they think they are traveling in the right direction."

For whatever reason, they became stuck in the snow and exited the vehicle. Mickelson told Aylworth that the cold temperatures in February froze the snowdrifts, which made it easier for the men to walk through. Another theory held by Mickelson in the article was that Madruga and Sterling collapsed during the walk and were left behind by the others. He believed that Weiher and Mathias made it to the trailer but was not certain what happened to Huett.

The article also provided some details about why the trailer was not heated. Mickelson said that there were butane tanks and some fuel oil outside the trailer. When the men arrived at the trailer, the butane tanks were probably covered in snow and not visible, but the fuel oil was on a stand that could be seen. Mickelson theorized that Mathias's Army training would have allowed him to start a fire if he could not figure out how to heat the trailer with the butane or fuel oil. According to Mickelson, Mathias left the trailer early, and that is why a fire was never started.

In the same article, Lance Ayers made a statement about why Ted Weiher never started a fire or tried to heat the trailer. "Weiher was deathly afraid of fire," said Ayers. Weiher's family house caught fire in the 1960s and he was forcibly removed from the house because he did not understand what the commotion was about. Again, according to his family, Weiher wanted a good night of rest more than leaving a burning home. Ayers told Aylworth that the Weiher family must have explained to Ted Weiher the serious nature of a fire and that he must have been afraid to start any kind of fire in the trailer.

Dallas Weiher Jr. was asked about a possible fear of fire, but he did not have any memories of his uncle being afraid. In fact, Weiher Jr. remembered that Ted Weiher carried around a lighter because he would occasionally smoke with Jackie Huett. Also, Weiher Jr. recalled that his uncle had a barrel for burning rubbish in the backyard of the Weiher family residence. Ted Weiher would call someone in local government to see if trash burning was permitted. Weiher Jr. remembered that his uncle had a low awareness of danger.

Ayers also believed that Mathias was in the trailer briefly, and he may have been the one who lit the candle. He also stated that it seemed that Weiher was able to survive in the trailer for some "eight to thirteen weeks" before he died.

Mathias's fate was still up in the air when the article was published. Mickelson told Aylworth, "The chances are pretty slim that he will be found. If he's someplace like down in Soapstone Canyon, where nobody goes, I don't think we'll find him." Both Ayers and Mickelson still speculated that foul play was a possibility, but they lacked any evidence to point in that direction.

Foul play was also discussed in a March 6, 1979, article by Cathleen Decker in the *Los Angeles Times*. Imogene Weiher, Ted's mother, was interviewed, and she shared the same theory she had shared with other family members that the five were forced up the mountain road by someone. Also, Imogene Weiher shared that couldn't stop thinking about the Yuba County Five, which led to many sleepless nights. "I keep wondering what happened that night, why they left Chico and went up there," said Weiher. "Then I get to thinking how long [Ted] was there… how cold he was… and I just can't sleep."

The case was still weighing heavily on Lance Ayers as well. He told Decker, "I'll live with this until I quit the department… and I'll remember it for the rest of my life." Decker stated in her article that Ayers sounded "sad and weary." Ayers shared that he was keeping in touch with the families, and a few months before he spoke with Decker for her article, he had attended the funeral of Melba Madruga. One year after the men disappeared, Ayers was still trying to figure out this incredibly bizarre mystery. "It's my baby and I'll have it until I solve it. It will haunt us until we find out what happened."

တ

On March 28, 1979, in an area west of Forbestown and south of Lake Oroville, a dog returned home after a day of wandering in the nearby woods. The owner was horrified when they discovered that the dog had in its mouth what appeared to be a human hand. The Butte County Sheriff's Department was contacted, and there was a possibility that the hand belonged to someone who went missing in the woods. One theory was that it belonged to Gary Mathias.

Butte County's Search and Rescue team began an investigation of the area, and more bones were discovered scattered in a location not far from where the dog's owner lived. Bones from a leg, arm, and spine were discovered. Some of the fragments were sent to Chico State University to be examined by an anthropologist.

Authorities were quick to dismiss that it was Mathias's hand because it was found in an area that was nowhere near the areas where the remains of Weiher, Madruga, Sterling, and Huett were found. The hand was from an adult male or female, according to investigators, and it was decomposed. However, investigators believed the bones had been in the location for several months or longer. Also, investigators determined from the bones they had collected that the person was approximately five-foot-three inches in height, which was shorter than Mathias.

Essie Hiett went missing near Oroville in February 1978. She was five-foot-five inches in height, and she was still missing when the bones were discovered. A skull had not been located and searchers were hoping to find it so they could get dental information for any missing persons.

A few days following the discovery, an anthropologist at Chico State University determined the bones were that of a primate and not human. An explanation of why the bones of a primate would be discovered in the woods was not provided.

୧୨

It was May 1979 when the Yuba County Sheriff's Department received a call from the San Juaquin, California Sheriff's Department. A man named Paul Morris (pseudonym) contacted them and said he saw a man matching the description of Gary Mathias hitchhiking. Morris told the

San Joaquin Sheriff's Department that he once resided in Marysville and was certain he saw Mathias get into a pickup truck. Morris had written down the license plate, and he gave it to the officers. The Yuba County Sheriff's Department was informed that the San Juaquin Sheriff's Department would track down the owner of the pickup truck to see if he could remember the name of the hitchhiker. No additional information was provided in the case files.

Meanwhile, Slater Judd Jr. was still submitting letters to the Yuba County Sheriff's Department. In a letter from Judd Jr. dated March 5, 1980, he warned the department that the rogue Marine renegades were still terrorizing California. Judd Jr. went on to claim that the Sheriff of San Mateo, California, had knowledge about what had happened to the missing men. According to Judd Jr., the truth was being covered up and there were documents and testimony to prove the renegades were terrorizing Judd Jr. and his family.

He informed the sheriff's department that he had been in touch with a U.S. attorney's office in San Francisco, and the lawyer was also concerned. The letter stated that when he personally stopped by the attorney's office, a judge in the building collapsed during a session. Judd Jr. theorized that the judge had been threatened by the rogue Marines, who also had been harassing the judge for years.

A newspaper clipping was included with the letter. It was a 1980 article from the *San Mateo County Times*, and it was titled "Sheriff to Attend FBI Seminar." If Judd Jr. believed he had some sort of smoking-gun evidence with that article, he was sadly mistaken.

❧

Perhaps the most chilling post-investigation encounter occurred during the late 1970s or early 1980s. Cathy Madruga, Jack Madruga's niece, was finishing up a day of work and decided to stop by a bar owned by her mother in Browns Valley, a small community to the northeast of Marysville. "I walked in, and the bar was completely full," said Madruga.

"I walked in to use the restroom. I walked in to the left and I'm checking the place out. There's a guy sitting at the end of the bar. He looks at me and I look at him. It was Gary Mathias."

Madruga swiftly made her way into the restroom and thought to herself, *Aw shit, that's Mathias.* She knew she needed to act quickly to inform her mother, who was working, but not be noticed by the man she saw in the bar. Madruga caught a glimpse of the man she believed to be Mathias, who was still seated in the bar, and immediately located her mother. Madruga discretely asked her mom to step aside with her in a back area of the bar, and that's when she dropped the bombshell. The authorities were called and Madruga decided to see if the man was still around. "He was out that door before we could get back out front," said Madruga. "I know it was him."

Browns Valley is in Yuba County, so Cathy Madruga contacted the Yuba County Sheriff's Department, and they scheduled a meeting not long after her sighting. Lane Ayers had stayed in touch with the family, according to Madruga. She recalled meeting with three people at the Sheriff's Department to discuss her Mathias sighting.

"They had me come in and look at mugshots," recalled Madruga. She remembered that they had placed multiple images of Mathias in a mix of a bunch of pictures, but she was successful in picking Mathias out ten times. "Ten times. They said, 'Okay,' and then they told me—now this came from the officer's mouth—that I wasn't the only one that had seen him," said Madruga. She was informed that someone saw him at a Denny's restaurant and a Montgomery Ward department store, and she even had another encounter with Mathias at a 7-Eleven convenience store. "He was coming out as I was pulling in. Now, I swear on my mother's grave it was him. If I made a mistake, then God forgive me. I feel bad for the family. I feel bad. I know who I saw. In my heart, it was Mathias who I saw."

Madruga's interview with the Yuba County Sheriff's Department is not in the case files. The other sightings Madruga was told about are not there either. The sighting of Mathias hitchhiking by Paul Morris was the only post-June 1978 sighting claim on file.

❧

Bill Sterling's family was dealt a massive blow on October 18, 1982, when David Sterling, Bill's brother, was killed in an accident in Yuba City. It was 2 a.m. when David Sterling was riding his motorcycle and collided with a tractor-trailer. At the time of his death, David Sterling was twenty-nine years old. People around town knew him as "Goober," and it was the second death of a child that Jim and Juanita Sterling had to deal with in four years.

❧

Jim Grant had left the world of law enforcement sometime around 1980 and was a real estate agent who specialized in homes that were solar-heated. On August 22, 1985, Grant was awakened by pains in his stomach, but everything had subsided within a few hours. Grant decided to get ready for the day because he had a 1 p.m. appointment to show a house. He went to take a shower and collapsed. He was later discovered and transported to a local hospital, where he was pronounced dead. Jim Grant was only forty-three years old.

Jack Beecham, who served as undersheriff under Grant, stayed in law enforcement and eventually became the commander of a California program known as the Campaign Against Marijuana Planting (CAMP) during the mid-1980s. CAMP was a statewide program with officials at the federal, state, and local levels that aimed to eradicate the illegal growing on public and private land. "It was huge. Marijuana planting and the violence associated with it," said Beecham. He would be with CAMP for roughly six years.

Tom McGarry was living in the Berry Creek area from 1979 into the early 1980s, and it was a hotspot for marijuana planting. He lived with his cousin and her husband on a property that had sixty acres, while his neighbor, Joseph Schons, lived on an adjacent property that had some eighty acres of land. "It was pretty rugged terrain covered with manzanita," said McGarry. "It wasn't the easiest place to get around. It was all dirt roads."

Living in the Berry Creek area allowed people to get away from the hustle and bustle of cities. It was a different way of life up there, and some individuals decided that there was money to be made by growing marijuana. However, there was the constant threat of being caught by authorities, being robbed, or possibly being killed by rivals. Two articles, "Trigger-Happy Growers Make Their Own Laws" and "Butte Authorities Declare War on Dope," were included in the June 21, 1982, edition of the *Sacramento Bee*. Both articles were written by Jim McClung, and they examined the lawlessness of the illegal drug industry in areas like Butte County, where McGarry lived.

McClung's article noted that the Butte County Sheriff's Department had suspected that from 1978 until 1982, there had been an estimated twelve murders tied to drugs in their county. It was reported that there were approximately one hundred individuals in Berry Creek involved in growing marijuana or running a drug lab, with about ten percent of them identified as "survivalists" who wore camouflage and armed themselves with weapons such as AR-15s. This created a dangerous environment, and law enforcement reported that visitors in the Plumas National Forest, PG&E utility workers, and US Forest Service Workers said they feared for their safety if they accidentally stumbled upon someone's secret growing area or drug lab.

Growing was a dangerous undertaking because law enforcement could swoop in on a moment's notice and confiscate the plants. Also, there were thieves who didn't think twice about stealing someone else's harvest. To many in the area, it was worth the risk because a grower could net anywhere from $10,000 to $40,000. Adjusting for inflation at the time of publication, those harvests would be worth anywhere from $30,000 to $122,000 for growers today.

Butte County conducted a major raid of Berry Creek during the summer of 1981, and they reportedly destroyed one hundred thirty-three planting areas. Law enforcement knew where to go because they had used aerial surveillance. Some of the growers allegedly shot at an aircraft used for spotting illegal growing, and there was an additional fear that officers would be shot at if they tried raiding certain properties.

Joseph Schons was still living in the Berry Creek area in 1981, and Tom McGarry recalled some incidents involving Schons and illegal growing. Not every resident was involved in the business, but those who were knew it was wise to plant in hard-to-find spots and to keep their mouths shut around certain individuals. Apparently, someone did not inform Schons of these unspoken rules. "He did not endear himself to the locals," recalled McGarry.

There were a few times when McGarry would see Greg Malone on the Schons' property. McGarry never had any interactions with him but would watch him from a distance. "I saw him out there making a ton of noise. A heavyset guy, not a mountain man."

One incident McGarry recalls with Joseph Schons took place sometime around October 1982. An intoxicated Schons drove up to the property where McGarry was staying with his cousin and her husband. Schons was highly agitated and yelled something from the car to the husband about something that was allegedly said about Cindy Schons. An angry Schons got out of the car and went up to the husband, which surprised McGarry. The husband, in McGarry's opinion, was a legit tough guy. Words were exchanged, Schons was shoved to the ground, and McGarry said that the husband told Schons to get back to his house and stop harassing people.

Schons drove back to his residence, which was up the hill from where McGarry and the others lived. "The next thing we know, Joe Schons is shooting a rifle at us. [I think] it was a .22, but it's hard to tell," McGarry said. McGarry remembers that his cousin and her husband were frightened because there were children in the area, and they made sure to get the kids to safety. There were some other people in the vicinity, and McGarry recalled they took cover.

During the shooting, McGarry grabbed a rifle and got Schons in his scope. "My friend is like, 'Don't shoot him,' and believe me, I would have been happy to do so." The Sheriff's Department was called, and they came up to confront Schons. Another officer showed up at the Schons property, and they eventually left without arresting Schons, which irritated McGarry since Schons was shooting wildly at innocent bystanders and didn't get into any kind of trouble. McGarry was certain after that moment that Schons was a police informant, "probably the worst in the world," in his opinion.

The Schons shooting story was corroborated by another individual who was there that day. They did not go into detail about the incident but mentioned that Schons was crazy to do such a thing.

℘

The main story involving the five in the 1980s was the 1985 petition by Ida Klopf to administer the estate of Gary Mathias, which was valued at the time at $7,000 or $19,000 when adjusting for inflation at the time of this publication. An article about the petition was featured in the December 21, 1985, edition of the *Appeal-Democrat*. In the article, the petition from Klopf states that the investigators told her family that Mathias had died in the Plumas and that his remains were carried away by wild animals. The article was written seven years after Weiher, Madruga, Sterling, and Huett were found but did not shed any light on new clues or theories.

During that time, certain family members knew that the story of the five was no longer newsworthy. Television during the 1980s allowed people the opportunity to have their unsolved cases featured on network programming. "I had [written] to *Unsolved Mysteries*," said Dorothy Weiher-Dornan. "They wanted to take the case, but the Mathias [family] wouldn't allow it, and they're the only ones who could allow it because their son hadn't been found. Our case had been solved, but not to my satisfaction." Following up on this, I contacted some people who had worked for *Unsolved Mysteries* in the 1980s and 1990s. They did not recall the story of the Yuba County Five because so many requests were submitted to them. One person interviewed for this book believed it may have been the Sterling family that voiced additional objections to the story being televised.

ↄↄ

The Yuba County Sheriff's Department was contacted in January 1990 about human remains found in the Arizona desert. Law enforcement from Phoenix found the skeletal remains of an unidentified person. A note in the Yuba County Sheriff's Department file stated that the remains had been in the desert for three months. Tests showed the person was probably forty-five to fifty years old and they had died the year before. If Gary Mathias was alive, he would have been thirty-seven years old. The Yuba County Sheriff's Department noted that it wasn't Mathias that was found because the remains did not match the age or the time frame.

It was December 1994 when a sergeant at the Yuba County Sheriff's Department received written information from another member of the department. Someone reported to the Yuba County Sheriff's Department in 1994 that Todd Morgan (pseudonym) had admitted to the deaths of several people during a church service in Yuba County sometime between September and October.

According to records from the Yuba County Sheriff's Department, this witness stated that Morgan admitted to some major wrongdoings in his life. One incident he confessed to was that he was responsible for the deaths of "two out of seven retarded males in the hills about seventeen years ago." Morgan also said he burned a man to death over a drug deal and that he also killed a girl. Another crime he admitted to was throwing a body off the Bullards Bar Dam into the New Bullards Bar Reservoir. That location is to the southeast of Lake Oroville.

From what the witness reported, Morgan made some very serious and disturbing claims. The first was a reference to the missing five. The burning admission may be related to the death of former Gateway Director Donald Garrett. The death of the girl could be related to the disappearance of Essie Hiett or possibly tied to the deaths of Valerie Lane or Doris Derryberry. Morgan did not specify anything with the body at the dam. Could that have been Mathias or Hiett?

The Yuba County Sheriff's Department sent someone to speak with the witness who reported the confessions from Morgan. What the Sheriff's Department learned was that the claimant had heard a story from someone who attended the church. The claims turned out to be rumors, and there is no mention of an attempt made to contact Morgan. When questioned in 2021 about the information in the report, a former member of the Yuba County Sheriff's Department mentioned in the report had no recollection of Morgan's alleged admissions or any kind of investigation.

Sixteen years after Weiher, Madruga, Sterling, Huett, and Mathias went missing, there was a possible lead, but it was nothing more than conjecture. Also, in 1994, the Gateway Projects closed its doors for good in June due to the economy and bad press about claims of fund mismanagement and safety issues.

∾

Some of the parents of the five passed away during this time. Jim Sterling, Bill's father, died unexpectedly in August 1991 at the age of seventy. Imogene Weiher passed away on March 20, 2002, at the age of seventy-nine. It was 2005 when Ida and Robert Klopf both passed away; Robert in February at the age of seventy-eight, and Ida in March at the age of sixty-nine. These parents all died not knowing what really happened to their sons.

∾

The 1990s was a time when people first had access to email and the internet. People around the world were connected easily. Information could be uploaded and shared with countless users in seconds. The story of the Yuba County Five eventually made its way online. It is impossible now to find the first entry about the case on a forum or website. There are some things that we do know. Information about Gary Mathias being a missing person was added in 2004 to the Charley Project, a missing persons database with over fourteen thousand cold cases. An entry for Gary Mathias was also made in July of 2007 at the Doe Network, an organization for unidentified and missing persons.

We do not know if a family member, law enforcement, or someone familiar with the story put the data online. Maybe they believed that doing so would generate some attention. A best-case scenario could have been someone coming forward anonymously with information. Maybe they remembered something, didn't say anything then, and were more comfortable doing so online.

☙

Lance Ayers passed away at the age of sixty-three on June 30, 2010, in Marysville. His obituary was the first item I found online when I did a search for Ayers after reading Cynthia Gorney's 1978 article for the *Washington Post*. I felt defeated for a moment because a valuable source was no longer with us.

It was sad that he passed away before the story of the Yuba County Five returned to the spotlight. Ayers spent a great deal of time working the case. His death was a massive blow when it came to institutional knowledge.

By 2010, more resources were available to researchers and online sleuths. Newspapers were scanned and their text was searchable. Websites dedicated to genealogy were full of valuable resources. People were developing podcasts about unsolved cases and eerie mysteries for fans eager to explore a story once considered forgotten.

CHAPTER TWENTY-FOUR: 2017–2023

While this is the first book I have written, I have published a few comic books and a graphic novel for an independent publisher based in the Midwest. One requirement for their writers and artists is that they make themselves available for a certain number of conventions per year. The reason is that connecting with new readers at conventions is important to the success of an independent company.

It was July 2019, and I was selling my comics at the Florida Supercon at the Miami Beach Convention Center. I was sitting next to David Hayes, a fellow writer I had met a few years earlier at a signing event at a comic book shop in Grand Rapids, Michigan. Hayes has written various comics, graphic novels, and novels. At the time, Hayes was the head of the novels division for the company that published my comics. The event was packed, and our table was very busy with fans of comic books and horror novels. Across from our table was Michael Beck, the actor who played Swan in the cult classic film *The Warriors*. He was busy talking to fans and signing memorabilia.

During a brief lunch break, I asked Hayes if the company would ever consider publishing a book of true crime. He wanted to know what case I was researching, and I told him about the Yuba County Five. The story captured his attention, and he told me to move forward with a book. Having his blessing was an exciting moment. Writing a book had always been on my bucket list.

There was a three-issue comic book project that had to be completed first. I was coordinating everything with the artist and letterer. We were hoping to have everything ready for print by the end of 2019 so it could be part of the 2020 solicitations. Basically, comic books and graphic novels need to be presented to the distribution company so they can promote the book to store owners. Smaller press companies rely on this form of promotion so they can compete with larger companies.

I didn't have anything on my agenda for 2020 in terms of writing. It seemed like a good year to travel and do research for the book. It was now the end of February 2020, and I was driving to Chicago with Hayes to sell some comic books at C2E2, a major comic book and pop culture convention. We discussed the Yuba County Five book and chatted somewhat about a disease that was in the news. Fellow attendees planned on having plenty of sanitizer, and we discussed whether we should shake hands with people. I was focused on the book and considering traveling to California that summer to look over the files at the Yuba County Sheriff's Department.

COVID-19 and wildfires in California changed everything that year. My research was done from home, but I made plenty of progress and made some important contacts with law enforcement, the families, and other Yuba County Five researchers.

The Yuba County Five was the topic of podcasts, articles, and original video content before the COVID-19 shutdowns. In 2020, the story continued to gain momentum and the case was being discussed around the world.

❦

In January 2017, Juanita Sterling, Bill's mother, passed away. She was remembered fondly by a friend as a kind person and a very religious woman. Whatever was thrown her way never broke her faith. She, too, died without knowing the truth behind her son's disappearance and death. Sadly, the case itself was months away from a resurgence on social media.

Finding the first podcast or original video content about the Yuba County Five is no simple task because podcasts and YouTube channels tend to come and go. The first discussion may have been the July 2017 episode of *The What If? Podcast*. The earliest uploads to YouTube may have occurred later that same year. *The Trail Went Cold* posted a video titled "The Yuba County Five" on November 29, 2017, and on December 1, 2017, a video titled "Beyond the Snowstorm: The Yuba County Five" was uploaded to the *Dark Curiosities* channel.

From that point, other YouTube channels focused on the case. Creators from all over the world were fascinated and puzzled by this mystery. Views for these videos range from a handful to millions. A 2023 YouTube search result showed over four million people watched a video about the case on the *Nexpo* channel on YouTube.

Podcasts were examining the case in 2018 and have continued to do so since it became buzzworthy. Perhaps one of the most famous early podcasts was the July 10, 2018, episode of *Stuff You Should Know*. Statistics for these podcasts are not readily available, but several true crime podcasts have discussed the five and offered theories.

The Yuba County Five were also discussed on Reddit, a site where topics are submitted for discussion. The stories are voted up or down by the community. Reddit does have various entries for the case, and one posted in 2018 has over thirty thousand upvotes with some two thousand comments from Redditors or users of the site. *The What If? Podcast* credited Reddit for discussing the story. A post was made there on July 15, 2017, titled "The American Dyatlov Pass. Five young men abandon a warm, safe car and disappear into the night."

The original videos, podcasts, and discussions on Reddit have given new life to a case that was considered lost. Commentators have offered theories or added valuable questions. This has been invaluable and has motivated individuals to conduct their own research to write books or articles about the case.

જ

A two-day story about the Yuba County Five entitled "Out in the Cold" was run by the *Sacramento Bee* on February 26th and 27th, 2019. It was written by Benjy Egel, a reporter who grew up in the Sacramento area. Egel had joined the newspaper in 2015, and his story was a front-page feature on both days, including an interview with former Undersheriff Jack Beecham.

Egel had discovered the case on Reddit. "I was looking around for story ideas like I do every morning when I was covering breaking news just to see what was happening and I saw something about this curious unsolved case from forty years ago or so," said Egel. His interest was piqued, and his editors gave him the go-ahead to pursue the story.

Jack Beecham was the first person Egel tracked down, and it was Beecham who got Egel in contact with the Yuba County Sheriff's Department. Steven Durfor was sheriff at the time and declined Egel's request to access the files for his article. However, Durfor was retiring, and Wendell Anderson ended up winning the 2018 election as sheriff-coroner of Yuba County. Egel recalled that Anderson had a different attitude and allowed him access. Anderson basically told him, "'Yeah, it's been a cold case for forty years. If you think you can drum up something on it, go ahead.'"

Egel reviewed boxes of files in a conference room at the Yuba County Sheriff's Department. He was delighted to discover some pieces of information that had not seen the light of day for over forty years. There were rules of course for Egel to follow. "I couldn't take any photos, I couldn't make any copies, but I could write down whatever information I needed from the boxes." Someone from the department was there to monitor Egel while he conducted his research. After three hours of research, an individual walked into the conference room and informed him that they needed to use the room. He was kicked out for the day but returned a few weeks later to complete his research.

Sacramento Bee readers were treated to what Egel described as a "deep dive" into the case of the Yuba County Five. "I think there was a really solid response from our readership," said Egel. He was pleased that a forty-year-old cold case made the front page and loved how it was a two-day story.

Jack Beecham was also interviewed for Egel's article, along with Dallas Weiher Sr.. Both were of the same opinion that Gary Mathias had something directly or indirectly to do with the disappearance of the five. Egel recalled Beecham's theories and Mathias's involvement. "He didn't want to go accusing anyone of anything particular, but it seemed clear to him, and I think to me, this wasn't the missing five. It was four and one." Egel went on to add, "Gary's mental disabilities were significantly different from the rest of the boys and with his violent past and some of the circumstances surrounding the bodies being found and the disappearance. Yeah, Jack thinks Gary was involved in some way."

"Out in the Cold" was truly a career highlight, according to Egel. It was not his first front-page story at the *Sacramento Bee*, but it was a project he pursued on his own with the support of his staff. The article was a finalist for the California News Publishers Association (CNPA) yearly awards. It was the first major article in a newspaper about the Yuba County Five since 1979. Most importantly, it is the first written piece to use the actual case files as reference material.

❧

Cynthia Gorney's 1978 article for the *Washington Post* is the first stop for Yuba County Five researchers and enthusiasts. Her work has been referenced since 2017, and she is surprised and delighted that the story has returned to the spotlight. To Gorney, it is an odd story that resonated with people in a certain way.

When interviewed for this book, Gorney was asked what she thought happened to the five on the night they went missing. "The only motivation for something like this that made any sense to me is somebody just going delusional." In her opinion, it wasn't a theft, nor was it anything of a sexual nature. Nothing added up to her, but she believed that it could be traced back to Mathias having some sort of psychotic episode. For Gorney, she thought that the explanation was that "somebody [was] convinced that he's saving his friends from the forces of evil or taking them to Valhalla or something."

✍

I received an email late in 2021 about a television series called *Auto/Biography: Cold Cases*. It airs on Motor Trend and examines cold cases with an automobile connection. They wanted to interview me for the show. The plan was to interview me over Zoom or one of those programs. I put on a dress shirt and tie and spent roughly an hour answering their questions. It was great knowing *Auto/Biography: Cold Cases* was going to examine the case of the Yuba County Five. This was the first television show, to my knowledge, to examine the disappearance of the men.

The episode was released in early 2022, and I watched it with my wife. It turned out to be a great episode. *Auto/Biography: Cold Cases* is available on various streaming platforms, and I had to spend some extra time helping my parents and in-laws find the show on a platform they used.

Also launched at this time was the *Yuba County Five* podcast by Mopac Audio. It is a seven-part podcast series hosted by Shannon McGarvey. I was interviewed for the series, but most importantly, it has interviews with members of the Weiher, Madruga, Huett, and Mathias families. Jack Beecham and Avery Blankenship from the Yuba County Sheriff's Department were also interviewed for the series. Drew Beeson, author of *Out of Bounds: What Happened to the Yuba County Five?* was interviewed too. The podcast received incredibly positive reviews from listeners, and it is the podcast to go to for understanding the story.

☙

It was late August 2022 when human remains were discovered by hikers near Oregon Creek in eastern Yuba County. The area was described as "steep and remote" by the *Appeal-Democrat,* plus it was part of a dense forest going toward Tahoe National Forest. As the news spread in the community, some of my contacts began texting me information about the discovery of the remains. They were found near a community called Camptonville, which is sixty miles south of Rogers Cow Camp. I reviewed a map and wondered if Mathias was the one that was discovered. A follow-up text from one of my contacts said the remains had been in the wilderness for less than a year. It turned out to be someone who vanished in May 2022 while out driving. The person's vehicle was also found following an exhaustive search by the Yuba County Sheriff's Department.

For a moment I felt that someone had found Gary Mathias's remains and the final chapter of the Yuba County Five case would be resolved. Some people I have interviewed for this book believe Mathias died in the Plumas National Forest in 1978 and was never discovered. When I asked Avery Blankenship, who worked with the Yuba County Sheriff's Department during the disappearance, if he believed Mathias perished in 1978, he said he did. Blankenship believes Mathias was the last guy in the trailer with Weiher. "You cannot military tuck yourself into bed," said Blankenship. "[Weiher] was either suffering or he was dead, and [Mathias] walked away, and maybe one of the others went with him."

"He's not alive, I know that," said Tammie Phillips, Mathias's sister. Four families have the remains of their loved ones, and she has been waiting for some forty-five years to receive news about the discovery of Mathias's remains. "I knew it was foul play from day one." Phillips tries to make a yearly journey to the Plumas to remember Mathias and the others. She leaves flowers and brings five balloons. They are released and sent off into the skies to remember Weiher, Madruga, Sterling, Huett, and Mathias.

Mark Mathias, Gary's brother, has also been waiting for news about the discovery of his brother's remains. "I got a call in the nineties, I can't remember exactly what year, but it was from a Yuba County detective, and he asked if I wanted to keep the case open, and I'm like, 'Yeah, my brother has never been found.' That was the last thing I ever heard from them." A letter in the case file at the Yuba County Sheriff's Department dated 2006 was a questionnaire for Mark Mathias to complete and submit. The Yuba County Sheriff's Department wanted to know if Mathias believed his brother to still be missing and to include any additional information that would be helpful. The contact address was redacted, so it is hard to tell if the letter was mailed to the correct address. An Application for Release of Information is included with the letter for Mark Mathias. It was completely redacted, and it is unknown if he completed the form. Two documents from 2019 and 2021 from the Yuba County Sheriff's Department are also included in the file, and they both state that Gary Mathias is believed to be a victim of foul play. No further details are provided in the letter.

Nearly one year after my interview with Mark Mathias, the Yuba County Sheriff's Department reached out to him and Tammie Phillips to get their DNA on file. They agreed, and now the DNA is on file to match any unsolved discoveries or future discoveries. The Yuba County Sheriff's Department has stated since 1978 that foul play was a possibility regarding the disappearance of Weiher, Madruga, Sterling, Huett, and Mathias.

CHAPTER TWENTY-FIVE:
THEORIES

David Hayes believed in this project back in 2019, and some two years after I began my writing journey, he messaged me to see how the book was coming along. He wanted to know if I needed any assistance because of his background. I knew him through creating comics but didn't really know much about him professionally. Hayes is a consulting criminologist, author, and academic. He is a doctoral student in forensic psychology at Walden University and teaches communications and psychology at several colleges, law enforcement organizations, and within the Michigan Department of Corrections.

I sent him my research files to review. He messaged me sometime later and asked if he could call and discuss the case. "I have a lot of questions," said Hayes in a message. I told Hayes I'd give him a call, and we discussed the Yuba County Five for close to two hours, which is not unusual for me.

Hayes reviewed the files and shared his professional opinions. "Non-intellectually disabled adults are at a five percent risk of personal victimization, whereas intellectually disabled adults are a twenty percent risk," said Hayes. He also stated, "Individuals with developmental disabilities don't often recognize danger in time and may misinterpret social cues, etc."

I have spent hours upon hours discussing the story with Shannon McGarvey and Drew Beeson. McGarvey dedicated countless time interviewing the family, law enforcement, the media, and various experts for the 2022 Mopac Audio *Yuba County Five* podcast series. She also dove into the case files from the 1978 investigation provided by the Yuba County Sheriff's Department.

Beeson reviewed newspaper articles about the men and interviewed family members for his book *Out of Bounds: What Happened to the Yuba County Five?* It was Beeson who found Tom McGarry, Schons's old neighbor. McGarry had commented online about the case, and Beeson successfully tracked him down for an interview. Beeson has continued to study the case following the publication of his book. He has a YouTube channel that discusses various mysterious cases, including the Yuba County Five. I have a great deal of respect and appreciation for McGarvey and Beeson.

I have also connected with other researchers who understand that the Yuba County Five case is far more complex than what has been told via podcasts and social media. They are Anthony Dunne from England and Eduardo Colella from Argentina.

Anthony Dunne reached out to me on social media and wanted to discuss the Yuba County Five. I was a bit apprehensive at first, but we chatted on social media. He knew the case well, and that eased my mind. A few colorful individuals have reached out to me during this book-writing process, but Dunne is a dedicated researcher who has done his homework. He is twenty-seven years old and lives in Lancashire, a county to the northwest of Manchester. His day job involves manual labor, and during the evening, Dunne is a personal trainer. Somehow, he has found time to conduct his own Yuba County Five research.

"I feel like I can relate to some of the five men as I'm around a similar age to some of the guys when they disappeared and live in an area kind of like Yuba City and Oroville." The community where Dunne lives has issues with crime like Oroville and Marysville did during the 1970s. Dunne has played in a band and works with his father, so there is the music and work connection with Gary Mathias. Also, Dunne played basketball in school.

Dunne was introduced to the case by *Bedtime Stories*, an animated YouTube channel dedicated to true crime, urban legends, and odd mysteries. "I remember watching the 'Boys from Yuba City' episode right after their 'Dyatlov Pass' episodes and feeling both incredibly saddened and intrigued by the case," said Dunne. "I have younger cousins who are on the autism spectrum and an older relative who suffers from schizophrenia, which made the Yuba [County Five] case more impactful to me."

This interest led Dunne to a three-year investigation into the story. Dunne completely understands why Beecham has referred to the case as being "bizarre as hell." He has reached out to Beeson and has even been able to briefly discuss the case with a few family members. "I firmly believe all five men were forced or manipulated to go up that mountain road. There's no doubt about it." Dunne is not sold on Gary Mathias being the one behind the disappearance. "Personally, I don't [believe that]. I think he might have been in the wrong place at the wrong time, just like his friends, or a target for someone to come after."

Eduardo Colella discovered the story via *Bedtime Stories* and enjoyed the *Yuba County Five* podcast. "I feel a personal connection with the case because, unfortunately, the missing persons issue is no stranger to me," said Colella. His uncle disappeared in 1976, and in 2005 a close friend vanished. "As we say in Argentina, 'Last time we saw them alive, so we want them back home alive.'" Colella understands what the families of the five have experienced. "Personally, I believe that this is the worst torture you can put anybody through. Not knowing what happened. Harboring hopes for a happy ending, no matter how silly or unreal they might be."

Nothing about the case makes sense to Colella. He is intrigued by the mystery and plans on writing a book about the Yuba County Five in

Spanish. On the forty-fifth anniversary of the disappearance of the men, I joined Beeson, Dunne, and Colella on YouTube for a live discussion. Family members were online watching, and they sent us messages of support. That was wonderful because their blessings are beyond important. I was part of the discussion for the first hour, but the other three discussed the case for an additional hour.

Talking to David Hayes, Drew Beeson, Shannon McGarvey, Anthony Dunne, and Eduardo Colella has been critical in developing theories about the case. These discussions have led to new thoughts on the disappearance.

ε⁄ͻ

We have no data or evidence to explain why the Yuba County Five vanished in the Plumas National Forest. Additionally, there is no concrete explanation as to why the men walked to the trailers near the Daniel Zink Campground and perished. Theories are aplenty. Gary Mathias had some sort of psychotic episode. Someone convinced the five to pull over while driving home and forced them up to the road near Rogers Cow Camp. Chico State fans may have encountered the five on the highway, a chase ensued, and they ended up in the Plumas trying to ditch their tormentors. Gary Mathias wanted to visit friends in Forbestown. They simply got lost on their way home and it was an unfortunate tragedy.

The purpose of this chapter will be to examine theories regarding why the men exited the highway to the Plumas, abandoned the car, broke into the trailer for safety, and perished. These are simply theories to try to make sense of what happened. Theories can lead to answers. It is believed by some that at the time of this book's publication, someone (or some people) who are still alive know what really happened that evening. What occurred possibly involves another person or group of people. We will examine that as well, but it should be noted that these theories are based on speculation. This story has no easy answers.

Some of my contacts for this case told me that in Yuba and Sutter Counties, there are people who have heard some chilling tales of what happened to Weiher, Madruga, Sterling, Huett, and Mathias. The stories are heartbreaking. People will gladly tell you about them, but only anonymously. One person told me that there's a mentality in the region that if you speak to law enforcement, then there are dire consequences. In their opinion, nobody wants to be viewed as an informant, and that belief is firmly entrenched in the minds of many residents in areas like Marysville and Olivehurst.

●ʅ

Understanding the friendship dynamic of the five is important to developing theories about the case. Weiher, Madruga, Sterling, Huett, and Mathias knew each other in some capacity. As a group of five, they had been acquainted for a year and a half, according to the records at the Yuba County Sheriff's Department. Weiher and Huett had known each other since the early 1970s and would regularly do things together as friends. Weiher and Mathias lived on the same street and the families were acquainted. Madruga and Sterling were close friends; it was not reported how long they had known each other. The five would occasionally venture out as a group to Sacramento or Yuba City to play miniature golf or to watch basketball games. The files do not show any record of the group driving to Chico for any reason. A few family members interviewed for this book were under the impression that all or some of the five had traveled to Chico in the past. At least one newspaper article found for this book does have a family member mentioning previous trips to Chico. It is important to note that, based on some interviews, Jack Madruga had experience driving to Chico.

When questioned by law enforcement, Melba Madruga, Jack's mother, was familiar with Bill Sterling but did not know him that well. She did not have any interactions with Ted Weiher, Jackie Huett, or Gary Mathias, according to the case file. Other family members had similar experiences.

Dallas Weiher Jr. knew Jackie Huett because he was good friends with his uncle. "He was a nice guy, a very sweet disposition. A good guy.

Absolutely." Weiher Jr. also recalled that Huett wasn't much of a talker, and he remembered Jack Madruga the same way. When remembering Bill Sterling, Weiher Jr. said, "He was very pleasant, very helpful, a nice person as well." However, Weiher Jr. never met Gary Mathias so he has no memories of him.

Tom Huett remembers his brother hanging out with Ted Weiher and has few, if any, memories of Jack Madruga, Bill Sterling, or Gary Mathias. When asked if he remembered Jackie doing anything with the group, Tom Huett replied, "They'd bowl, they'd ride around and just hang out." Tom Huett would drop his brother off at various places around town. He said Jackie would only do something with the group if Weiher was going. Jackie would make sure that he would be home for dinner, but Weiher would call on his behalf to let the Huetts know if they would be home later than expected. Tom Huett said Jackie and Ted Weiher would meticulously stick to their plans and not deviate from them.

☙

The main link to the disappearance of the five is Gary Mathias. A report in the Yuba County Sheriff's Department file from 2006 is listed as a supplemental investigation. The detective who wrote it states, "Upon review there did not appear to be any leads that were not followed until the end." There are two letters in the Yuba County Sheriff's Department's file from 2019 to 2020 that states Gary Mathias was believed to be a victim of foul play. Both letters state that Mathias's disappearance was a "missing persons/homicide" case. It was reported in the press in 1978 that they believed in some way that foul play was involved. There is nothing on file from Jack Beecham, Avery Blankenship, or Lance Ayers that discusses any theories regarding foul play and how it connects to the disappearance. Foul play has been viewed as one of two possibilities, either done to the group by an outsider, or by Gary Mathias.

A few parents interviewed by law enforcement in 1978 said they had reservations about their sons hanging out with Gary Mathias. They knew he was schizophrenic and had a reputation around town for getting in trouble with the law. People knew about Mathias's criminal record and believed he was capable of snapping at any time. Information gathered by the Yuba County Sheriff's Department showed that Mathias had turned his life around following a string of incidents from circa 1971 to circa 1975. He was seeking mental health help and was taking medication. Mathias was enrolled at Gateway and was part of the basketball team. He was working at his stepfather's business and living at home.

When questioned by law enforcement, Ida Klopf said her son was doing well. Some of the information she provided to law enforcement revealed some peculiarities, though. Klopf said that Mathias would ask his stepfather, Robert Klopf, permission to go to bed, eat food, or take a bath. She also admitted to Yuba County investigators she had no idea her son was going to a game on February 24th. Mathias had left the house without identification, but his mother told investigators that he had somewhere between $10 and $15 cash on him. Ida Klopf would later speak to the press and give the impression that she knew her son was going to the game in Chico.

Eyebrows are raised when I review information provided by Robert and Ida Klopf. For example, there are times when they said they did not know Gary Mathias was going to the game, and other times they shared that they were aware of the trip. Also, Robert Klopf stated to reporters that Mathias was probably at the bottom of Lake Oroville. That statement is eerie and very strange. Why would he be at the bottom of a lake? Did Klopf know the fate of his own stepson?

Gary Mathias visited his grandmother, Viola Watterman, in Oregon in January 1978 and promised her he would return in the summer. A letter was sent to Watterman by Mathias a week before he disappeared, and it did not mention anything about his summer plans. The report on file with the Yuba County Sheriff's Department stated that Mathias would take a bus to Oregon to visit his grandmother.

Schizophrenia has been the reason why Mathias has been viewed as the main suspect. He has been thought of as a ticking time bomb that exploded the night the men went missing. Sheilagh Hodgins wrote in an article titled "Violent Behaviour Among People with Schizophrenia" that people with schizophrenia will commit assaults, but murders committed by schizophrenics are extremely rare. A stigma has been attached to schizophrenia, and it has led to unfair judgments of those who suffer from it. Also, it should be noted that studies show people who are diagnosed with schizophrenia are more likely to be victims of violent crimes.

It was January 1978 when Gary Mathias had a confrontation with a man named Farren DeLozier. Married to Connie Huett, Jackie's sister, DeLozier told the Yuba County Sheriff's Department that Mathias had punched him in the face at a party for no reason. DeLozier admitted he retaliated and hit Mathias in the face multiple times before the fight was broken up by several people. An acquaintance of DeLozier's informed him and Connie that Mathias was involved in a similar fight a month or two before at another party. It was not reported who Mathias hit, and the person who hosted that party could not be reached for comment by the Yuba County Sheriff's Department.

One person interviewed for this book was surprised that DeLozier didn't retaliate further following the sucker punch from Mathias. The person, who wished to remain anonymous, said that the DeLozier family was a tough bunch and people did not mess with them. If they did, then they would be in a world of trouble. That contact was skeptical of the story of the fight because they believed DeLozier would have put Gary Mathias in the hospital for a sucker punch.

There is a possibility that the fight with DeLozier or with the unnamed person could have fueled some sort of hatred toward Mathias. Revenge may have been planned, and it is possible that it culminated the night the five went missing. DeLozier or the unnamed person might have learned about the men's trip to Chico and decided to drive there to see if they could find Mathias at the game. There have been rumors of a confrontation between the five and an unknown subject or group outside of Behr's Market in Chico. These rumors have no solid evidence. The men may have been followed and somehow forced off the road near Oroville.

From there, it is possible they were told to drive on the Oroville-Quincy Highway to a designated spot, which ended up being the road near Rogers Cow Camp in the Plumas National Forest.

ↂ

Forcing the men off the road or forcing them to drive to a designated spot in the Plumas would have taken more than one person. Madruga was known for driving his car where he wanted and under his terms. Madruga also hated driving on unpaved and rutted roads because he feared damaging his Mercury Montego. Someone familiar with the roads in Plumas during the 1970s remembered the road past Mountain House was gravel. The road where Madruga abandoned his car was in even worse condition as it was rutted and there was snow. Someone had carefully driven the car up the road until it became stuck near the snow line. The road where they abandoned their car led to nowhere. A window on the Montego was reportedly left partially rolled down and the car was unlocked. Those who knew Madruga said that was out of character. He was someone who made sure his car was locked and the windows were rolled up. When Madruga's remains were found, his keys were on him. This led some to theorize that Madruga decided or agreed to abandon the Montego and begin walking or running.

Some images exist of the Montego the night it was discovered in the Plumas. They are not individual but on a digitized sheet of negatives. The quality is not great, which is frustrating, and careful examination of the images does not prove or disprove a window was rolled down. A woman playing in the snow at the Rogers Cow Camp area the weekend of February 24th and 25th, 1978, remembered seeing the Montego. According to the woman, she did not recall any windows being rolled down. Were the windows rolled down by someone else at a different time? Was the information from the witness correct?

What we do know is that the Montego was near Rogers Cow Camp. The Yuba County Sheriff's Department had spoken with a teacher named

Joanne Martin; she told them that the men lacked "abstract reasoning ability" where they could function normally if given positive input and direction. Someone gave them orders, and they were followed. It is very doubtful the men would have driven to a remote location for no reason.

According to David Hayes, after he read Martin's statement to law enforcement, he understood that "they would respond to clear direction and would reason out any action one step at a time and not holistically." He added that "her informal diagnosis is very close to what modern professionals would consider autism, and her appraisal of how the boys would behave is the one that should probably be given the most credence."

Hayes agrees with family interviews about some of the five being on the autism spectrum if diagnosed today. "The reported development disabilities appeared to be those akin to autistic behaviors, including preferences for routine, unintentional social blunders, comfort in taking language literally, assistance in understanding expectations, etc."

☙

I spoke to a few people about the Plumas, and they told me some stories of confrontations they'd had in the area. One man recalled taking a motorcycle ride up there during the day. He decided to take a different route and was met by a truck stopped in the middle of the road at an angle. The driver had a gun and asked the man what they were doing. He said to the driver that he was just riding around up there having fun. He was told to go back home. That person thought there might have been some marijuana growing going on nearby.

I spoke with another person who lived in the Berry Creek area at one time. They had lived there years after the men went missing. Crime was a constant issue for them, and it seemed that the allure of living in the Plumas in peace was just a fantasy.

The five may have driven to the Plumas because of a direct order or because of some sort of deception. Perhaps they were there because they felt it was a safe haven. It is possible they did not know the dangers associated with the area.

உ

A scenario that was theorized but not clearly expressed was someone with a gun threatening the five. The parents were asked by investigators how their sons would react if threatened by someone with a gun. The parents surmised that their sons would comply with orders and not try anything to subdue the individual with a gun.

The gun theory is traced to a claim that shells were found near the Montego when it was discovered. Jack Huett Sr. told Mopac Audio he was at Rogers Cow Camp the night the car was found and discovered thirty-aught-six shells that he handed to Lance Ayers. Hunting is legal in the Plumas, but a record of those shells was not in the report, and there was no proof they were linked to the case.

A few of the parents added that their sons were not fond of the dark. Madruga and Weiher were known for being nervous or uneasy in the dark, plus Weiher would want someone with him as company. Also, the men did not like snow and cold weather. They didn't hate snow but just did not express any interest in doing activities in the snow. Madruga and Huett were known to do things outdoors with their families in warmer weather, like swimming, fishing, and camping. Sterling was known to avoid certain outdoor excursions with his local singles group.

The gun theory was brought up to understand why all five men abandoned the vehicle near Rogers Cow Camp. Someone or something made them all leave the car behind. The car could have provided some warmth while it was running, although gas would have to be conserved. They were also capable of pushing the car out of the snow. However, it was never stated if any of the five had experience with a car that had been stuck in the snow.

Mountain House would have been their closest destination for help that they were aware of. Since Mountain House is no longer standing, it is difficult to determine the exact distance from Rogers Cow Camp. Communities to the south of Rogers Cow Camp are Junction House,

Brush Creek, and Berry Creek. A walk to Junction House from Rogers Cow Camp is roughly three miles, a walk to Brush Creek is roughly eight miles, and a walk to Berry Creek is roughly fourteen miles. From what Joseph Schons told investigators, the walk to Mountain House was equal to the distance to Brush Creek, and the men could have made the walk in three hours or less. They would have passed Mountain House, along with various homes, to get to Rogers Cow Camp. The men would have also passed homes in the Plumas. There were opportunities to stop and ask for directions or request to use a phone if they were hopelessly lost.

❧

The location where the Montego was abandoned is beyond comprehension. When the five got into Madruga's car to leave Chico, they took California Highway 99 out of town. At a location south of Chico and north of Oroville, the highway splits in two. One route is a continuation on Highway 99 south toward Yuba City. The second is a connection to State Route 149, a short drive to then connect to California Highway 70 going south toward Marysville.

For the men to drive to the Plumas, the most logical route is the Oroville-Quincy Highway. It is part of State Route 162 that goes through Oroville. Madruga would have been able to exit from Highway 99 and Highway 70 and connect to State Route 162, which becomes the Oroville-Quincy Highway in Oroville. The easiest exit would have been from Highway 70 into Oroville. They could connect to State Route 162 from Highway 99, but it would be a six-mile drive east to get to Oroville.

But why get off the highway to Oroville? One possibility is the fact that someone in the car needed to use the restroom, and either Madruga or someone else knew of a place to stop in town. There is the possibility that the person who wanted to look for Mathias in Chico followed them off the highway into Oroville and confronted the five at the place where they stopped for the restroom. Another scenario would be that the five stopped somewhere, and there was a confrontation with a person or group of people. Maybe someone or a group recognized one or all five, and there was some sort of previous unfinished business that had to be solved in the parking lot. Also, the five could have run into a stranger or group of strangers somewhere, and they began harassing the men for whatever reason.

To avoid a fight, the five could have jumped into Madruga's car and tried to lose their tormentors. This may have led to a plan to take back roads home to avoid any further issues. As reported, a map of California was out and in the front seat. The maps were not Madruga's but Sterling's. If the map was in the front seat, then Sterling could have been riding on the passenger side and navigating. Juanita Sterling claimed her son was good at reading maps.

While it is likely that they drove a different route to lose someone, it is important to note that the Oroville-Quincy Highway is a winding road, and speeding along it would be dangerous due to sharp turns. Madruga has never come across as a reckless driver.

൭

I have reviewed some maps of California from the 1970s that were published by the California Department of Transportation. Interstates and state highways are shown, but not all are equally detailed. I examined one 1978 map and traced the route from Chico to Oroville. State Route 162 or the Oroville-Quincy Highway ends once someone has crossed the Bidwell Bar Bridge over Lake Oroville. The roads in the Plumas are not shown, and roads leading to Forbestown are also not shown. Forbestown is not even listed on the map.

A California road map from 1970 I reviewed showed Forbestown and the roads leading to it from Oroville. Also, the Oroville-Quincy Highway was shown going through the Plumas past places like Berry Creek, Brush Creek, and Bucks Lake. It did not show anything regarding the side roads that the men ended up on near Rogers Cow Camp.

The map used by Sterling is not available for viewing by researchers. If the map he used had State Route 162 ending past the Bidwell Bar

Bridge, then it could have been guesswork by Sterling to navigate the roads. Sterling may have believed that one of the roads would link back to Highway 70, which would have them heading south toward home. If he had a more detailed map, he could have navigated more easily through the Plumas or directed Madruga to turn around and get back to the highway.

There is a possibility that the Oroville-Quincy Highway was closed at a certain point. This was not discussed in an article or in the case file. I did speak to someone with knowledge of the Plumas, and their memory of the area during the winter is that portions of the highway were closed off due to the snow, making travel impossible. If this did happen, then Madruga could have turned his car around and returned to Oroville. There are spots on the Oroville-Quincy Highway where someone can easily pull off to the side and get back on the road going the other direction.

The Bidwell Bar Bridge should have been a landmark that alerted the men that they were nowhere near Marysville or Yuba City. There were opportunities to turn around before and after the bridge. For some unknown reason, they kept driving.

"You can't end up where those guys ended up by accident," said Tom McGarry, the former neighbor of the Schons I spoke with. "You can't say, 'Oops, how'd I end up here?' You're going up and up and up. There ain't no mistake in that. You gotta do that deliberately." McGarry still follows the case via blogs and videos. He is beyond perplexed with some of the comments made by people about the Plumas. "You can tell they have no idea what they're talking about," said McGarry. In his opinion, people underestimate the ruggedness of the Plumas. Also, McGarry believes the five were sent in that direction for a reason.

What surprised him was that they drove past Mountain House. In McGarry's opinion, if they kept going beyond Mountain House, then there was something going on and it was not good. McGarry described the area past Mountain House as a no-man's-land, and the road where they abandoned the car was an odd choice. According to McGarry, the road they chose was probably an old logging road. "If you went up the wrong logging road, you would be going up the mountain, and the road would end."

That is exactly the type of road Madruga drove up until the Montego became stuck in the snow. McGarry said that the car did not have four-wheel drive, and that was something you needed to get around that location. Even with four-wheel drive, McGarry said that those roads were tough to traverse. Joseph Schons was stuck on the same road as the five. His Volkswagen Beetle was not the best choice for those Plumas roads either. It seemed to some to be beyond coincidental that on the night of February 24, 1978, he was up there stuck in his car too.

When I discuss the case with families and fellow researchers, we try to guess how much of Schons's story about seeing the Yuba County Five on that road was factual. Known for public intoxication and spinning tall tales, Schons is an unreliable narrator. His actions and words dug a proverbial hole from which he could not escape.

What is known is that Schons was at his residence in Berry Creek, which he referred to as a summer place. The family, according to Schons, lived in Rancho Cordova near Sacramento. The driver's licenses for Joseph and Cindy Schons on file, however, stated they resided in Berry Creek and not Rancho Cordova.

There are two known times Schons was interviewed by the Yuba County Sheriff's Department, and his stories varied. His first interview was with Undersheriff Jack Beecham over the phone. Schons told Beecham he was driving seven to eight miles north of Mountain House toward Bucks Lake when he got his Volkswagen stuck in mud and snow. He mentioned nothing about stopping at two different establishments for beers. The second interview was in person with Yuba County Detective Bud Cozine at the Oroville Medical Center.

Schons remembered more about the evening of February 24th and the morning of February 25th during the second interview. What surprised Cozine the most about Schons was that he was very lively and animated when discussing what happened to him in the Plumas. When Cozine pressed for details, Schons had an attitude change and went on the defensive. He was no longer animated, according to Cozine. "I get the feeling you guys think I know something about these dudes," was a statement Schons made, which was out of character, according to Cozine.

Schons informed Cozine that when he was admitted to the hospital, he was overly emotional and crying. It was difficult for him to communicate with anyone. That statement is interesting. Schons may have witnessed something that upset him. He may have felt remorseful for his actions that night. Schons could have frightened the men or screamed obscenities at them. Something went wrong that night. And we will never know the truth.

Cozine interviewed witnesses at Mountain House, people who helped Cindy Schons, and Cindy Schons herself. When reviewing all the interviews, a few things stick out and require further examination.

Joseph Schons did stop at the Brush Creek Bar on February 24th then went to Mountain House to drink more beer. The case files do not contain interviews with anyone at the Brush Creek Bar. The interview at Mountain House was with owner Josephine Berman. It was Berman who served three beers to Schons and recalled him talking about dogs biting people. When Schons was interviewed by law enforcement, he said he heard whistling as if someone were calling for a dog. Larry Nelson (pseudonym) lived up in the Plumas and was in the area near Rogers Cow Camp, where he saw the Montego and the Volkswagen both abandoned because he was doing some cross-country skiing in the area. Schons told Cozine that when he was experiencing his heart attack, he had defecated and vomited near his vehicle several times. Nelson told Cozine that he did not see or smell vomit but saw what he believed to be animal waste, possibly from a dog.

"I should have done this two years ago," Schons reportedly said at Mountain House. More than one witness at Mountain House interviewed by Cozine recalled this statement. They also remembered Schons said nothing about a heart attack or a Mercury Montego stuck on the same road. He mentioned nothing about the men vanishing in the night or anything about the people he claimed were in the pickup truck. What did he do that should have been done two years ago?

Schons's heart attack story has numerous issues. When someone experiences a heart attack, there are a variety of symptoms. Schons claimed he was sweating, plus he was vomiting and defecating frequently. Men who are having a heart attack will have pain in areas such as their chest, neck, and jaw. Vomiting is a symptom, and from what Schons explained, there was a pain in his chest.

To stay warm, Schons claimed he went into his Volkswagen and rested for roughly four to five hours. Drew Beeson, the author of *Out of Bounds: What Happened to the Yuba County Five?* doesn't buy Schons's story because of one key issue. The Volkswagen Beetle that Schons was driving had an air-cooled engine, which would not have provided heat if the car had been running while idle. Beeson said those types of cars need to be in motion to produce heat.

Schons may have spent ten hours in his car resting and waiting for help. Temperatures in the Plumas were below freezing, and his car was not producing heat. That is roughly ten hours of exposure to dangerous temperatures while suffering a heart attack at a four-thousand-foot elevation. Schons claimed he walked some eight miles from the Rogers Cow Camp area to Mountain House. This journey apparently took additional hours to complete in the cold. His story seems implausible. Researcher Anthony Dunne is not sold on the heart attack story and questions why it took Schons a ridiculous amount of time to decide to walk to Mountain House. It should have been the first thing he attempted instead of getting into his car.

Schons did not ask for an ambulance or someone to drive him to the hospital when he arrived at Mountain House. Witnesses said Schons did not mention a heart attack.

A possible theory is that Schons may have taken a dog into the Plumas and abandoned it, or worse, at some location near Rogers Cow Camp. The conversation at Mountain House about dogs biting people and possible animal waste near the car is all we have in the way of clues. The whistling noises allegedly made by people during the late hours of February 24th or early hours of February 25th are also interesting. Schons said the noises were like someone calling a dog. Another possibility is that Schons let a dog loose and it ran into the Plumas. Perhaps Schons stayed in his car to wait for the dog to return. Investigators made nothing in the way of comments about a dog or animal tracks near the car.

Did the Schons family own an aggressive dog? Was there a neighbor's dog bothering Schons? Did Schons lose a dog because he had too much to drink?

A possible scenario is that after Schons did what he did to the dog, he went back to his car and realized it was stuck. Perhaps it was there he developed an elaborate story about checking the snow line and having a heart attack.

Schons told some investigators he wanted to see the snow line, and some newspaper reports said he was checking on a vacation cabin. Beeson said that he researched the area and discovered there were no vacation cabins owned by Schons. The family resided in Berry Creek and that was their only cabin.

Interviews and research done for this book revealed neither Schons nor his family were the outdoor types. Schons could have simply asked anyone at Mountain House if they knew anything about the snow line. Josephine Berman thought it was unusual that Schons drove north from Mountain House toward Rogers Cow Camp. She knew those roads were less traveled and were problematic for drivers. Berman stated Schons knew better than to go that way because if he did get stuck, then he'd be in trouble because hardly anyone would be up that road that time of day.

Berman also stated that she never saw Schons walk down the hill on the evening of February 24th because she was very busy at Mountain House. It has been theorized that Schons could have deliberately driven his car into the snow to get it stuck. Schons may have walked down the road, met up with someone around Mountain House, and driven to Oroville. A possible theory could be that Schons might have been looking for someone to drive him to his car in the Plumas. The person who would drive Schons that way could have been robbed at gunpoint. This has been theorized as a fate that the five met when they drove into Oroville.

"It has always been my gut feeling [Joseph] Schons was somehow involved with this disappearance," said Beeson. "His story changed multiple times and it was noted that he was in the area at the time of the disappearance." Beeson is frustrated by the unbelievable stories of Joseph Schons in the press.

There are some who view Schons's stories as an attempt at the reward money. The families offered a $1,000 reward early in the case. Schons could have heard about this and may have created a story to appease the families and get the money. Simply stating he saw the men run into the Plumas was perhaps what he thought was a way for him to provide enough information.

What we do not know is what percentage of Schons's story about the night of February 24th is true. His stories varied in the press. Did he really see the Montego and the men abandon the car? Did he really see a pickup truck? If he did see anything, then did the people in the pickup truck threaten Schons? Who were the people in the pickup truck? If the pickup truck story is true, then why were they following Madruga? Did something occur in Oroville, and it ended with a chase into the Plumas? Was something planned to find Madruga and the others in Chico or possibly on the highway home? While we cannot know if Schons's story about a pickup truck is true, there are people who believe that a certain individual and some coconspirators were part of a chase and attack on the five.

Many have been interviewed for this book, and not everyone interviewed is quoted or referenced. Some have spoken to me off-record concerning their theories. There are people still afraid to talk about the foul play aspect of this case. While many see Joseph Schons as a bumbling drunk who elaborated when given the chance, they do believe that Schons did see a pickup truck that night. In their opinion, the pickup truck was linked to a man named Todd Morgan.

Morgan reportedly confessed in a Yuba County church circa 1994 that he had committed a series of heinous crimes. One of them included the deaths of "two out of seven retarded males in the hills about seventeen years ago." The 1994 Yuba County Sheriff's Department's report was not the first time I heard about Morgan. His name came up during the first phone call I had with a contact who assisted me with research. Morgan's name popped up again and again as I was examining this case. The only problem is linking him to the truck and to the Plumas on February 24th, which has been almost impossible.

Also, it was rumored that Morgan did not work alone. Various other names have come up in conversations, and those questioned about Morgan's involvement believe he worked with two other individuals that evening. While it is difficult to link Morgan to that night, it is even more difficult to get people on the same page about the pair that allegedly aided Morgan.

What problem did Morgan have with the five? The main theory is that Morgan had an issue with someone in the car due to some personal matters. The two apparently did not get along, and the rumor is that Morgan wanted to make an example of this individual. Perhaps Morgan took two accomplices with him in a truck and tried to find the five in Chico or on the highway home.

There is another theory, but like the first one involving Morgan, there is no evidence. Two of the five allegedly made comments to someone about Morgan harassing women at the Gateway Projects. It is not known if the two spoke with anyone at Gateway about the harassment or if the comments made their way back to Morgan.

What has been theorized about Morgan has come from people who, in most cases, do not know each other. Again, Morgan's involvement is just a rumor, and there is no evidence. The only thing that has been stated many times is this theory. It will not go away. Rumors can travel at the speed of light while the truth moves at a painstakingly slow pace.

Morgan was arrested numerous times following the disappearance of the five. One incident occurred months after the disappearance and involved Morgan shooting at a residence that was occupied at the time. One of those who were shot at was believed to be the owner of a pickup truck. Some of the people I have spoken to about the case believe Morgan did this to silence witnesses. It could also be purely coincidental.

A parent of one of the five reportedly had a confession letter placed in their mailbox. It was written by someone who was supposedly in the pickup the night the men disappeared or knew a great deal about what allegedly had happened. The writer was not one of the men in the house shot at by Morgan. Rumors around the Yuba County area are that the author was ready to speak to the Yuba County Sheriff's Department about Morgan and his accomplices. At some point following the writing of the letter, however, the author died under unusual circumstances believed to be caused by an overdose. It should be known that the person who wrote the letter had had numerous run-ins with the law and had a known substance abuse problem. Their reliability is under question. However, some have stated off the record that the individual was far more reputable than Morgan.

The issue with the pickup truck theory is that it all depends on Schons telling the truth. If so, then we do not know why the five were being followed. If Morgan wanted to go after the men, then why waste time and gas by driving to Chico or Oroville? Couldn't Morgan have settled the score in Yuba County? Morgan would have had to arrive at the game, locate the men, and follow from a distance before making his move.

Researching this case uncovered another suspect who may be the driver of the pickup truck. Like the Morgan theory, this is simply based on observation. Ben Richardson (pseudonym) was reportedly a pickup truck owner who had been tangled up in a violent confrontation that involved a chase in a pickup truck. Richardson was arrested but out on bail during the disappearance. He lived in the area, and his wife had given birth recently for what that's worth.

Richardson's name was discovered on social media. He was mentioned in a post, and that led me to do some research. I have found no link between Richardson and the men. There is no known history between this man and the group. Attempts were made to link Richardson to Schons or Morgan, but no connections were discovered. Again, all we have is coincidence.

⁂

We do know that Gary Mathias had a fight with Farren DeLozier a month before he went missing. Mathias had a fight with another person as well, who was not named in the investigation. Would DeLozier or the other person want to go after Mathias? Was their pride damaged following a sucker punch from Mathias?

This is like the Morgan theory. Why would someone drive to Chico to go after Mathias? They simply could have gone after him in Yuba County. Did the person or persons chasing the men know the Oroville area and the Plumas? Were they following the men the night they vanished?

We do not know if DeLozier owned a truck at the time the men went missing. DeLozier was arrested in the early 1970s for stealing a pickup truck from the Sacramento area. Of note, Farren DeLozier assisted the Huett family in searching the Plumas for the missing men.

ભ

The Montego was driven to a spot in the middle of nowhere where it became stuck. The men abandoned the car and fled into the wilderness yet the car could have been freed easily by five people.

Shannon McGarvey, the host of the *Yuba County Five* podcast, researched Madruga's 1969 Mercury Montego and the route it took from Marysville to Chico and from Chico to the Plumas. According to McGarvey's research, the 1969 Montego averaged sixteen miles per gallon with a tank capacity of twenty gallons. That means the car would go two hundred forty miles with a full tank of gas.

When law enforcement examined the car, they noticed it had a quarter of a tank of gasoline. McGarvey is unsure if Madruga had a full tank of gas after visiting the Mico Station in Yuba City before the game in Chico. It was reported that Madruga and Sterling were at the station but not the others. In the report from the Yuba County Sheriff's Department, Jackie Huett was the last to be picked up, and he lived on Erle Road in Marysville.

The trip to Chico State from Huett's home is an estimated fifty-five miles, with just over a mile added for a detour to Behr's Market. We do not know where the men parked that evening, so we are assuming they drove to Behr's from a parking lot at Chico State. After that, the drive to the spot near Rogers Cow Camp is roughly fifty-five miles. That's one hundred eleven miles. That trip would have left them close to half a tank of gasoline.

If Schons's story is true, the Montego pulled up the road, stopped, and all the occupants exited the vehicle. What might have happened is that the vehicle pulled up the road and got stuck. The car could have been running, keeping the men warm. They may have decided after a while to walk away from the vehicle, knowing it was stuck. There could have been a plan to look for a pay phone and call for help.

Another scenario is that someone could have siphoned gas from the car. If Schons' car was out of gas, then he could have tried siphoning gas from Madruga's car if he had the ability to do so. Or Cindy Schons and one of her helpers could have siphoned gas from Madruga's car to get the Volkswagen started.

Madruga comes off in interviews as someone who was very particular about his car. Alcohol was not allowed, and he avoided roads that were in bad shape because of possible underbody damage. Was Madruga watchful over his gas gauge? If he knew there was only a quarter of a tank left, then why did he drive up the abandoned road? A map was out in the car, and surely one or more of the men had to know they were far from Marysville.

"They had no history of getting lost, and all things, including the weather, was normal when they left Chico," said Drew Beeson. The journey from Chico State to the Plumas makes no sense when considering the route. Newspapers from Chico and Oroville were reviewed for accident reports on Highways 70 and 99, and nothing was mentioned. The case files also did not show any road closures or accidents that would have diverted traffic from the highway into Oroville. The idea that the men simply were lost does not make for a strong theory.

Occam's razor is a philosophical rule where the simplest explanation is perhaps the correct explanation. This has been used in videos and podcasts about the Yuba County Five case. While this is a puzzling case, those who use Occam's razor believe the five either got lost coming home from Chico or Gary Mathias had some sort of schizophrenic episode.

The theory of the five being lost has already been discussed in this chapter. The route they took from Chico to the area near Rogers Cow Camp is not a straight shot. They had to exit the highway and drive into Oroville. This took them east, and at some point, they crossed the Bidwell Bar Bridge and drove into the Plumas.

Gary Mathias's desire to visit friends in Forbestown has been a theory from law enforcement since the beginning. The friends were interviewed, and they had not seen Mathias in years. Cathy Madruga's experience with those friends was one of a booby-trapped area with suspicious characters living on properties with chain-locked sheds. The Yuba County Sheriff's Department never reported that the area was booby-trapped, nor did they claim that the people who knew Mathias were suspicious.

It is unlikely that Jack Madruga would have agreed to make that trip. Forbestown is less than one hour's drive from Chico. It would have been another hour to drive from Forbestown to Marysville. What would Gary Mathias need in Forbestown? Some of the five men were very specific with their plans, and deviating from them was pretty much out of the question. The basketball tournament the next day was very important, and getting a good night's sleep was necessary.

As Drew Beeson mentioned earlier, the men had no known incidents of getting lost while driving. They successfully made a trip to and from Sacramento on Thursday, February 23rd, for basketball practice. Madruga drove the men to the practice facility. Highway 99 and Highway 70 merge together north of Sacramento. Coming home, Madruga had a choice to take Highway 99 or Highway 70 home. They did not get lost that evening or during other trips to Sacramento.

We do not know for certain if the five had been to Chico as a group before the night they went missing. Some family members believe they drove there before to see a game at Chico State. None of the interviews mentioned anything about previous group trips to Chico. Madruga had been to Chico in the past, according to interviews.

Could Gary Mathias have persuaded Madruga to take the route he took to the Plumas? Was Mathias having a psychotic episode that resulted in the men abandoning the car? Mathias has often been viewed as the person responsible for the fate of the five. However, it is important to review the evening of February 24th in some detail.

Ida and Robert Klopf, Mathias's parents, said he was on a regiment of medication and doing well. He worked with Robert Klopf on the 24th and was left at home while the Klopfs ran out to pick up dinner. Mathias walked over to Weiher's house and was picked up by Madruga. The Klopfs claimed they did not know about the game at Chico State.

Mathias was in the car going up to Chico State. He was in the stands during the game and at Behr's Market, buying snacks. Bill Lee from the *Chico Enterprise-Record* saw the men in the stands seated near the UC Davis crowd. The only person that stood out to him was Weiher because Lee claimed he was "unusual in his behavior." Whatever the behavior was is not reported. The case file does not show any records of an individual contacting the Yuba County Sheriff's Department or the Butte County Sheriff's Department about Mathias's behavior at the game. When interviewed, Mary Davis, the clerk at Behr's Market, only recalled Jackie Huett out of the five. If Mathias was going through psychosis, then nobody stepped forward with any kind of information to support that.

Mathias could have had some sort of delusion that they were being followed or in some sort of imminent danger; he could have been having hallucinations that night. Although he was on medication, it did not mean that Mathias wasn't experiencing some common issues related to schizophrenia. He could have convinced the others to go into the Plumas and abandon their car. From there, they walked along a road in the cold and snow until they found the trailers near the Daniel Zink Campground.

Madruga once abandoned Weiher and some others in Sacramento because they were getting on his nerves. If Mathias had a delusion about something, then he would have had to do some serious work convincing the others. Ted Weiher wanted to be in bed at a specific time and was known to blow a fuse if pushed far enough. Bill Sterling had a major confrontation while institutionalized. If Mathias posed a threat to these men, then it seems likely that someone like Weiher could have handled Mathias on his own, let alone with all four of them working together. There is a possibility that they could have pulled the car over and made Mathias get out. A drastic move, but if Mathias became violent or highly agitated, then the others could have stopped somewhere to let him out and walk it off.

Mathias's mother told investigators that she did not know anything about the game in Chico. Mathias was living at home, and Ida Klopf said that her son would ask permission to eat and bathe. Was this something that Mathias did on his own, or was he living somewhere with incredibly strict rules? If Mathias went to a game without asking permission, then would he be grounded in some way? Would his stepfather not allow him to go to the basketball tournament?

Mathias may have realized he was in trouble on the way home. He may have asked Madruga to drop him off somewhere. Mathias had walked hundreds of miles from Oregon to California, and maybe he would make the trip to his grandmother's home. He made the trek once while unmedicated.

A map was out in the car and placed in the front seat, which suggests that Sterling was riding on the front passenger side. If this was the case, then Weiher, Huett, and Mathias were in the back seat. Jim Sterling, Bill's father, told investigators that they knew someone who had a cabin near Bucks Lake. The Oroville-Quincy Highway leads to Bucks Lake, which is northeast of the Daniel Zink Campground.

Little is known about Bill Sterling. If he was navigating, then what was his plan? Juanita Sterling, his mother, said her son was good with maps. If the men were being followed, then maybe Sterling believed he could lose them in the Plumas or find a safe place to hide there. There was a quote attributed to Juanita Sterling in a newspaper article where she claimed Jack Madruga never used Highway 70 when going to Chico. She never mentioned this to investigators or another newspaper.

Highway 70 begins north of Sacramento and goes north toward Marysville, where it continues north past Oroville. At Wicks Corner, the highway curves east and goes into a twisty northeast drive toward the Nevada state line. Perhaps Sterling decided they could drive through the Plumas and connect to Highway 70 near the town of Quincy. It is also possible that Sterling believed side roads in the Plumas connected them to Highway 70. If Sterling was great at reading maps, then he should have suggested they turn around and go back through Oroville to get back on the highway home.

What we also know about Sterling is he was institutionalized as a youth into his teenage years. There was a major confrontation during that time with another patient. Juanita Sterling said her son could be a danger to others if they got in his way. Did someone upset or anger Bill Sterling that evening? Was he frustrated about being lost?

What is peculiar about Sterling is that his mother refused to share his autobiography with law enforcement. She said it contained grammatical and spelling errors, plus there was some private family information she did not want revealed. An April 17, 1978, edition of the *Oroville-Mercury Register* included a letter from Juanita Sterling in the "Letters to the Editor" section. She wanted to know who wanted to hurt her son and his friends. To her knowledge, Bill did not have any enemies and was a kind soul. There was a quote in the article from his notebooks that read, "I want to be there when he [Jesus] come back that day when Gabriel blow his horn and God march us to heaven to live eternal." That is possibly the closest we will see of Sterling's personal writings.

☙

A window was reportedly rolled down on the Montego when it was searched by investigators. It has been said that the rolled-down window was on the driver's side, which means that someone could have approached the car to speak with Madruga. If Gary Mathias was seated behind Madruga, then Mathias could have been the one they wanted to speak with that night. This also leads to a theory that the person doing the talking convinced all five to get out of the car.

For whatever reason, the five got out of the Montego and walked some twelve miles to the trailers near the Daniel Zink Campground. They walked uphill to get to their destination and not downhill. Footprints were found near the car when it was discovered, but it is hard to tell if they were from the five or from other people.

An individual with knowledge of the Plumas informed me that it is easy to get turned around and lost in the Plumas, especially during the winter. If a Sno-Cat plowed a path to the Daniel Zink campground, then the men may have followed that path in hopes of finding someone to help them. The same person who informed me about the Plumas was very certain that the Sno-Cat plowed a path toward the trailers. They were new trailers, and it was important to get the snow off the roofs so there wasn't any structural damage.

A walk from Rogers Cow Camp to Daniel Zink was mapped out at twelve miles, so they may have spent four to five hours walking in the snow and cold. Not one person was wearing proper clothing, nor did they have winter hats or gloves. This was a dangerous walk because hypothermia would have been minutes away from doing serious damage to the men mentally and physically. Wet clothes, exposed skin, and cold temperatures were a dangerous mix, which also led to frostbite for at least one of them.

We have no idea how long these men were walking in the Plumas before they broke into the trailer. These Forest Service trailers were stocked with food, fuel, and supplies. They were used by Forest Service employees and those who needed to be in the area for an extended period. Someone broke a window to gain access to the trailer. The C-rations were found, and someone used a P38 can opener to open at least one of the cans. The others were painstakingly opened with a "church key."

We know Ted Weiher made it to the trailer, and there is proof Gary Mathias was there because his shoes were found inside. Some are sure that Jackie Huett was in there as well since he never left Weiher's side. There is less certainty that Jack Madruga and Bill Sterling made it to the trailer. It is possible that Madruga and Sterling could have lagged behind and perished.

However, Weiher, Madruga, Sterling, and Huett had close friendships. Weiher and Sterling were friends, and we know Sterling and Madruga were good friends. To allow one or two people to fall behind seems unthinkable, but we do not know how much hypothermia had impacted their rationale. Given their lack of proper winter attire and below-freezing temperatures, hypothermia would have set in rather quickly.

Weiher was found on a bed, and a candle in the trailer had been lit at some point. The broken window was near where Weiher was found; there appeared to be no attempt at covering it up. Also, the fuel to heat the trailer was never used. Books and cardboard were available but never set on fire to keep anyone warm or to make a signal. If a helicopter was over the area, then did anyone try to signal it?

There is a belief among some family members that some of the five may not have made themselves known for one of two reasons. The first could have been the fear of getting in trouble for breaking into a trailer. The second could be the fear of getting the attention of the person or people responsible for their disappearance.

Weiher lost roughly eighty to one hundred pounds while in the trailer. The cause of his death was ruled to be pulmonary edema. This can be from traveling at a high elevation or by any trauma to the chest wall. Lying flat causes difficulty breathing because of the collection of fluid in the lungs, and untreated pulmonary edema leads to heart failure. Weiher's weight loss means he may have not eaten or only ate a small amount of food while in the trailer. Others, possibly Mathias and Huett, may have been the ones who ate the C-rations. More importantly, how did the men survive without access to water? It has been theorized that the men melted snow or ate snow for hydration since there was no running water in the trailer. Weiher may have survived a month and would have had to have had some water and some food to survive.

If Mathias and Huett were in the trailer, then it is possible Mathias left first to look for help. Weiher's shoes were missing, but Mathias's shoes were in the trailer. Mathias could have put on Weiher's shoes, left, and possibly succumbed to the elements. This would have left Huett with

Weiher. Some believe Huett was there when Weiher passed away. The event was possibly too traumatic, so he left and died of exposure.

It is debated if Madruga and Sterling were in the trailer. Some believe the others would not leave these two behind. One theory is all five made it to the trailer and Mathias decided to go out on his own for help. When he did not return, Madruga and Sterling decided to go out for help. When they did not return, Huett left once Weiher had passed away.

Ⅎ

This was a simple trip to Chico to watch a college basketball game. They successfully drove to Sacramento the day before for basketball practice. We do not know if they were familiar with the school in Sacramento. If not, then that should disprove the theory that these men got lost on a ride from Chico. If Madruga was familiar with Chico and Sacramento, then why would their February 24th trip put them in the middle of nowhere?

Saturday, February 25th, was an important day because of their basketball tournament. They wanted to be home on the 24th to be well-rested. Uniforms were laid out. They were to meet at the Montgomery Ward in Marysville on Saturday to be transported to the event.

Gateway Gators coach Robert Pennock was a no-show at Montgomery Ward, according to a report by Lance Ayers. Pennock claimed he was running late that day and drove to the event directly from his residence. Ayers found it odd that Pennock made no attempt to contact the families or law enforcement about the fact that the five men had not shown up. Pennock made no efforts to reach out to anyone that day or at all in the first two weeks. Pennock was asked by Ayers if it was odd that nobody reached out to him, and he was nonchalant.

Pennock claimed law enforcement never contacted him about the 1975 incidents at Gateway and the murder of Donald Garrett. These incidents were reported by the press, and Pennock's vehicle was set on fire during that time. In contrast, reporting suggests that these incidents, including the murder, were taken very seriously by law enforcement and the local fire department.

The murders and arsons were unsolved at the time of the disappearance. Did the five run into Weirdo the Fireball Freak in Chico? Was that person paranoid because he thought they knew his identity? Did he take action to silence the men that night?

こↄ

These theories have no concrete evidence. Everything is speculation and rumors. I've done my best to go over these theories in my head. I try to find holes in them. There are too many questions. It is difficult to put together a concrete answer.

Some family members have their own theories. They vary in ways, but foul play and/or coercion are part of most of them. I've spent time talking to some family members about their theories. It's been even more important to listen during those times because I'm talking to people with forty-five years of experience with this case.

One person I wanted to find was Debbie Lynn Reese. As I stated already in this book, she received numerous odd calls in March 1978 from a man claiming he knew what happened to the men. He told her he had hurt the five and that they were all dead. Reese's telephone number was not listed, which added to the mystery.

Shannon McGarvey from Mopac Audio helped me track down Reese. I called her and she had no memories of those phone calls. I was baffled by that admission. There are some creepy and unsettling things I remember from thirty or forty years ago. Reese was a bit surprised someone was calling about the Yuba County Five. I explained to her it had gained popularity on social media. She kindly answered my questions to the best of her ability, and she has spoken with me on the phone a few times since.

It was August 1976 when Reese, along with her husband, were involved in a small plane crash near Shelter Cove, California. It's a Northern California community in the King Range National Conservation Area along the Pacific Ocean. Reese survived the crash but sustained broken bones in her back. Others on the plane did not fare as well. She made a difficult two-mile walk to get help for those still stuck in the plane and badly injured. The walk was not only difficult due to her injuries, but the terrain in the area was rugged. She did eventually find help. Reese understands what the men went through in the Plumas trying to find assistance and shelter. The mystery behind their disappearance baffles her.

During our conversations, Reese confirmed her telephone number was unlisted. While researching this book, it was discovered that Reese and Farren DeLozier were acquaintances. It is unknown if DeLozier knew Reese's number and made those suspicious calls. Some have questioned the story Reese provided investigators. Those who question it believe she may have wanted the reward money provided by the families or the *Sacramento Bee's* Secret Witness. The Yuba County Sheriff's Department asked Reese to record the caller, but it never happened. In the file for the Yuba County Sheriff's Department is a note that states Farren DeLozier owned a red pickup truck at one time during the early 1970s.

∾

It was close to sunset when I drove to Oroville for a second trip to the Plumas National Forest. My first trip was during the morning hours, and I did not experience what the men had the night they vanished. Also, during my first trip, I was discussing my research with Brian Bernardis and Lyndsey Deveraux during the ride. On this second trip I was able to take in the beauty of the Plumas for the first time, plus I was a bit startled by the terrain.

I crossed the Bidwell Bar Bridge and parked. The sunset was over Lake Oroville, and it was magnificent. I felt guilty for enjoying the beauty. The purpose of my drive was to retrace what happened to the men on February 24th. I was overwhelmed. There was no way those guys drove to this location by accident. Something had to be going on that night, but I had no idea how all of this happened. I felt like I had failed the five and their families. They had faith in me, and I thought I would somehow find something to help with the case. Maybe I had and didn't know it at the time. There was nothing to accomplish feeling sorry for myself, so I drove up into the Plumas.

The trip felt longer this time because I was driving alone. Dusk covered the land, and it was amazingly beautiful. The roads wound up higher and higher. My thoughts were with Jack Madruga, and I was anxious. I wondered what was going on in his mind that night. I thought of the others as well. Did they realize things had taken a turn for the worse? I passed numerous locations where they could have turned around. A deer crossed the road in front of me. It was in no hurry.

I made it to the former location of Mountain House. It was dark and the stars were out. It was wonderful seeing the stars without light pollution from the city. The road heading up to Rogers Cow Camp was closed and I wasn't taking any chances. I pulled over and turned off the lights. Words cannot describe how dark it was. I had no idea how the men left their vehicle and walked some twelve miles to the Daniel Zink Campground area and found shelter. I couldn't see anything in front of me; it was truly unnerving. Also, cell service was nonexistent in that area, and of course hadn't existed when the five went missing.

I turned the car back on and noticed something. The gas tank registered a quarter of a tank. I swear on my life, it was a quarter of a tank. It was an eerie moment. The drive out of the Plumas seemed to take longer. The men would have driven over the Bidwell Bar Bridge at night, and I wanted to know if there were lights on the bridge. There weren't, but I could make out the bridge. I shook my head. Something went down that night.

I am convinced Ted Weiher, Jack Madruga, Bill Sterling, Jackie Huett, and Gary Mathias experienced some type of threat from a person or group of people on the evening of February 24, 1978. The incident happened in Oroville and the five somehow got away in Madruga's car. Sterling navigated while Madruga drove. Their plan was to lose the person or group in the Plumas National Forest. Sadly, Weiher, Madruga, Sterling, Huett, and Mathias were found, forced out of the car, and were sent off somewhere. At some point, they ended up at the trailer, where they perished.

The person or group that was behind this act is unknown. There are suspects I have in my mind, and some will stay there for the time being. Those who were part of the group that was behind this knew the men were going to Chico for a game and decided to act against one or more of the five. I believe the target was Gary Mathias. The motivation was either the sucker punch at one of the parties or some unsettled issues. It explains why Mathias was never found and why Weiher and Huett never signaled for help.

CHAPTER TWENTY-SIX: CONCLUSION

One evening during dinner, my wife asked if I knew how I would end this book. I told her I had a plan, but when I started to work on this chapter, I found it difficult to write. There is a personal sadness that this is the end of the writing journey. Friendships were created, and there have been some moments that I have cherished. It is rewarding knowing this book will be in the hands of those interested in the case and those who remember the case. My biggest hope is that someone has their memory jumpstarted and they recall something important about the incident. Perhaps that memory brings some kind of closure to the families and investigators.

It has been forty-five years since Ted Weiher, Jack Madruga, Bill Sterling, Jackie Huett, and Gary Mathias vanished during their trip home from Chico. The story of the Yuba County Five has experienced a great deal of interest online, and family members are pleased that people care about what happened to their loved ones. Cathy Madruga, Jack Madruga's niece, was caught off guard when the case returned to the spotlight. "I had no idea. I don't have a computer or a cell phone." She relies on family and friends to update her on what is being posted. It was between 2017 and 2019 when people reached out to her again about her uncle's death.

Cathy Madruga has in her possession a Madruga family history. The entry for Jack Madruga notes he was murdered in 1978, and she believes that to this day. It is still upsetting for Cathy and others to talk about. Some have decided not to discuss it with anyone. Others are willing when they feel up to it.

"It's fascinating," said Dorothy Weiher-Dornan when asked about the case and its return to the spotlight. Weiher-Dornan takes time to read articles on it, but it's hard because each one makes her cry. She admits she's a crier, but there's no shame. Life's been tough, but Weiher-Dornan is a fighter. She had been married for forty-two years when her husband passed away. She has "beautiful kids and grandkids." When I interviewed her in 2020, she was waiting on a great-grandchild.

Dallas Weiher Jr. moved away from California and is an associate pastor at a small church. He spends his Thursday and Friday nights working junior varsity and varsity high school football games as an announcer and spotter. "Bless their hearts," said Weiher Jr. when talking about the team. There was a time they had one win in four years. Weiher Jr. has not given up hope on the team. The same can be said about the Yuba County Five.

"Intriguing, the mystery of it," said Weiher Jr. "It's so mind-boggling. Baffling. It doesn't make any sense." Mopac Audio reached out to him sometime in 2017 or 2018 to discuss the case. It was the first time he had spoken about it in decades. It turned out to be an overwhelming and emotional experience. He has only caught a few videos or podcasts since, but he did listen to the *Yuba County Five* podcast by Mopac Audio. There is an audio clip of Imogene Weiher on the podcast. Weiher Jr. said he was listening in his truck and had to pull over. It was the first time he'd heard Imogene's voice in years. It was truly a moving experience. While Weiher Jr. appreciated *Yuba County Five*, he believes other podcasts are way off base. Weiher Jr. doesn't have time for half-baked theories or wrong information being stated as fact. He's not sold on Gary Mathias being the culprit, because Weiher Jr. believes his uncle Ted would have pummeled Mathias if he got out of line.

Dallas Weiher Sr. never left the Marysville area. He is a well-known softball player and was a sheriff's reserve deputy for the Yuba County Sheriff's Department. "If Ted were still alive, he'd probably be living with me," said Weiher Sr. with a hearty laugh.

"One of my biggest gripes is that no one ever talked to me about it," said Gary Mathias's brother, Mark Mathias, when first interviewed for this book. The Yuba County Sheriff's Department never interviewed him in 1978, and neither did the press. It would be forty-two years before anyone reached out to him to learn more about the case and Gary Mathias. He had a similar experience as Dallas Weiher Jr., where he finally got to speak with me about something he never really had the chance to talk to anyone about publicly. Revisiting the past is exhausting for Mark Mathias, but he wants people to know the real Gary. When he was interviewed for this book, he wanted to know if Tammie Phillips would be involved. He was pleased when I told him his sister was also participating.

"I don't believe for a minute that Gary is still alive," said Tammie Phillips. She will not give up on finding her brother's remains. Also, she will not give up on making sure the right story is out there about Gary and that people understand he did what he could to deal with his schizophrenia. Phillips also wants to adopt a section of highway in memory of the five somewhere along the Oroville-Quincy Highway. "I'm going to ask [Plumas County] if I can put up a sign to honor their lives and I will come and clean the area monthly." She said she would clean a mile herself on both sides of the road if needed. She also reads articles, listens to podcasts, and watches original videos about the case. They tell the same story about the men, how Gary had schizophrenia and that is the reason he is responsible for their demise. Something else happened that night, and the truth will reveal itself sooner than later, in her opinion.

Claudia Huett learned the truth about what happened to Jackie Huett when she began dating Tom Huett. She met Jack Sr. and Sara and they eventually started talking about Jackie. The more she got to know them, and sometimes after a few drinks, they would discuss the case and what they believed happened. Claudia Huett fell into the rabbit hole of the Yuba County Five. Not only is she knowledgeable of the family history, but she has Sara's collection of newspaper clippings, audio recordings, and other items. Claudia feels privileged to be part of their family.

"I don't know of anyone that could speak ill of them," said Claudia Huett when remembering Jack Sr. and Sara. They were the last of the Yuba County Five parents to pass away; it was February 2018 when Sara died and May 2019 when Jack Sr. died.

Jack Sr. and Sara Huett were alive when the story of the Yuba County Five resurfaced. Huett Sr. is the only parent of the five ever recorded for an interview during the resurgence of their case. He was interviewed by Mopac Audio at Tom and Claudia Huett's home. Clips of the interview are featured on the *Yuba County Five* podcast.

Huett Sr. was asked if Gary Mathias had anything to do with the disappearance of his son and the others. "I don't think that," said Huett Sr. After Jackie Huett's remains were found, Huett Sr. spent four or five days in the Plumas trying to find Mathias's remains of. The weather was getting warmer and Huett Sr. remembered law enforcement calling off the search for Mathias. "I still think that he's just at the bottom of [Lake Oroville]. Where the hell did he go?"

Huett Sr. believed foul play played a role in the disappearance of the five. He heard the rumors about the group being chased into the Plumas by a group of men in a pickup truck. There was another rumor that Gary Mathias was tossed into Lake Oroville and the men in the pickup were involved. Huett Sr. told Mopac Audio that he informed Lance Ayers about Mathias being tossed into Lake Oroville. Ayers, according to Huett, didn't seem too sure of the theory and the discussion ended there. Huett Sr. and Ayers had a great deal of respect for each other, but Huett Sr. wasn't satisfied with the overall investigation. "Yes, I'd like to see an answer. They dropped it like a hot potato."

What also bothered Huett Sr. was the fact that he believed all five were treated differently because of their intellectual disabilities and mental illness. "Most [people] thought of them as stupid, dumbass kids. They were grown men and when you get cold… you do something about it." Huett Sr. searched the trailer where they found Weiher and discovered fuel and matches. It was his opinion that, for those who made it into the trailer, there was some sort of personal struggle about being in there and breaking the law. "They wouldn't break it. I know they wouldn't." Also, Huett questioned the trailer being locked. He was at the Daniel Zink Campground and noticed a window in the door was broken. Glass was discovered outside the trailer, not inside.

Everything about that case stuck with Huett Sr. until his dying day. It is difficult when parents must bury their children. It is even more difficult when parents must bury their children never knowing why their children disappeared and died.

☙

While the mystery of the Yuba County Five has never been solved, there was one cold case that did finally see justice. It was 1973 when Doris Derryberry and Valerie Lane were assaulted and murdered in Yuba County. DNA evidence was preserved, and in 2016, new technologies led to the arrest of two men. Avery Blankenship, a member of the Yuba County Sheriff's Department that I interviewed for this book, told me their disappearance was the one case he wanted to see solved in his lifetime. He worked on the case, and it bothered him for decades that it became a cold case. Both men were sentenced in 2017 for the assault and murders.

Essie Hiett, the missing woman from Olivehurst, is still classified as a cold case. Hiett disappeared less than two weeks before the men. A possible suspect was announced in 2015, but that person was eventually ruled out.

☙

Imagine, one of the most perplexing and baffling mysteries of the 20th century occurred on February 24, 1978. Five friends who were Special

Olympics athletes from Northern California journeyed to a college basketball game to watch their favorite team. They had successfully made trips like this in the past. On the way home, they made a series of turns that led to them being stuck on a snow-covered mountain road in the Plumas National Forest. They were seventy miles in the wrong direction. All five got out of the vehicle and vanished into the darkness, the snow, and the freezing temperatures. Not a single member of the group was dressed for the conditions.

A drinker with a penchant for lying witnessed their last moments. Or did he? He saw another vehicle behind the car with the five. Or did he? It was hard for him to tell what was happening because he was suffering a heart attack. Or did he? The witness quickly moved out of the spotlight and stopped talking.

All or some of the men somehow walked twelve miles to a trailer, made their way in, and did what they could to survive. Cans of food were opened, but the heat was not turned on. Matches were in the trailer, but fires were not set to signal distress.

Their families frantically searched for them. Someone discovered their car and reported it to the authorities. Four county sheriffs' departments were involved, but all the expectations rested on the shoulders of one jurisdiction, Yuba County. Volunteers searched for the men in treacherous conditions. Helicopters and tracking dogs were used. They could not find the men.

Psychics were brought in to assist. People claimed to see the missing men in various locations, but their stories were either a case of mistaken identity or pure nonsense. In the end, the psychics and claimed sightings took time away from the investigation and frustrated investigators and families.

Months later, a group of guys riding motorcycles found the trailer. Four of the five missing men's remains were discovered. Funerals were held while the search continued for the fifth. The search was called off, and the case faded into oblivion for the time being.

Nearly forty years after the five went missing, their case was resurrected via podcasts and original creator content videos. It has caught the attention of many people around the world. They are fascinated by the case. Many are saddened by the whole ordeal and want to know what really happened the night Weiher, Madruga, Sterling, Huett, and Mathias vanished.

ℰ⁀ↄ

"I'll be working on my book." I don't know how many times I said that over the span of two years. My wife and kids were very patient and supportive. I spent many days and nights typing on the computer with my headphones on. At first, I did not know if I could get two hundred pages written for this book. Writing two hundred pages turned out to be a piece of cake. Cutting it down to a manageable size was much more challenging. Numerous paragraphs were removed during the editing process because I'm a Midwesterner who loves to ramble.

This journey began because I wanted to read a book about the Yuba County Five. The articles, podcasts, and original videos that I read, listened to, and watched back in 2018 only gave me the tip of the proverbial iceberg. This is a daunting case. I hope we receive answers about the fate of the men on that fateful night. Maybe this book will be the inspiration for that.

There were times when I would experience writer's block. I'd grab my headphones and play some of my favorite songs from 1970 to early 1978 as motivation. *Jailbreak* is a 1976 album by Thin Lizzy. It features the anthem "The Boys Are Back in Town." That is the song that gets me in the right mindset for writing this book. That intro hits me, and I think of Jack Madruga and his 1969 Mercury Montego. In my mind, he's driving around Yuba City or Marysville with Ted Weiher, Bill Sterling, Jackie Huett, and Gary Mathias. It's Saturday night, and the world is theirs. Maybe they will enjoy mini-golf or a trip to the roller rink. Perhaps they will meet some cute girls. Everything is wonderful in the world, and tomorrow they will play basketball.

ACKNOWLEDGMENTS

I was able to write this book only with the help of many people. This is the place where they receive my thanks and gratitude. It is hard to put these into the right words, so I hope everyone understands how much I appreciate your time, support, kindness, and encouragement. Some individuals are not going to be listed here because they have asked to remain anonymous. I will thank them personally. Maybe I already have. You never know.

Thank you to my wife Cathy and my children, James, Maggie, and Bea. Cathy took care of our family while I was off doing research or in another room interviewing someone on the phone for the book. That woman is truly a saint. My family has been very supportive of this project, and they have enjoyed walking in on me typing, yelling, "Are you still working on that book?!" They joke because they love, and I love them very much. You all were there for me from start to finish. You motivated me to go the extra mile and write a great book. This happened because you encouraged me to be the best person possible.

I also want to thank my parents, Jim and Patti Wright, along with my sister, Amy. They were excited about this project. My in-laws, Tom and Sharon Hancharik, have been asking for updates about my book for years and are huge supporters.

The families of the five have been tremendous assets and are all good people. We all met over the phone, and it has been a special journey. I plan on staying in touch, so you're stuck with me.

Thank you to Dallas Weiher Sr., Dallas Weiher Jr., Dorothy Weiher-Dornan, and Nelda Weiher. Your help goes beyond words—and thank you for giving me the chance to know the real Ted. I appreciate your kindness and prayers as well.

Thank you to Tom and Claudia Huett for giving me the chance to understand the real Jackie Huett. Also, you allowed me to know more about Jack and Sara Huett. The pictures and videos you sent me were a huge help, and I appreciate all the time you've given me to talk with you about the case. You two are a quick text away and that has been fantastic.

Thank you to Tammie Phillips and Mark Mathias. You have wanted the real story about Gary released to the public, and I hope people understand your brother better after reading this book. I know it was difficult to share some of the information, and I appreciate everything. You two were always a text or call away when I needed help with my research.

Thank you to Cathy Madruga for sharing stories about Doc and the Madruga family. You were truly the "old-school" one out of the bunch because you're only available via phone. You tell it like it is, which is very cool.

Thank you to the Yuba County Sheriff's Department for allowing me to have access to the original case files. Nathan Lybarger, Brian Bernardis, and Lyndsey Deveraux helped me out and were great resources of information. I appreciate you taking me to the Plumas and discussing the case with me. You all were incredibly helpful and accommodating.

Jack Beecham, Avery Blankenship, and Larry McCormack were gracious enough to allow me to interview them over the phone. They were great resources regarding the 1978 investigation from the perspective of the Yuba County Sheriff's Department. We had some great interviews. I never had the chance to know Lance Ayers, but his daughter, Terri Ayers, was kind enough to answer some questions about her father. Thank you very much.

Cynthia Gorney was the first person I interviewed for this book. She was very patient with a rookie true crime writer. Thanks for taking time out of your schedule for a quick but helpful interview.

Every book needs an editor, so I must thank the talented and diligent Colleen Alles for her work. Without Colleen, this book would be a rambling mess.

Chris Maas and Jonathan Beal were the first people outside of Yuba County I spoke to about this case. I appreciate your time and support. Also, you two introduced me to Shannon McGarvey. Thank you, Shannon, for all of your support and research regarding this case. You did a superb job with the *Yuba County Five* podcast and have been a trusted supporter during this project. We shared various articles, reports, leads, images, and phone numbers. Working with you and Drew Beeson at times was like the Hardy Boys and Nancy Drew working a case.

A thank you goes out to Drew Beeson, fellow Yuba County Five author. I really appreciate all the help you provided me with my research. We spent a great deal of time discussing the case over the phone, and our YouTube session was great. I was honored to be your first guest on your show. Thank you for the books as well. You have been a big supporter of my work, and that is awesome.

I need to thank David Hayes for his support of my book. He believed in it when I pitched him the idea in 2019, and has been following my progress closely. You were able to provide me with some helpful data and some great writing advice. Also, thanks for falling into the rabbit hole that is this case.

Sean Kael Williams helped me out with my research. Thanks for taking the time to speak with me on the phone, or by text or e-mail about the case. Your assistance is greatly appreciated.

Tom McGarry was someone who allowed me to know more about the Plumas National Forest and Joseph Schons. You are a true raconteur, and I still laugh when I look over our interview. Don't change. Thank you for your time!

As an archivist, I must thank the archivists and librarians who assisted me with this book. Gina Zurakowski from the Yuba County Library and Michelle Sandoval from the Sutter County Library assisted me by searching microfilm and city directories for requested information. You two are fantastic. Archives are awesome!

Anthony Dunne and Eduardo Colella deserve thanks for being supportive of my journey. It is refreshing to see there are other Yuba County Five researchers out there from different countries. You two are awesome. Also, thanks to Kenny Davenport-Slater for waiting so patiently for this book to be released.

A special thank you to Steven and Leya Booth at Genius Books for publishing this book. Thank you for believing in me and this project.

Printed in Great Britain
by Amazon

40018245R00185